Revolutions in Eastern Europe

Revolutions in Eastern Europe

Roger East

Pinter Publishers, London and New York

First published in Great Britain in 1992 by
Pinter Publishers Limited
25 Floral Street, London WC2E 9DS

British Library Cataloguing in Publication Data
A CIP catalogue record for this book is available from the British Library.

ISBN 0-86187-179-0 (Pbk)
      0-86187-169-3 (Hbk)

Library of Congress Cataloguing in Publication Data
Applied for.

Computer typeset by CIRCA Reference, Cambridge
Printed and bound in Great Britain

CONTENTS

INTRODUCTION

This book goes to press exactly three years after the Polish communist regime began its round table talks with the banned Solidarity movement. The changes since then, while they can never be "complete", have certainly been comprehensive. In 1989 there were eight "East European" states. One, the GDR, no longer exists, while another, Yugoslavia, has disintegrated into three, four or five parts. The region, which westerners might once mentally have lumped together as the "Eastern European bloc", is no longer in any sense a bloc. It may be unhelpful even to go on thinking of it as one region, for clearly there is at least a north-south divide. Nor can the adjective Eastern really be used with much meaning for these European states. After the dramatic break-up of the Soviet Union in 1991, there are 10 European states to the east of them. Prague and Budapest at least, like Berlin and Vienna, must be ranked with the capital cities of Central Europe once again.

The book tries to provide a clear record of this period of change. It seeks to set in context the main events of the collapse of communism in Eastern Europe, and the creation of the post-communist political systems.

It begins with a brief introductory chapter, contrasting the historical antecedents of the states which made up Eastern Europe between the two World Wars. Thereafter, the eight main chapters are arranged on a country-by-country basis. They have a consistent structure, so that it should be possible to refer easily to the relevant experience of other countries at any point.

Each of the country chapters begins with information on the geography and the population, and a short history, with the emphasis on the events surrounding the fall of the communist regime. In each case the constitutional changes are then identified, as is the impact of the revolution on the former ruling communist party. There is information on the main individuals and groups of the post-communist system, full election results for the period to the end of 1991, details of governments, and specific sections where appropriate for salient issues such as the dismantling of secret police systems and the treatment of minority nationalities. A comprehensive chronology completes the coverage for each of the eight countries.

The final chapter considers the new shape of Europe: its alliances and defence framework, its institutions for political and functional co-operation and for economic integration. There has been much speculative comment on how the former communist states are being fitted into, and are crucially affecting, what were once mainly West European and Atlantic structures. In keeping with the factual emphasis throughout this book, however, the final chapter once again concerns itself primarily with recording what has actually taken place, and with the attempt to arrange this information in such a way as to help distinguish the wood from the trees. As with the other chapters, it ends with a comprehensive chronology.

Acknowledgement is due to Carpress International Press Agency for the maps on pages 7, 20, 38, 62, 63, 87, 107, 135, 156, 157 and 173. For the text and chronology in the final chapter, and for the index, I am indebted to the assistance of Frances Nicholson, my colleague at CIRCA Reference. I would also like to thank my colleagues, past and present, who have worked to cover the events in Eastern Europe on the editorial team of *Keesing's Record of World Events*. I have drawn heavily on their labours in writing this book, and I gratefully acknowledge that debt, to Ian Gorvin most of all.

Roger East

Cambridge, February 1992

CONTRASTS IN PRE-1918 HISTORY

If too sweeping a generalization were made, about the common historical experience of the eight states of Eastern Europe prior to 1989, objections would rightly be raised. From a postwar political perspective, the first of these might be that only six were within the Soviet orbit, while Yugoslavia had taken a second road, and Albania of course was on its own. Then there is the obviously special case of the GDR.

Widening the focus, however, it should be stressed that the common thread is of very recent introduction. Looking at the European history of the seventeenth, eighteenth or nineteenth centuries, for example, it would be difficult to identify anything of significance, in respect of which one could begin to speak of Eastern Europe as an entity. There is very little in common, even between countries which are neighbours, in the national history of Poles and Czechs, or of Hungarians and Romanians. Apart, that is, from the experience of being for much of this time subject peoples.

Subject peoples of four empires, 1683-1918

During the period of the existence of the Habsburg empire as a great European power, a period which dates from the lifting of the Turkish siege of Vienna in 1683 to the reshaping of Eastern Europe after World War I on the basis of an unevenly applied principle of independent nationhood, there were four main centres of power. Two of these, Russia and the Ottoman empire, were external powers with East European dominions; the two others, Austria (latterly Austria-Hungary) itself and the progressively consolidated Prussia/Germany, were centred in the northern and western parts of the region.

Poland, itself formerly one of the great kingdoms of Europe and leader of the anti-Ottoman coalition which had relieved Vienna, was at the beginning of this period the only other independent power (apart from Swedish toe-holds in the north). The partitions of Poland, in 1772, 1793 and 1795, completed the dominance of the four empires. The period of the French revolutionary wars and the Napoleonic empire in Europe, profoundly influential in the fostering of liberal nationalism, was principally confined to the western half of the continent, although it was certainly disruptive of Habsburg rule, and involved the brief creation of the Grand Duchy of Warsaw (1807-13) and of the Illyrian Provinces under French rule in what is now Croatia.

Running through the list of our post-1918 states, only Poland had a history of direct Russian domination, confined between 1772 and 1815 to what is now its eastern fringe, but then extended by annexation through to Warsaw and Lodz. Their relations had been one of the great European rivalries in the fourteenth, fifteenth and sixteenth centuries, but the decline of the Polish-Lithuanian kingdom under its elective monarchy, after 1572, was hastened after Russia had eliminated, in the Great Northern War (1700-21), the strong Swedish influence on the balance of power. The areas formally annexed by Russia in the partitions of Poland were allowed some initial autonomy as the Congress Kingdom of Poland. The industries of Lodz and Warsaw became linked in with St Petersburg, however, in the earliest phase of Russian railway-building; the customs barrier was abolished (1851), and anti-Russian revolts were crushed in 1830 and 1863, after which the separation was altogether eliminated and Polish culture in the Russian sphere was suppressed. The war between Poland and Bolshevik Russia in 1920-21, if it was essentially an opportunist venture on the Polish side, nevertheless had deep roots in historical enmity.

What Poles had undergone at Russian hands since partition was similar in some respects to the experience of the Poles under Prussia/Germany. An emphasis on industrial development promoted the growth in particular of Breslau (Wroclaw) and Danzig (Gdansk), but in 1848 the incipient nationalist revolt was swiftly put down by German nationalists acting in the name of the Frankfurt Parliament. Less repressive was the experience of those whose homelands, in what is now southern Poland, came into Habsburg dominion. Here they kept some local autonomy and cultural freedoms, and even an independent republic of Krakow in 1815-46. This arrangement, initially due to Austrian and Russian differences over which side should annex it, allowed the old Polish capital and university centre to flourish as a haven for liberal and nationalist thinkers from all over the Habsburg empire, until Metternich in 1846 resolved to end their pernicious influence by annexation.

Poland is unique in respect both of having been partly under Russian rule, and of having been partly under German rule, in the pre-1918 period. Elsewhere, Russia's influence, if not its rule, was felt most keenly (apart from in 1848-49 when Tsar Nicholas's armies took on the role of repressive "policeman") in the eastern Balkans, as the far from disinterested sponsor of nineteenth century nationalism.

The wider context of this was the slow disintegration of the Ottoman empire, which for 500 years until the mid-nineteenth century extended over all of what became Bulgaria, Romania (apart from Transylvania), Serbia (apart, again, from a area, now Vojvodina, under Hungarian rule in the Habsburg empire), Macedonia, Montenegro and Albania.

Serbia's was the first nationalist revolt, ultimately unsuccessful in the Napoleonic era in 1804-1813, but leading to autonomy in 1830 and independence in 1878 (this being the precursor to the struggle for Greater Serbia and the liberation of all the South Slavs from Habsburg and Turkish rule).

The provinces of Moldavia and Walachia gained the status of autonomous principalities within the Ottoman empire at the end of the Crimean War, from 1856; they were unified in 1861, declared their independence in 1877 during the Russo-Turkish war, and were recognized, as independent **Romania**, in 1878 at the Treaty of Berlin.

In **Bulgaria,** where the experience of Ottoman rule was much more direct and culturally and economically intrusive than further north, there was a revival of cultural nationalism in the late eighteenth century, based on the identity of the Orthodox Church, which was eventually able in 1870 to constitute itself independently of the authority of the Greek patriarch. The church, with Russian encouragement, launched an agitation for national independence, and in 1876 an uprising was brutally crushed, but the Russian victory in the Russo-Turkish war gave them the ability temporarily to dictate the settlement terms, which they used to establish a "Big Bulgaria", from the Danube to the Aegean, under the Treaty of San Stefano (1878). Russia was seen by the other main European powers, however, as having gained an unacceptable expansion of its Mediterranean influence under this settlement, and was forced to back down. Later in the year the Treaty of Berlin cut down Bulgaria both in size (so that it no longer reached south to the Aegean) and in status, leaving it as a principality nominally within the Ottoman empire. The country's subsequent history, to 1918 (it achieved full independence in 1908) and indeed beyond, was dominated by the ambition of restoring the San Stefano frontiers, prompting its involvement in the Balkan Wars of 1912-1913, which also made **Albania**, at least on paper, an independent state .

The boundary between the Habsburg and the Ottoman empires had been pushed north and west by Ottoman military power, whose invading forces crushed a peasant revolt in **Hungary** in the early sixteenth century. The last onslaught, in the mid-seventeenth century in the reign of Sultan Mehmed IV, reached Vienna in 1683. Pushing back the Turkish armies thereafter, the Habsburgs had reconquered Hungary (to whose throne the Habsburg dynasty had acceded in 1526) by 1699, and added to their empire at Ottoman expense in the subsequent decades notably in Transylvania and, temporarily, in northern Serbia. Hungary, with its powerful and reactionary Magyar aristocracy dominating the countryside and a middle class nationalist element of growing significance in Budapest and other cities, swiftly acquired and jealously guarded a high degree of autonomy under the Habsburg empire. Ultimately it obtained equal status with Austria and a Dual Monarchy (from 1867) under which only defence and foreign affairs were handled jointly.

It was Hungary which exercised the Habsburg dominion not only over Transylvania but also over **Slovakia** and **Croatia**. Unsatisfied with limited autonomy from 1868, Croatian nationalism was essentially anti-Hungarian in its initial conception (see also under 1848 below), and oriented towards Yugoslav aspirations, as in neighbouring Serbia (although Croats were mainly Roman Catholic, whereas Serbs were mainly Orthodox).

Within the Habsburg empire throughout this period were the **Czech lands** of Bohemia and Moravia. The Habsburgs had acceded to the Czech throne in 1526 and crushed the rebellion by Czech nobles at the Battle of the White Mountain in 1620. The rise of a middle class Czech nationalism, in conflict with German national aspirations in an increasingly urban and industrialized environment, was held in check by Habsburg authority, bureaucracy, and, on occasion, armed force.

The "year of revolutions": 1848 in Budapest, Prague and elsewhere

The turbulent events of 1848, across Europe's major capitals from Paris through Germany to Prague and Budapest, reflected the widespread frustration felt against the stifling conditions (both economic and political) of conservative and authoritarian regimes. It was a moment when middle class intellectuals and nationalists, inspired by liberal ideologies and by the news of what was happening in neighbouring capitals, proclaimed their right to independence and their faith in parliamentary structures. Their revolts were fuelled by economic recession, unrest and unemployment, the failure of harvests, and the consequent food shortages in the cities.

In Budapest in March, the Diet, responding to news from Paris and the urgings of the poet Petofi and the lawyer and editor Kossuth, adopted the so-called March Laws, claiming the right to a government responsible to the Diet. The Emperor Ferdinand initially accepted, but then exploited the divisive nationalisms within the Hungarian lands (including Transylvania, Croatia and Slovakia), encouraging the governor of Croatia to lead military moves against the Hungarian rebels, in return for the promise of Croat autonomy under Habsburg protection. Kossuth's citizen's defence forces held them off, but when Russian armies were brought into play in defence of the existing European order, they put down the Hungarian rebellion in August 1849.

By this time the Russian army had already occupied Walachia, where liberals in Bucharest had wrung concessions from the Turkish governor. In Prague it was the Austrian armies which bombarded and crushed the 1848 rebellion. Here the events had been sparked off by the Slav congress and by Czech nationalist demonstrations in June, in which the wife of the Austrian military commander was accidentally killed.

The heroic age: looking further back for national independence

It was the events of 1848-49 which gave Hungary its nationalist hero figure Kossuth, set alongside St Stephen, the first Hungarian king in the year 1000 at the start of the great age in Hungarian national history. For Poles the heroic age was the period when the Polish and Lithuanian kingdom of the fourteenth and fifteenth centuries was the greatest power in Europe, its lands reaching down to the Black Sea. The Czechs had their own cohesive state, formed in the tenth to twelfth centuries (whereas Slovakia was under Hungarian rule from the ninth century), and a Czech monarch, Charles IV, who in 1346 became Holy Roman Emperor. Czechs also look back proudly to the religious reforms and associated national feelings stimulated by the Czech priest Jan Hus, who challenged the authority of Rome and was burned at the stake in 1415, provoking protracted resistance to the authority of the Emperor Sigismund.

Further south, Romanians claimed a special link with the glory that was Rome; Bulgaria was a powerful empire in the tenth century before the rise of Ottoman power. Serbia too had an empire in the mediaeval period, which reached its height in the mid-fourteenth century, but was overthrown by the Turks at the Battle of Kosovo in 1389 (a date whose commemoration by the Albanians of Kosovo is thus a highly potent symbol of national divisions). Croatia had a period of independent existence in the tenth century, but was thereafter joined to Hungary. Albanians remember as their national hero Skanderbeg, the leader of a Christian revolt against Turkish rule in 1443-1468.

The contrast in religious traditions

Christianity spread throughout Eastern Europe in the ninth and tenth centuries. Albania, compulsorily Islamized after the defeat of Skanderbeg, is the only country with a Muslim majority, although there are important numbers of Muslims in Yugoslavia (Albanians in Kosovo, and the Muslims of Bosnia-Hercegovina). There was a sizeable Muslim population, mainly Turks, in Bulgaria, although it has been much reduced by "assimilation", persecution and the exodus to Turkey in 1989 [see Bulgaria chapter].

The main line of religious division is that between Orthodox Christianity, dominant throughout the southern part of Eastern Europe, and Roman Catholics. Orthodox Churches dominate in Bulgaria, Romania, Serbia and Macedonia. Catholics are greatly in the majority among Croats, Slovenes and Slovaks, and overwhelmingly so among Poles; they also form a majority in Hungary (and Transylvania), but alongside numerous Protestants. The Czechs are mixed as between Catholics and the Hussite and other Protestant denominations. Of the eight countries in this book, only the former GDR was by a large majority Protestant (Evangelical).

Agrarian and urban societies

A major contrast in pre-1918 history is to be seen between those countries with a significant urban population and experience of the nineteenth century European industrial revolution, and those which had remained largely unaffected (and which generally continued to be so until the all-consuming efforts of the postwar Stalin-influenced communist regimes to build a heavy industrial base).

In the former category are Germany, parts of Poland and Hungary, and the Czech lands in particular. In the forefront among the great industrial areas of Europe prior to 1914 were Bohemia and Silesia, while Warsaw and Lodz in the Russian part of Poland, and Danzig/Gdansk and Breslau/Wroclaw in Posen (German Poland), and Brno in Moravia, were major industrial centres. Kosice in Slovakia had iron ore and a metals industry, and Budapest and other Hungarian cities were industrial producers, notably of textiles.

Although northern Bulgaria had a significant textile industry, Romania had petroleum and Serbia its coal mining, the urban population in Bulgaria was still only about one third of the total population in the 1930s, and the proportions in Romania, Yugoslavia and Albania were even smaller.

Diplomatic alignments in 1914

Nationalism in the Balkans, as has been so often said, provided the spark for the European war in 1914, the continental conflict which was then widened to become World War I. Germany and Austria/Hungary on the one side comprised the so-called

Central Powers; Serbia and Russia were on the other side with Britain and France (the Entente or Allied Powers). The line of cleavage in Eastern Europe at the outset thus ran through Poland, east of Slovakia and Hungary, and south of Croatia and Slovenia.

Turkey joined the Central Powers later in 1914, as did Bulgaria the following year, and in 1916 Romania entered the war on the Allied side. Only Albania remained neutral. It was the defeat of the Central Powers, and the collapse of the Russian empire, which opened the way for the redrawing of the map of Europe.

ALBANIA

The official name of the country was the Albanian People's Socialist Republic (*Republika Popullore Socialiste Shqipërisë*) from 1976 until 1991. It was renamed as simply the Republic of Albania on April 29, 1991.

Geographically Albania, part of the Balkans, is a mountainous country whose population is principally concentrated in the comparatively fertile western lowlands along the Adriatic coast. Its land area, of 28,748 sq. km, and population, of only some 3,100,000, made it by some way the smallest of the eight independent European countries under Communist rule in the post-1945 period. About one third of the population live in urban areas, and Tirana, the capital, is the only substantial city, with a population of about 225,000; other main towns, with 60-80,000 inhabitants, are the port of Durrës and Elbasan, Shkodër, Vlore and Korçë.

There are significant numbers of Albanian-speakers, amounting to 40 per cent of the total, living in Yugoslavia to the north [see under Yugoslavia]. Albania itself is relatively homogeneous in ethnic terms. The most important minority group, Greek-speakers, numbered approximately 50,000; there is also a Macedonian minority. The country, once mainly Muslim (with Orthodox and Roman Catholic Christian minorities), was officially proclaimed as atheist under the communist regime, but many preserved their Muslim or Christian allegiance in private worship, and re-emerged when mosques and churches were allowed to reopen from late 1989 onwards. The Albanian language comprises two dialect groups, the dominant one (Tosk) being associated with the southern part of the country, the other (Gheg) with the north.

In modern history, as the Ottoman empire lost control of the Balkan region Albania attained a nominally independent status in the course of the Balkan Wars (1912-13), but was effectively swallowed up in wartime military occupation; in the settlement which followed the 1914-18 war, it was restored to independence, within boundaries fixed in 1921. Ahmet Zogu, a conservative chieftain, made himself ruler of the country by conquest in 1924 and took the title of King Zog four years later. His regime aligned itself with fascist Italy, but collapsed under Italian military intervention in April1939.

When Italy pulled out of World War II the Nazi German occupation of Albania began (in late 1943). The Germans found both the terrain and the people hostile, and, in general retreat, had pulled out of Albania by the summer of 1944. For this the partisans were quick to claim all the credit. In fact, much of their activity during this period consisted of internecine feuding. The communists, led by Enver Hoxha and identified by British military intelligence as the most worthwhile of the rival partisan groups, emerged in the ascendant; Hoxha became prime minister at the head of a communist-dominated coalition government in November 1944, and formally pro-claimed a republic in January 1946.

Under Hoxha, Albania became more and more isolated over four decades of hardline Stalinism, characterized externally by dramatic rifts first with Yugoslavia (1948), then with the Soviet Union (in 1961 over the Sino-Soviet split), and in 1977-78 even with China, effectively the last option for international Marxist-Leninist solidarity and aid. Hoxha, whose name, image, works and monuments became all-pervasive through the cult of his personality, sought to glorify Albania's isolation as a mark of its integrity in pursuing the one true road to socialism. Private property was banned, religion officially abolished (in 1967), and foreign economic assistance renounced; opponents of Hoxha were dealt with in ruthless purges. The last of several leading party members to commit suicide (as the official accounts described it) was Mehmet Shehu, in 1981 after 27 years as prime minister.

Before Hoxha died in April 1985, he had groomed for the succession (and installed as President) his protégé Ramiz Alia, whose apparently smooth takeover seemed to hold out only the most limited prospect of reform. The country's international isolation, even if it was now slightly relaxed in respect of contacts with the west, provided a barrier against any spread of the epidemic of glasnost and perestroika. Rumours suggested that the main internal challenge to Alia might still be from a hardline faction around Hoxha's widow Nexhmije; and the East European *annus mirabilis* of 1989 ended without the tide of change engulfing Albania. Alia in January 1990 professed to see no parallels between the situation in Albania and the demise of the "revisionist" regimes of Eastern Europe, whose ruling cliques had "compromised and soiled the legitimacy of the socialist state". 1990, however, was to show that Albania was no exception, merely backward in following the same broad trend. In Albania as elsewhere, the monolithic communist state could not endure, in the circumstances of economic failure and the spread of a popular belief that the regime was not after all invulnerable. For the first half of 1990, the debate (albeit under pressure from demonstrations and industrial unrest) largely represented a victory of the reformers over the hardliners within the party hierarchy. This period saw the lifting of the ban on religion, and limited political and economic liberalization. The absence of any non-communist political experience, and the absolutist nature of the regime in the Hoxha years, made it difficult for opposition to find an initial focus for more fundamental demands. In the latter part of that year, however, new political forces grew in confidence in their challenge to the regime, holding out the promise of liberal democracy and a better life through an aid-backed rush for a free market economy.

Shkodër in the north, closest to the Albanian community in Yugoslavia, had been the location of the first demonstrations in late 1989. When these spread to Tirana, efforts to repress them were more visible internationally. Mindful of the East German precedent, and of the importance which young people attached to a new promise of freedom to travel abroad, thousands of young men in July 1990 sought refuge in the West German, French and Italian embassies. By letting these first asylum-seekers go, the regime hoped in vain to flush out what it wanted to see as the problem of "anti-patriotic elements". Students and workers now mobilized in mass demonstrations, wringing out further concessions but still pressing for multi-party elections. The poll held in March-April 1991 revealed the extent of support for the opposition's newly-formed Democratic Party in urban areas, even if the conservatism of rural Albania left the communists with a clear overall parliamentary majority. For Alia there was personal humiliation when he was roundly defeated in a Tirana constituency, and the election soon proved a hollow victory for his party. The haemorrhage of the mass exodus continued, with young Albanians flooding into Italy despite all that country's efforts at discouragement; a general strike in May compelled the regime to concede the formation of a "pluralist" government the following month (which survived, amid growing tensions, only until the opposition Democratic Party pulled out in December). The last half of 1991 saw repeated disagreements over legislation which would bring fundamental economic change, and a growing agitation against the remaining power of entrenched former communists, notably in the media. Indications from by Ramiz Alia, in failing health at the end of 1991, that he would not seek to go on as President, merely confirmed the fact that the "old order" had passed. It remained unclear how the rejection of the Albanian brand of communism would translate into a new form of government. There were to be fresh elections in 1992. The victors would then face the increasingly apparent real difficulties of managing a transition to a free market economy, in a society separated by a daunting gulf from any standard of international competitiveness.

The principal personalities of Communist rule

Enver **Hoxha** (1908-85). A southern Albanian from Gjirokaster, Hoxha joined the communist party in the 1930s while at university in France. Returning to Albania in 1936 as a French teacher after abandoning his studies in law, he joined a Marxist group in Korçë to organize against the regime of King Zog. In 1941 Hoxha was chosen as first secretary-general of the newly-constituted Albanian Communist Party. It was the resistance struggle which brought this small group to prominence through the National Liberation Movement and National Liberation Army, thanks in part to Hoxha's charismatic leadership and ruthlessness. In power from 1944 (he formally relinquished in 1954 his government post as prime minister, but not the first secretaryship of the renamed Party of Labour of Albania), he consolidated his personal supremacy in a series of purges beginning with the "pro-Yugoslav" faction (Hoxha himself having always been associated with the rival Albanian nationalist standpoint). Hoxha oversaw the creation of a Stalinist centralized power structure and command economy, but fell out with the Soviet leadership over the Sino-Soviet split in 1960-61, whereupon Khrushchev denounced the "bloody atrocities" of his purges. Ever more xenophobic in the cocoon of his personality cult after the break with China in the late 1970s, Hoxha in 1982 denounced his long-time associate Mehmet Shehu (who had died in mysterious circumstances the previous December) for having been a US, Yugoslav and Soviet agent since the war; further purges were reported in the succeeding years. When Hoxha died in April 1985 his personality cult remained intact and his widow Nexhmije continued to wield much influence as a hardliner in the party central committee, chairing the umbrella Democratic Front until December 1990. The violence of attacks on the statues and symbols of Hoxha all over Albania in 1991 underlined the extent to which the communist period had been defined by his omnipresence; Nexhmije was expelled from the party in June, and she and other hardliners were arrested in December 1991.

Ramiz **Alia** (b. 1925). Albania. Head of State. Born in Shkodër to poor Muslim parents, Alia joined the communist partisans in his late teens to fight the German occupation, both in Albania and in neighbouring Yugoslavia. His record and responsibilities in the National Liberation Army marked him out to become a prominent leader of the party youth movement in the postwar period, rising within the party to full membership of the politburo and secretariat in 1961. He was a leading proponent of Albania's "cultural revolution" in the 1960s, and Hoxha's chosen successor after the death of Mehmet Shehu. A full member of the Politburo from 1961 and Head of State from 1982, he assumed real power as PLA first secretary after Hoxha's death in 1985. His approach was initially to proceed with cautious reforms, while preserving the Hoxha cult. Persuaded only in the course of 1990 that a desperate economic situation and growing popular protest required more rapid change, he effectively marginalized the hardline elements in the party, and took the gamble of allowing other parties to contest the 1991 elections. The PLA's success in those polls in March-April, securing a two-thirds majority in an Assembly which duly re-elected him as President, proved only a punctuation point in the party's loss of its controlling position. The writing was on the wall in the party's effective defeat in urban areas, and Alia himself lost humiliatingly in a Tirana constituency. As President he was debarred under the new interim constitution from holding party leadership posts, which he duly resigned in early May. On Jan. 1, 1992, he had, but survived, a heart attack.

Adil **Çarçani** (b. 1922). A party member from wartime resistance days and a politburo member from 1961, he was Shehu's successor as prime minister from 1982, and was identified with the early, cautious reform moves under the Alia regime in 1985-90. Given responsibility for forming a government with a fresh "reformist" image in December 1990, he was replaced two months later in the immediate pre-election turmoil.

Fatos **Nano**. A young economist brought into the government in December 1990, Nano was made prime minister by Alia in the provisional government formed immediately before the March 1991 elections, and in the post-election government in May. The following month, however, this government made way for the "pluralist" administration of Ylli Bufi, and when the PLA was renamed the Socialist Party at its June 1991 congress Nano was elected party chairman, simultaneously relinquishing his government post as minister of foreign economic relations.

Ylli **Bufi** (b. 1949). The prime minister from June to December 1991, heading Albania's first coalition "government of national stability", Bufi, a PLA member, was a chemical engineer before Alia brought him into the government as part of the July

1990 changes, when he was given charge of the ministry of foodstuffs and light industry.

Constitutional changes

Albania in the Hoxha period had two constitutions, that of January 1946 under which the monarchy was formally abolished and the People's Republic of Albania proclaimed, and that of Dec. 28, 1976, which renamed the country as the People's Socialist Republic of Albania, defined it as "the state of the dictatorship of the proletariat" with the PLA as the "sole leading political force", and specified that, in building socialism, Albania relied primarily on its own efforts.

A commission set up in November 1990 was charged with reviewing the constitution.

A new draft constitution was presented to the Assembly on April 25, 1991. Its major provisions were adopted four days later on an interim basis, pending completion of the full legal process of approving the new constitution. Replacing and invalidating the constitution of 1976, the interim constitution renamed the country as simply the Republic of Albania (i.e. dropping the adjectives "Socialist" and "People's"); it defined the country's new political system as "democratic and juridical, based on social equality, the defence of freedom and the rights of man, and political pluralism".

Position and status of communists

Party name

The ruling communist party operated under the name Party of Labour of Albania (PLA—*Partia e Punës te Shqipërisë*) from 1948 (the time of the purge of the "Titoists") until June 13, 1991, when at its 10th congress in Tirana (a session characterized by unprecedented condemnations of Hoxha) it was renamed the Socialist Party of Albania. The original party, formed in November 1941 when the Comintern instructed Yugoslav communists to bring together Albania's various Marxist groups in a single party (comprising a few hundred students and intellectuals), had been known as the Albanian Communist Party until 1948.

A group claiming to be the ideologically legitimate successor to Hoxha's party was constituted as the Albanian Communist Party in late 1991, as approved by the Justice ministry on Nov. 9. The party spokesman acknowledged links with the Association of Enver Hoxha Volunteers.

Legal status

There had been no legislation as of end-1991 banning communist activity. The arrest in December 1991 of a number of former communist leaders, including Nexhmije Hoxha and long-serving politburo member Rita Marko, related to accusations of corruption while in office. Trials of "blockmen", as former party officials were known, was a principal demand of the Democratic Party when it withdrew from the government at the beginning of December 1991.

Workplace organization

The official party ideology had dominated the Central Council of Albanian Trade Unions, the only legal federation, which consisted of four main unions divided broadly according to economic sectors. There were union branches in each workplace. In December 1990 the Central Council declared that it would in future act independently of the PLA. The strike activity of 1991 gave rise to the creation early that year of an umbrella Union of Independent Trade Unions of Albania (UITEA) chaired by Valer Xheka, whose demands spilled over from the economic into the political sphere as part of the pressure for an end to communist domination.

Party assets

Most of the property of the former PLA was nationalized by government decree on Nov. 1, 1991.

Ideological orientation

The PLA in power was dedicated to a centralist ideology in which the industrial proletariat was theoretically the principal focus of the revolution, but which also claimed the representation of the interests of the peasantry as a major plank of its programme. It isolated itself successively from the Titoists, from Soviet-aligned regimes (which it regarded as practising dangerous revisionism), from the Chinese (guilty since 1977 of "hegemonism" and then of restoring capitalism), from "degenerate bourgeois" Eurocommunism, and, at least until 1990, from *glasnost* in the Soviet Union (which encouraged the libelling of Stalin and other Albanian-acknowledged Bolshevik revolutionary leaders). In its reform guise from late 1990 the PLA under Alia came to accept abandonment of the party's right to a "leading role", and the need for liberal economic reforms. As the Socialist Party of Albania from June 1991, it was ostensibly committed to privatization and rapid conversion to a free market, but was still accused by its opponents of obstructing the radical measures they believed to be essential to that end.

Electoral significance

The Democratic Front, the communist-controlled umbrella organization, was the only body allowed to put up candidates at general elections up to and including that of Feb. 1, 1987, and was regularly recorded as winning 99.9 per cent in 100 per cent turnouts. In the first (and, as of end-1991, the only) multi-party elections in March-April 1991 the then PLA won 169 out of 250 seats, with over 60 per cent of the first-round vote and clear dominance in the rural areas, but much less success in the urban areas, where the fledging opposition's agitation had so far been almost exclusively concentrated.

Principal non-communist parties

The **Democratic Party** (DP) was formed on Dec. 12, 1990, and formally legalized a week later; it proved itself the leading opposition force in the 1991 elections (principally in the capital and major towns), on a platform including private land ownership (with the possibility of foreigners buying land), the depoliticization of the army, and "shock therapy" for a rapid transition to a market economy. The DP's supporters placed much reliance on the expectation of massive Western aid in the event of its winning the elections; rumours of the existence of a US "blank cheque" were rife. The DP's main leaders were the charismatic and increasingly stridently anti-communist Sali Berisha, the academic Gramoz Pashko and, as secretary-general, Eduard Selami. The party entered the pluralist "national stability government" formed by Ylli Bufi of the PLA in June 1991. In late September 1991, at the first DP national assembly in Tirana, Berisha, backed by those in the DP who favoured the rapid ousting of communists from positions of authority throughout Albanian society, withstood the suggestion that he should step down as party leader and was elected chairman by a large majority. In early December he risked a party split by pulling the DP out of the Bufi government.

The **Republican Party** contested the 1991 elections in 165 constituencies, and took three posts in the June 1991 coalition government, from which it pulled out in December. Its leader was Sabri Godo. Together with the DP and the **Social Democratic Party** it formed the opposition alliance within the June-December coalition government.

Smaller interest groupings participating in the elections identified themselves as the **Ecology Party** chaired by Namik Hoti, the **Agrarian Party** chaired by Meno Gjoleka, the **Omonia** organization (representing ethnic Greeks), the **Party of National Unity**, the **Women's Union**, the **Youth Union**, the **Democratic Front** and the **National Veterans' Committee**. Parties continued to proliferate in the subsequent months.

Elections

Legislature

Under the communist regime a unicameral People's Assembly, with 250 members, was elected every four years from a single list of candidates, by universal suffrage of those over 18 (with turnouts generally recorded as at or near 100 per cent). The last two such elections were in November 1982 and February 1987.

The electoral system for the multiparty elections in March-April 1991, again for a 250-seat Assembly, involved contested single-member constituency elections, with first round ballots on March 31, and a second round run-off on April 7 or 14 in 19 constituencies where no candidate had secured an overall majority.

March-April 1991: election of Assembly			
	1st round, March 31	2nd round, April 7&14	Total
PLA	162	7	169
DP	65	10	75
Omonia	3	2	5
National Veterans' Committee	1	-	1
Total	231	19	250

Presidency

Under the communist regime the People's Assembly elected the Presidium whose president (Omer Nishani from 1946 to 1953, Maj.-Gen. Haxhi Lleshi from 1953 to 1982, then Ramiz Alia) was nominal head of state.

Under the interim constitution adopted on April 29, 1991, the newly-elected People's Assembly on April 30 elected Ramiz Alia to the new post of President of the Republic; a token PLA opponent, Namik Dokle, received two votes against 172 for Alia, while 71 votes (corresponding to the entire opposition) were ruled invalid. The President was C.-in-C. of the armed forces, appointed the government and had powers to dissolve the People's Assembly or to declare a state of emergency.

Governments since the end of the communist monopoly on power

After the March-April 1991 elections, Fatos Nano, the prime minister in the provisional government formed in February, formed a new government which won a parliamentary vote of confidence on May 12. Mass protests backed by hunger strikes, however, led to further change within weeks.

On June 12 a new "national stability government" was formed, headed this time by Ylli Bufi, and nominated by the PLA but designated an "apolitical government". It included 11 PLA members, nine proposed by the DP (including DP leader Gramoz Pashko as deputy PM , minister of defence Perikli Teta and minister of finance Genci Ruli), representatives of the Republican Party, the Social Democratic Party and the Agrarian Party, and nine non-party members. The Bufi government resigned on Dec. 6, 1991, after the withdrawal of the main opposition party representatives.

On Dec. 18, 1991, the former food minister Vilson Ahmeti, a 40-year-old non-party engineer who had been a junior member of governments since 1987, formed a new coalition administration pending the holding of fresh elections now brought forward to March 1992.

Security and human rights issues

The disbanding of secret police services

As part of a May 1991 reorganization of what had been the Interior Ministry (involving the creation of a Ministry of Public Order), a new state body was also set up, the National Security Committee, to replace the former secret police or *Sigurimi*.

The trial began on Dec. 4, 1991, of four Shkodër police and communist officials, charged with responsibility for the death of DP supporters at demonstrations in the town in early April. The case had become a *cause célèbre* in the arguments over whether former communist leaders should be put on trial for their actions; a parliamentary commission had already found, on April 25, that responsibility for provoking the Shkodër violence lay with the security forces who had baton-charged a peaceful demonstration. The Procurator General had been dismissed on the insistence of the Assembly in May, and caretaker interior minister Rrapo Mino strongly attacked, over the Shkodër affair.

Political prisoners

A pardon was approved on Jan. 5, 1991, for 202 people currently serving prison sentences for "agitation and propaganda against the state" and for "attempted defection abroad". The People's Assembly ordered that all other cases should be reviewed. Under continuing pressure from the Forum for the Defence of Human Rights, a general pardon was announced on March 12, and on July 2 Alia signed a further decree pardoning the last political prisoners.

On Sept. 30, following a hunger strike in Tirana by former political prisoners, the Assembly passed a law on their amnesty, rehabilitation and compensation.

Religious freedom

Religion had been "abolished" in 1967, when the regime announced that Albania was the world's first atheist state. This was explicitly confirmed in the 1976 constitution. In practice, even in a state with such totalitarian intentions, the repression of public worship did not mean the eradication of religious belief or even of some private observance of both Muslim and Christian ritual.

The ban on "religious propaganda" was lifted in May 1990 as the political climate shifted towards greater liberalization, and, significantly, religious toleration was one of the key signs of the relaxation of political controls signalled by Alia in early November 1990. This was soon followed by the first services, beginning (on Nov. 16) with a Catholic mass in Shkodër whose celebrant, Archbishop Simun Yubani, had been released the previous year after 22 years in prison. The first legal Muslim service, at Tirana's Etem Bey mosque on Skanderbeg Square, took place on Jan. 18. 1991, attended by several hundred worshippers and watched by a crowd numbering many thousand.

CHRONOLOGY

January 1946. Proclamation of a republic, with Enver Hoxha as its leader.

1948. Albania's quarrel with Yugoslavia is followed by purges of alleged "Titoists".

1961. Criticism of the Soviet policy of peaceful coexistence with the West, articulated at the ALP congress in February, indicates Albania's support for China in the developing Sino-Soviet dispute. Purges of pro-Soviet elements begin in May; the breach between Albania and the Soviet Union is highlighted at Soviet party conference in October, and Albania leaves Comecon; diplomatic relations with the Soviet Union and East European countries are broken off by the end of the year.

1967. Religion is officially abolished.

1974-76. Widespread purges are reported, apparently directed against opponents of Hoxha's attacks on the Soviet line in East-West detente; the former defence minister is executed in September 1974.

January 1976. A new constitution is introduced, enshrining the increasingly isolationist and inward-looking policies which characterize the previous 31 years of Albania's "building of socialism".

July 1978. The ending of Chinese aid, after a dispute in which Hoxha accuses the Chinese of harbouring aspirations to seek hegemony.

December 1981. The death of prime minister Mehmet Shehu is officially described as suicide. More purges in the top party leadership are reported over the next three years.

April 1985. Hoxha dies and is succeeded by Ramiz Alia.

January 1990. After the upheavals of 1989 across Eastern Europe, the party leadership asserts that there will be no similar pressures for change in Albania which Alia describes as a society of justice, free from social conflicts or national oppression. Nevertheless, he puts forward a package of economic and political liberalization measures, including production incentives to workers and the idea of choice between (PLA-approved) candidates in elections, amid the first reports of signs of internal unrest, especially in the north.

17 April 1990. Departing from the regime's previous isolationist stance, Alia speaks of Albania's desire for "friendly relations with all countries", at a party plenum which also approves limited economic reforms.

7-8 May 1990. Reforms of the legal system and penal code are approved by parliament, as is the lifting of the ban on "religious propaganda".

7-9 July 1990. Changes in the party politburo and the government are seen as strengthening the position of a more reform-minded faction and removing hardliners. Alia, announcing the changes, places particular stress on gradual economic reform; later in the month artisans are permitted a degree of "free enterprise" trading, and restrictions on foreign investment are modified.

9-13 July 1990. Thousands of asylum-seekers who have taken refuge in foreign embassies are given passports and allowed to leave Albania.

30 July 1990. Diplomatic relations are restored with the Soviet Union.

25 October 1990. Ismail Kadare, a leading Albanian writer previously regarded as a supporter of the regime, seeks political asylum in France, expressing the belief that Alia has "no intention of emulating the political reforms of Eastern Europe".

November 1990. The party leadership supports constitutional reform and encourages religious tolerance; the first (Catholic) service is held on Nov. 16.

11 December 1990. As pro-democracy demonstrations spread from Tirana to other towns, five hardliners are dropped from the 11-member party politburo (with a government reshuffle following later in the month), and Alia announces that opposition parties will be permitted.

12 December 1990. The formation of the Democratic Party is announced.

23 December 1990. A new Forum for the Defence of Human Rights is set up, campaigning for the release of all political prisoners, and the official trade union federation declares its independence from the communist party.

11 January 1991. Up to 1,000 coal miners go on strike at the Valias mine near Tirana; the strikes spread to other sectors, despite government concessions on pay and

working conditions, until new industrial relations legislation is rushed through the parliament on Jan. 23.

16 January 1991. The government agrees to postpone Albania's first free multiparty elections from Feb. 10 to March 31—a concession to the opposition, which had otherwise threatened a boycott.

18 January 1991. Several hundred people in central Tirana attend the first legal Muslim religious service since 1967.

31 January 1991. Two young economists, Fatos Nano and Shkelqim Cani, are promoted in a government reshuffle.

9 February 1991. Thousands of people are prevented by police from leaving the port of Durrës on ferries to Italy.

20 February 1991. President's rule is declared (with an interim government formed two days later in which Fatos Nano becomes prime minister), in response to the opposition demand for the resignation of the Çarçani government in the run-up to elections. On the same day, tanks are deployed in Tirana after student-led protestors march down the boulevard from the university to the central Skanderbeg square and pull down the statue of Enver Hoxha, chanting "Hoxha-Hitler". A hunger strike is called off when the outgoing government agrees to the university dropping the name of Enver Hoxha, but attacks on his monuments continue in succeeding days, with several deaths reported on Feb. 23 and numerous arrests.

27 February 1991. Private ownership of cars and motorcycles is legalized, although such things remain effectively unavailable in Albania and their importation unaffordable for ordinary people. Other restrictions symbolizing Albania's isolation, such as the prohibition of beards as an "alien manifestation", have been lifted in the various liberalization measures since late 1990.

8 March 1991. With thousands of Albanians arriving in Italy in seized cargo boats and fishing boats, the Italian government orders its navy to prevent them reaching the port of Brindisi; about 2,000 are subsequently persuaded to return, and others are moved to refugee camps.

15 March 1991. Diplomatic relations with the USA are restored after 45 years.

31 March 1991. First round of multi-party elections, in which the communist PLA shows its domination of the rural electorate; the main opposition Democratic Party, despite its strong showing in the main towns, concedes defeat on April 1.

2 April 1991. Anti-communist rioting breaks out in Shkodër, apparently set off by opposition disappointment over election results; at least four people are shot dead by police, and the DP calls a general strike to commemorate them on April 4.

7 and 14 April 1991. Completion of elections in constituencies where second-round run-offs are necessary.

10-17 April 1991. First meetings of the new People's Assembly in which the PLA holds a two-thirds majority; the DP boycotts the opening session, demanding the exposure of those responsible for the killings in Shkodër the previous week, and on April 25 a parliamentary commission blames the security forces for provoking the violence.

29 April 1991. A new interim constitution supersedes that of 1976, no longer designating Albania as a Socialist People's Republic but simply as the Republic of Albania.

30 April 1991. The new Assembly elects Ramiz Alia as President under the interim constitution; the opposition's 71 votes are all declared invalid.

3 May 1991. A new PLA government formed under Fatos Nano wins a vote of confidence in the Assembly. On May 10 Nano announces his programme, and commits his government to introducing a free market economy, but it survives less than a month as strike actions and popular anti-communist protests intensify.

4 May 1991. Alia resigns from the party leadership in keeping with the new constitutional requirements of his election as President.

29 May 1991. Diplomatic relations are re-established with the UK, although a dispute remains unresolved over Albanian gold, recovered from Nazi Germany but held in London since the war pending the payment of compensation for two British ships sunk by mines in 1946.

11-13 June 1991. The PLA holds its congress in Tirana, criticizes Hoxha, expels old guard leaders and renames itself the Socialist Party of Albania. Fatos Nano is elected as new party chairman on June 14.

12 June 1991. Ylli Bufi, named as prime minister on June 5, announces the formation of a new "government of national stability" in which the communists will for the first time share power with opposition parties.

17-18 June 1991. The Italian government sends back some 800 of the increasingly unwelcome Albanian would-be emigrants, warning that all who have not found jobs or been recognized as political refugees will be repatriated under new immigration rules after July 15.

22 June 1991. US Secretary of State James Baker promises humanitarian aid during a one-day visit on which he receives an enthusiastic popular welcome in Tirana.

4 July 1991. Bufi meets the Pope in the Vatican and it is agreed that diplomatic relations will be restored (which is done on Sept. 7).

22 July 1991. EC Commissioner Frans Andriessen visits Tirana, after which the EC agrees to mount a food and medical aid programme.

5 August 1991. The government begins its programme of handing back land to peasants, intending that the operation should be completed within six weeks.

13 August 1991. A Soviet embassy is opened in Tirana.

25 August 1991. Anti-communist demonstrations resume in Tirana for the first time since the formation of the power-sharing government in June, and a sustained campaign focuses particularly on the control of the media by former party cadres.

28 August 1991. Italy announces a major emergency food aid programme, having refused entry to tens of thousands of new would-be emigrants and carried out a forcible repatriation operation in mid-August.

1 September 1991. Economic reforms include the creation of a national privatization agency, encouragement of foreign investment, and the linking of the currency, the lek, to the value of the European currency unit or ECU.

27 September 1991. The Democratic Party holds its first national assembly, at which delegates vote to back the increasingly confrontational leadership of Sali Berisha.

3 November 1991. Alia warns, with little effect, that police will intervene to stop strikes; industrial unrest and disturbances over food and energy shortages continue, as does the opposition's campaign over control of the media.

4 December 1991. Hoxha's widow Nexhmije and former politburo member Rita Marko are arrested to stand trial for corruption.

6 December 1991. Ylli Bufi resigns as prime minister after the withdrawal of key opposition participants in his five-month-old "national stability government".

16 December 1991. A new government under Vilson Ahmeti is sworn in, to administer the country pending the organization of fresh elections.

21 December 1991. Alia accepts March 1, 1992 as the date for fresh elections.

BULGARIA

The official name of the country was the People's Republic of Bulgaria (*Narodna Republika Bulgaria*) from 1947 until 1990. It was renamed as simply the Republic of Bulgaria on Nov. 15, 1990.

Geographically Bulgaria is a south-eastern outpost of Slav habitation in Europe. It lies to the east of Yugoslavia, and in between Romania, across the Danube to the north, and Greece and Turkey to the south. Although Bulgaria has a sense of closeness to

Russia, it does not share a common border except in that it lies on the Black Sea coast. Bulgaria covers an area of 110,912 sq. km (less than half the size of Romania or Yugoslavia); its population of some 9,000,000 (static or falling) is likewise dwarfed by that of Romania and Yugoslavia (both over 23 million) and is slightly smaller than that of Hungary. The most populated areas are in the fertile lowlands of the Danube plain, around the capital Sofia, the Black Sea coast around the fast-growing city of Varna, and from Plovdiv south-eastwards into Upper Thrace. Most mountainous is the Rhodope massif dividing south-western Bulgaria from Greece and Macedonia; the Balkan Mountains run in a line from north of Sofia to north of Stara Zagora. Sofia, with a population of 1,100,000, is by far the largest city, three times as big as Plovdiv or Varna. Officially nearly two-thirds of the population is classified as living in urban areas, the consequence of rapid migration to the main towns since 1945.

Bulgarians comprise at least 85 per cent of the country's population and speak a South Slavic language written with the Cyrillic alphabet. Few Bulgarians live outside the country's borders (setting aside the question of the kinship of Macedonians with Bulgarians) and the main minorities issue, an important one, concerns Bulgarian Turks. There are approximately three quarters of a million Turkish speakers (a difficult figure to assess reliably in historical terms in view of the controversial programme to "assimilate" the Turkish population in the mid-1980s, and the repression of mid-1989 which provoked a huge wave of emigration to Turkey). There are also about a quarter of a million gypsies in Bulgaria. The retention of the Pirin Macedonia district meant that there were some 200,000 Macedonian-speakers in the far west of the country as recorded in the 1946 census, but their language was officially classified as a Bulgarian dialect and their sense of distinct identity discouraged strongly in the assimilation campaign of the 1960s.

Larger parts of Macedonia now within Greece and Yugoslavia had come within Bulgarian territory, however briefly, in the pre-1918 period and during World War II, and the Bulgarian communist regime under Zhivkov was given on occasion to emphasising the country's ancient Thracian cultural antecedents in such a way as to suggest that Bulgaria had a historical, cultural and ethnic claim to Macedonia as a whole. The situation contributed to fuelling the periodic revival of tension with Yugoslavia, which both feared a Bulgarian claim and objected to Bulgaria's alleged suppression of the distinct identity of its own Macedonian population. The prospect of Yugoslavia breaking up into separate republics, as was apparently inevitable in the latter part of 1991, reopened the issue of how a separate Macedonian republic would relate to its Bulgarian (and indeed its Greek) neighbours.

Muslim ethnic Bulgarians, known as Pomaks, were compelled to abandon Muslim names in an assimilation campaign in the early 1970s; most Bulgarians with religious affiliations are Eastern Orthodox Christians, like prime minister Filip Dimitrov, although atheism was officially encouraged under the communist regime.

A defeated ally of the Central Powers in World War I, Bulgaria in the inter-war period continued to harbour ambitions of recovering access to the Aegean, a consideration which dominated its foreign policy alignment and would eventually lead to Bulgaria joining World War II on the Nazi German side. The two radical parties of the left, the Agrarians and the Communists, were the largest groups in the country's first parliament from 1920, but the Communists refused to join the Agrarian-led government of Aleksandur Stamboliski, until Stamboliski was killed in a coup d'etat in June 1923. In response the Agrarians and Communists launched insurrections, which ended in failure and the flight abroad of many party activists. The Communist Party was banned from 1924, and several of its leaders were executed. Elements of the party turned to terrorism, taking part in a bomb attack spectacular even by Bulgaria's violent standards in this period when they killed government ministers and over a hundred others in Sofia cathedral in April 1925. Others reorganized and were operating legally again within three years under the name Workers' Party. A succession of coalition governments during this period ended with another coup in 1934 and a short-lived military regime; the Workers' Party was driven underground for ten years, for most of which period King Boris maintained his personal dictatorship and concentrated on finding a way to recover the territory of "Greater Bulgaria", extending to the short-lived "San Stefano frontiers" of 1878.

Technically neutral but pro-fascist in 1939-41, Bulgaria allowed the German army to occupy its territory in February 1941, then joined the Axis powers the following month (and took part in the occupation of Yugoslavia), while still seeking to avoid involvement in war with the Soviet Union. King Boris was killed in August 1943, while partisan resistance activity against German forces and the pro-German regime intensified. The German army pulled out at the end of the year and Stalin called on Bulgaria to reverse its alliance and join the war on the Soviet side—which it did only after the Red Army attack in September 1944, and only after the coup in that same month in which the partisan Fatherland Front took power. Bulgarian communists subsequently made much of their involvement in assisting Yugoslav partisans to throw out the retreating Germans. The Paris peace conference in 1946 (as confirmed in the February 1947 peace treaty) allowed Bulgaria to regain southern Dobruja, previously annexed to Romania, but otherwise maintained its pre-war borders.

Under the conditions of Red Army occupation until the end of 1947, and with the West effectively prepared to write off Bulgaria to the Soviet sphere of influence provided that Greece was not allowed to go communist, Bulgaria's communists were able gradually to consolidate their control of the Fatherland Front. Pro-Axis leaders had already been purged in February 1945, removing the possibility of an effective opposition from the historical parties of the centre and right, and the abolition of the monarchy was confirmed by referendum in September 1946. Elections the following month gave the Fatherland Front a clear majority in the parliament, and the Communists a clear majority within the Front. Georgi Dimitrov, the veteran Comintern leader, had returned to Bulgaria after the war having spent 20 years in exile (the last 10 in the Soviet Union, where other Bulgarian communists had been among Stalin's purge victims); he now became prime minister. The Agrarians were the first of the party's possible rivals to be cowed and cut down by "salami tactics", and in September 1947 the Agrarian leader Nikola Petkov was executed after a show trial in which he was accused of treason. This same procedure was used two years later to purge the communist party itself of its so-called Titoist wing, consisting principally of those who had emerged from underground activity to join the wartime partisans, as opposed to those who had been in the Soviet Union with Dimitrov. Meanwhile the Social Democrats had been merged into the communist party in 1948 (when it reverted to the name Bulgarian Communist Party rather than Workers' Party), and the Fatherland Front further streamlined by the dissolution of smaller parties; from 1949 onwards it comprised only the BCP and a subservient Bulgarian Agrarian People's Union.

Under Dimitrov, rapid steps were taken to reorder the basis of Bulgaria's primarily rural economy, starting with the nationalization of private enterprises in 1947, and the drafting of a five-year plan for socialization of the whole economy, commencing in 1949. Bulgaria in that year became a founder member of Comecon, and accepted a role primarily as agricultural producer (but also supplier of specified industrial goods, notably fork lift trucks) under the concept of the division of labour within the socialist bloc. The collectivization of agriculture was pushed through in the late 1950s, partly responding to the misguided enthusiasm of elements of the then leadership, notably Vulko Chervenkov, for the supposed achievements of Chinese communes. An attempt was made, too, at a Chinese-style "great leap forward" for rapid industrialization, the ideological basis for this being the 1959 "Zhivkov theses".

Dimitrov had died in July 1949, as the "Titoist" purges were getting under way in earnest. The party leadership passed shortly thereafter to the Stalinist Vulko Chervenkov, who was eventually outmanoeuvred by Todor Zhivkov after a protracted period of rivalry within the party. Zhivkov's victory was confirmed by his success in allying himself with the theme of destalinization, in the ascendant in the Soviet Union under Khrushchev after 1956. Indeed, under Zhivkov Bulgaria distinguished itself as the most docile of all East European countries in following the Soviet line, in its internal politics, its economic management, and its foreign policy alike.

It was the attempt to go along with Gorbachev's reformist line after 1985 which eventually proved impossible for Zhivkov. His regime, while certainly capable of brutality (the existence of concentration camps was revealed after his downfall), had the image of a relatively bland dictatorship by East European standards. His power was exercised through a regional and local network of party barons, on an almost feudal model. It was, in consequence, an inherently conservative structure, with power at all levels in the hands of a "mafia" whose primary impulses were concerned with retaining their status and advantages. Zhivkov did have, admittedly, a propensity for announcing programmes of change which would have been far-reaching, had there been the real will to see them implemented. However, he tended to suppress rather than encourage initiative and intellectual purpose within his leadership coterie, lacking the capacity of someone like Hungary's Kadar to use and channel new ideas on running the economy.

Until the mid-1970s, Bulgaria's economy exhibited at least a pattern of sustained and rapid growth. Thereafter, however, it became increasingly apparent that it was structurally dependent on Soviet support, and threatened with financial crisis (a crisis which Zhivkov sought to conceal by selling on the world market the oil which Bulgaria was able to buy at concessionary rates from the Soviet Union). Misdirected investment had gone on industrial white elephants, while safety and pollution standards were so low (in Bulgaria and also across the Danube in Romania), and the environmental and health damage so apparent, that ecologists would be in the forefront of the slow-to-emerge Bulgarian dissident groups in the latter 1980s.

In an early effort to deal with the slowdown in economic growth, the Bulgarian version of a New Economic Mechanism at the beginning of the 1980s gave some official encouragement to a limited experiment in market socialism. Bulgaria also borrowed heavily abroad from the mid-1980s onwards, with the consequence that by the end of the decade the economy was saddled with a burden of foreign debt which it could not afford to service, still less to repay. A threefold challenge was presented by Gorbachev's reforms from the mid-1980s (to which Zhivkov was the first East European leader to pay lip service, but which he remained quite unprepared to follow through). Firstly, it became clear that the Soviet Union was neither willing nor able to go on propping up the Bulgarian economy, in view of its own desperate needs. Secondly, glasnost would mean allowing criticism, although Bulgarian intellectuals had hitherto been kept unusually docile. Thirdly, a Bulgarian perestroika would entail the grave political risk of demanding real and sustained sacrifices from the Bulgarian people.

There were some changes. In 1987 Zhivkov's "July Conception" was issued, apparently taking on board the Gorbachev approach; there were campaigns against bureaucracy, corruption and inefficiency. Decentralization was a theme of the party congress in January 1988, while parliamentary elections the following month allowed voters for the first time a choice between candidates (albeit all approved by the Fatherland Front). Then came signs of a retreat, with the dismissal from the party leadership in July of two prominent reformists (one of whom, Stoyan Mikhailov, had done the work in drawing up Zhivkov's "July Conception" the year before).

By 1989, as the economic situation deteriorated, Zhivkov was ready to resort to a blatantly chauvinist tactic, launching a fresh campaign of "assimilation" and repression of Bulgaria's Turkish minority. Already in 1984-85 this card had been used, in a campaign to abolish Turkish names. Now Zhivkov tried again to stress the national identity of his regime, to play on the still widespread fears and resentments rooted in five hundred years of oppressive Turkish rule. Effectively without consulting colleagues, he clamped down hard on demonstrations against assimilation in May, and in June 1989 challenged those who regarded themselves as Turks to go to Turkey. Over 300,000 did so before Turkey closed the border; Europe's largest postwar movement of population, a disaster for Bulgaria's international image, and a setback for food production, since many of the ethnic Turks were effective producers on fertile land.

It was reputedly this episode which drove foreign minister Mladenov to the point of preparing his "palace coup". This came on Nov. 9, in the wake of further adverse international publicity for Zhivkov's regime, generated by the suppression of human rights and environmentalist demonstrations while the CSCE was holding its conference on the environment in Sofia in October. Gorbachev had been briefed by Mladenov in advance; Zhivkov was astonished to find a majority of the politburo agreeing that he should go; and, next day, the announcement was made, with Mladenov taking his place.

Unexpected as this news may have been, it was immediately taken to mean that the tide of change in Eastern Europe had now reached Bulgaria. An outpouring of pent-up anti-Zhivkov feeling, but an absence of anti-Soviet slogans, were features of the demonstrations which followed.

The BCP under Mladenov, and with reformists rapidly brought into the leadership, moved rapidly to present itself as a party with a democratic future. The party's leading role was renounced, and free elections promised; the opposition had scarcely time to make these demands an issue. Grouping themselves together under the United Democratic Front (UDF), the disparate strands of the opposition did manage to win some concessions at the round table talks in early 1990, but were clearly not ready (despite conspicuous US assistance) for the election campaign in June. The communists, meanwhile, had reconstituted themselves as a democratic party of the left, proclaimed a commitment to market economics, voted in Mladenov as interim President, with Aleksandur Lilov becoming party leader, and adopted the name Bulgarian Socialist Party (BSP) in a symbolic break with the period before Nov. 9. The BSP won the elections—the only former communist party to achieve this in Eastern Europe (until the Albanian elections of 1991), and an apparent sign that Bulgaria was "bucking the trend".

Over the succeeding months, however, the real battle was joined. The BSP, in the face of continuing economic collapse, a sustained campaign of demonstrations and a growing independent trade union movement, was unable to govern effectively. If it was to construct a credible economic programme, one which would allow it to borrow internationally, it needed some co-operation from the opposition. The UDF refused that co-operation, protesting that the BSP, still entrenched in power, was simply seeking a way to weather the crisis. If it did so, the hour might pass for taking on the power of the *nomenklatura*, the officials, media chiefs, industrial managers and professionals who had flourished under the communist regime. And so the UDF held out for a non-BSP government, for fresh elections in 1991, for the exposure of corruption, and for the confiscation of party property.

It was brinkmanship, and it put back, by critical months, the start of market economic reforms in earnest. However, thanks to an all-party agreement at the beginning of 1991, an interim coalition under non-party prime minister Dimitur Popov was able to begin real steps to reshape the economy—although an acute crisis over the condition of outmoded nuclear power stations made an overhaul of the energy sector an even higher priority, and the threat of a nuclear disaster added to an already almost impossible agenda on the environmental front.

Despite the narrowness of their eventual election victory in October 1991, the UDF was in power at the end of the year. Bulgaria had its first ever post-war government without communists (or in this case ex-communists). The former UDF chairman Zhelyu Zhelev, who had been trying to portray a less partisan image in his role as interim president for the last seventeen months, was the clear favourite to win direct presidential elections in January 1992.

Stripped of the trappings of office, the socialists remained a force in opposition, far more so than elsewhere in Eastern Europe, but the moment had passed when they might have thought they could ride out the revolution. Legislation had gone through by the end of 1991 on the confiscation of BSP property; and, in another and more world-shaking revolution, communism had collapsed in Russia itself. The upheaval there in 1991 was of immense significance for all the formerly communist countries of Europe, but nowhere more directly so than in Bulgaria, where the communist regime had been the most closely linked to its Soviet parent, and where its socialist successors had at one time seemed the most likely to hold on to political power.

The principal personalities of Communist rule

Todor **Zhivkov** (b. 1911). A printer and son of a peasant, he won respect as a partisan fighter and organized the coup of September 1944 by which the Fatherland Front took power. Brought into the top party leadership by Chervenkov in 1954, he became the dominant figure by exploiting his position as first secretary and his talent for convincing the Soviet leadership of his malleability. By 1962 he was prime minister as well as party leader, and made the next three decades the Zhivkov era in Bulgaria, playing off or cutting down possible rivals, while always remaining a loyal follower of the Moscow line. Gorbachev, however, he apparently failed to convince, especially when, with the economy deteriorating and with few real results from his grand reforming projects, he clamped down on any Bulgarian *glasnost* and launched the fierce anti-Turkish campaign of mid-1989. Apparently astonished by the "palace coup" which toppled him that November, he believed at first that he would go into honourable retirement. This hope was soon dashed by the vehemence with which demonstrators denounced him. Nepotism, corruption and repression were laid at his door and he was arrested, soon to be further damned by revelations of the use of concentration camps under his regime—but attempts to make him stand trial were abandoned in 1991 because of his age and ill health.

Georgi **Dimitrov** (1882-1949). A unionist, revolutionary socialist, and member of parliament from the age of 21, Dimitrov was involved with the Comintern from 1919. Forced to flee Bulgaria after the abortive 1923 insurrection, he exemplified the international revolutionary activist of the 1920s. Arrested by the Nazis in 1933 and charged with involvement in the *Reichstag* fire, he made himself a celebrity by his defiant defence and acquittal. He was Comintern executive secretary from 1934 and based in Moscow until his return to Bulgaria to lead the Fatherland Front in 1944. In this role, and as prime minister from 1946, Dimitrov was the founding father of the communist regime, and ruthless in his elimination of opponents and possible rivals, giving way to Stalinists of lesser stature only because of his illness two months before he died in a Moscow sanatorium in 1949. Venerated by the regime and placed in a mausoleum in Sofia, Dimitrov's body was removed and cremated in July 1990, when an unexpectedly large crowd turned out.

Petur **Mladenov** (b. 1936). Born into a peasant family in Toshevtsi in 1936, Mladenov (whose father died fighting with the partisans) went to Sofia University in the late 1950s and then to the Moscow State Institute of International Relations. As foreign minister from 1971 until 1989, he became acutely conscious of how Bulgaria's international reputation was suffering from Zhivkov's nationalistic repression of ethnic Turks in mid-1989. He prepared the way carefully, both with Gorbachev and with fellow reformists in the party, for a surprise "palace coup" which ousted Zhivkov on Nov. 9-10. Mladenov himself then took on temporarily both the party leadership and the chairmanship of the State Council, resigning the former post (and thereby denoting the separation of party and state) before the party congress the following January. In April 1990 he secured election as interim state president, but resigned in disgrace when opponents produced video evidence that he had suggested using tanks against a December 1989 pro-democracy demonstration.

Chudomir **Aleksandrov** (b. 1936). Born in 1936, Aleksandrov had established himself by the mid-1980s as the politburo member most likely to spearhead political reform, but was then abruptly dismissed from the party leadership in July 1988 for criticising Zhivkov. Although not reinstated immediately on Zhivkov's overthrow in November 1989, he reappeared briefly in government as a Deputy Premier in Lukanov's BSP administration until the 1990 elections.

Constitutional changes

The so-called "Dimitrov" constitution or "people's democracy constitution" introduced in 1947 was made subject to a number of amendments in 1971, and was thereafter known as the "Zhivkov constitution". It provided amongst other things for increased powers for the President (a post which Zhivkov then took on).

The country was governed from April 1990 under interim constitutional arrangements, until the adoption on July 12, 1991, of a new constitution. This defined Bulgaria as a parliamentary republic and as a "democratic, constitutional and welfare state"; it also defined the proportional representation system for the subsequent elections, and required the direct election of the state president.

Position and status of communists

Party name

The name Bulgarian Communist Party (*Bulgarska Komunisticheska Partiya*), used by the ruling communists after the absorbtion of the Social Democrats in 1948, had first been used in 1919-24 by what had been the Bulgarian Workers' Social Democratic Party (Narrow Socialists), the designation of the communists after the 1903 social democrat party schism. During the inter-war period, after the BCP was banned in 1924, there had been a legal Workers' Party in 1927-34, and thereafter an illegal Bulgarian Workers' Party (Communist), many of whose leaders were in exile in the Soviet Union. This name had been retained within the Fatherland Front from 1943 to 1948.

The Fatherland Front continued to exist throughout the period of communist power as a nominal alliance of the communists, the Bulgarian Agrarian People's Union and "independents", with a common list presenting the only candidates at each election.

After the overthrow of Zhivkov and the introduction of a multi-party system, the BCP's congress in January-February 1990 decided that the party needed a new name symbolizing the "clean break", and the title Bulgarian Socialist Party (BSP) was adopted in early April 1990 after a referendum among party members. Petur Dertliev, the veteran Social Democrat and long-term opponent of the communist regime, failed to prevent them adopting this name and had thus to differentiate his own party as the Bulgarian Social Democratic Party.

A small "rump" Bulgarian Communist Party continued in existence, while a group of some 30 dissenting radical reformers from the old BCP formed an Alternative Socialist Party.

In November 1991, after losing its parliamentary majority in the October elections, a BSP group within the Assembly decided to designate itself as the Parliamentary Union for Social Democracy.

Legal status

The constitutional right to a "leading role" was renounced by the BCP central committee on Dec. 13, 1990, and the National Assembly voted through on Jan. 15 the change to the relevant Article 1 of the constitution. The BCP and its successor BSP remained legal and full participants in the political system, although there were minority voices (notably Ahmed Dogan, the ethnic Turkish lader of the Movement for Rights and Freedoms) calling for the party as a whole, and not just the disgraced Zhivkov and some of his close associates, to be "put in the dock".

Workplace organization

Under pressure from the opposition in the round table discussions, the party in February 1990 conceded the abolition of workplace cells and those in the armed forces, colleges and media. Organization was henceforth to be on the basis of residential area units. A bill passed in October 1990 debarred members of the army, police and judiciary from party membership.

Union organization under the communist regime had been monopolized by the BCP-controlled Central Council of Trade Unions, which was reconstituted on a separate basis in February 1990 as the Confederation of Independent Bulgarian Trade Unions, while the opposition independent union movement *Podkrepa* also established itself.

Party membership

Party numbers under Zhivkov had fluctuated, as a consequence of the various purges, generally somewhere in excess of one million. A figure of 984,000 in early 1990 had dwindled by November 1991 to 476,840 BSP members.

Party assets

The BSP in government delayed dealing with the controversial issue of party property, suffering unpopularity and the anger of demonstrators who set fire to its Sofia headquarters in August 1990. The UDF, once in government itself in late 1991, brought in legislation on the confiscation of party property which, by the end of the year, had been passed but which the BSP was seeking to refer to the constitutional court.

Ideological orientation

From the time of its first post-Zhivkov congress in early 1990, the party declared itself "destalinized" and no longer Marxist-Leninist (although still Marxist), emphasizing a commitment to multi-partyism and, in the economic sphere, to a "socially oriented market economy". Within its concept of "democratic unity" it recognized within the party the existence of "different political tendencies". The principal such tendencies were the predominant group around party leader Lilov (and his successor Videnov), whose formulation for the BSP was "a modern left-wing socialist party", and a minority of more reform-oriented social democrats. Aleksandur Tomov, leader of the radical Movement for Democratic Socialism (Demos) within the BSP, who had stood against Lilov for the party chairmanship in September 1990, was, as deputy premier, the highest-ranking party member in Popov's coalition "government of national stability" from December 1990 until the party's election defeat the following October. Georgi Pirinski was the unsuccessful social democrat faction candidate for the chairmanship in December 1991.

Electoral significance

The electoral monopoly of the Fatherland Front before 1990 ensured the BSP some 270 seats in the 400-member People's Assembly, and the Front of near 100 per cent support in what were recorded as near 100 per cent voter turnouts.

The BSP won an overall majority with 211 out of 400 seats, and 47.15 per cent of the vote, at the Grand National Assembly election in June 1990. It fell back to 106 out of 240 seats with 33 per cent of the vote in October 1991.

Principal parties in the post-communist period

The **United Democratic Front** (UDF) was formed in December 1990 to bring together the disparate strands of the democratic opposition to BCP rule. Committed to a rapid switch to a market economy, and heavily and overtly supported by US advisers at the June elections, it was nevertheless unable to mount a sufficient challenge to the BSP outside urban areas, and finished in second place with 144 out of 400 seats (and just under 38 per cent of the vote). Thereafter it seized the initiative, however, in preventing the BSP from retaining its power and influence. A notable feature of the post-election period was the creation of the so-called "cities of truth" by demonstrators encamped outside government offices, in Sofia and elsewhere. The first UDF chairman, the conciliatory-mannered sociologist Zhelyu Zhelev, was elected interim President in August 1990, after Mladenov's disgrace and a deadlock in the Assembly between mutually unacceptable BSP and opposition-backed candidates. Petur Beron, a biologist and a founder member of the environmentalist Ecoglasnost, succeeded as UDF chairman upon Zhelev's resignation (to become President) in August. In December 1990 Beron himself resigned, and was replaced as UDF chairman by the Green leader Filip Dimitrov, amid allegations from within UDF ranks (notably by the *Podkrepa* leader Trenchev) that Beron had acted as a police informer under the former communist regime. Beron had been criticized for supporting UDF participation in a coalition, but despite his departure the UDF did support the coalition formed by non-party prime minister Popov, until the October 1991 elections, when it won the highest percentage vote (34.36 per cent) and the most seats (110 out of 240) and went on to form a minority government.

Podkrepa (Support), the independent trade union founded and led by Konstantin Trenchev, was a powerful force in bringing the country to a state of effective paralysis and demanding the rooting out of BSP power bases. It had worked initially underground, and then affiliated with the UDF, later opposing any involvement in coalition talks with the BSP. The Confederation of Independent Trade Unions elected as its chairman in February 1990 Kryustu Petkov, who also belonged to the independent Podkrepa Labour Council.

While Filip Dimitrov took on the UDF leadership as its first prime minister, other Greens were closer to the Federation of Democracy Clubs, which formed a **Liberal Party** in November 1991 with Petko Simeonov as its chairman.

The **Bulgarian Social Democratic Party** won only one seat at the June 1990 elections. Its leader Petur Dertliev, put forward by the UDF for the country's presidency in July, was strongly opposed by the BSP, which eventually agreed to vote instead for the UDF chairman Zhelev.

The **Bulgarian Agrarian People's Union** (BAPU or BZNS) led by Victor Vulkov declined to participate in the BSP government in early 1990, but also resisted the idea of merger with the UDF. It contested the elections as a separate party, winning 16 seats in 1990 but losing representation altogether in 1991, after a spell in the coalition "pluralist" government. In July 1990, backed initially by BSP votes, Vulkov had come within three votes of election as interim president, before the successful compromise choice of Zhelyu Zhelev.

The **Nicola Petkov faction** of the Agrarians, led by Milan Drentchev, broke away from the main BAPU or BZNS after the fall of the communist regime and allied itself at first with the UDF, but had split away again by the time of the 1991 elections, as part of a complicated realignment among the factions competing for a dwindling number of Agrarian votes.

The **Movement for Rights and Freedoms** was formed to defend the rights of ethnic Turks in the face of the Bulgarian nationalist feeling whipped up in the latter years of communist rule. It put on a strong showing in both the June 1990 and the October 1991 elections (emerging as the third largest group in parliament on both occasions), while having to counter the repeated suggestion that it should be debarred as an ethnic-based and militarized body.

The post-communist political leaders

Zhelyu **Zhelev** (b. 1935). President on an interim basis from August 1990, Zhelev was expected to win a mandate to continue in office in the January 1992 direct elections. He had first come to prominence as a sociologist critical of the communist regime in the 1970s, emerging in late 1989 as a leader of the UDF, but was sufficiently conciliatory in manner to win BSP backing as a compromise candidate for the Bulgarian presidency after Mladenov's disgrace. Keeping himself to some extent above partisan quarrels, he helped steer through the formation of an interim coalition under the non-party leadership of Dimitur Popov in December 1990, and the construction of a programme for reforms which would create a market economy.

Filip **Dimitrov**. A former academic and vice-president of the Greens within the UDF, Dimitrov became UDF chairman in December 1990 and prime minister, at the age of 36, after the October 1991 elections. An Orthodox Christian on the right wing of the UDF, he had conducted an energetic campaign, and set out his priorities as economic stabilization, the control of inflation, more rapid privatization, and the confiscation of BSP party property.

Dimitur **Popov** (b. 1935). Prime minister in the transitional government from December 1990 until the October 1991 elections, he was formerly a judge in Sofia and was chosen as premier as a non-party compromise candidate.

Andrei **Lukanov** (b. 1938). The reform communist appointed as prime minister in the first post-Zhivkov government in 1990, Lukanov had backed Mladenov's "palace coup" the previous November, and was seen as a down-to-earth political operator as well as a well-educated technocrat and linguist. The son of a former politburo member, he was born in the Soviet Union, educated at the Moscow State Institute for International Relations, elected to parliament in 1976, and appointed by Zhivkov in 1987 as minister of foreign economic relations. It was to Lukanov that the responsibility fell, after the 1990 elections, to try to bring the opposition into a governing coalition under his leadership; an attempt which he eventually abandoned to form another short-lived and hamstrung BSP-based government in the autumn of 1990. At the December 1991 party congress he was dropped from the party's supreme council.

Aleksandur **Lilov** (b. 1933). The BSP party leader from early in 1990 (i.e. elected at the January conference, before the name change from the original BCP), Lilov withstood a challenge from more radical reformers to win re-election at the September congress, but stepped down in December 1991, with the party now confined to opposition, and with Zhan Videnov as his designated heir. A Moscow-educated literature graduate from a poor peasant family, he had become a member of the BCP politburo in 1974, but was effectively sidelined by Zhivkov in 1983-89 as head of the Institute for Modern Social Theories.

Zhan **Videnov** (b. 1959). The successor to Lilov as BSP leader in December 1991, Videnov was elected with his predecessor's second-round support as a younger generation representative of the left socialist wing, against the challenge from Georgi Pirinski of the more reform-minded social democratic wing. He was a graduate of the Moscow Institute of International Relations and a specialist in foreign economic relations.

Ahmed **Dogan**. A philosophy professor in his mid-30s, Dogan became leader of the Movement for Rights and Freedoms, the political voice of Bulgaria's embattled ethnic Turkish minority. Dogan also proved an especially vocal advocate of "putting the whole BSP in the dock" for the crimes of the Zhivkov era.

Elections

Legislature

Under the communist regime a unicameral National Assembly with 400 members was elected for a five-year term from a single list of candidates, by universal adult suffrage (with turnouts generally recorded as just under 100 per cent). The last two such elections were in 1982 and 1986, after which date changes were made to allow voters a choice of approved candidates.

The electoral system for multi-party elections on June 10 and 17, 1990, for a 400-seat Grand National Assembly, was agreed at the round table talks. It provided for half the seats to be elected in single-member constituencies (81 of which required a second round run-off on June 17 because no candidate gained an overall majority), and half to be distributed among the parties on a proportional representation basis, with a 4 per cent minimum threshold. Each voter had two votes. Turnouts were recorded as 90.8 per cent of the 6,977,000 eligible voters on the first round, and 84 per cent in the second round run-offs.

For the 1991 elections (originally scheduled for Sept. 29 and then rearranged for Oct. 13) the July 1991 constitution established that there would be a 240-seat Assembly, with all candidates elected on a proportional representation basis, parties being again required to pass a 4 per cent minimum threshold. A total of 38 parties and groups put up candidates, and the turnout was recorded at 83.87 per cent.

Presidency

The 1971 constitutional arrangements provided for the National Assembly to elect a State Council, whose president (Zhivkov) was in effect head of state. On Nov. 17, 1989, Mladenov was elected to this office in place of the deposed Zhivkov.

In the interim pending agreement on a new constitution, Mladenov was elected President by the Assembly on April 3, 1990. His disgrace and resignation in July meant another such election, in which a two-thirds majority was required, this time by the new Assembly. The BSP and UDF put up mutually unacceptable candidates (respectively Chavdar Kyuranov and Petur Dertliev) and the agrarians put forward their leader Viktor Vulkov. There were five inconclusive rounds of voting on July (respectively Chavdar Kyuranov and Petur Dertliev) and the agrarians put forward their leader Viktor Vulkov. There were five inconclusive rounds of voting on July 24-30. Finally, on Aug. 1, the compromise candidacy of the UDF chairman Zhelev was unopposed and he won 284 of the 389 votes cast.

The July 1991 constitution provided for the direct election of the President, and polling was scheduled for Jan. 12, 1992, with a second round on the following Sunday if no candidate secured an overall majority.

General election results

June 1990 National Assembly elections		
Party	percentage*	seats
BSP	47.15	211
UDF	37.84	144
MRF	6.03	23
Agrarians	8.03	16
Others		5
Total		400
October 1991 National Assembly elections		
BSP	33.14	106
UDF	34.36	110
MRF	7.55	24
Agrarians	3.86	0
Others	21.09	0
Total		240

*Percentages in June 1990 are distributed only among parties qualifying for proportional representation seats by exceeding the 4 per cent threshold; other smaller parties could,and did, win constituency seats.

Governments in the post-Zhivkov period

Three communist-led or BSP-led goverments were formed after the fall of Zhivkov. The first of them, approved by the National Assembly on Nov. 17, 1989 (i.e. the day on which it also approved Mladenov as President), was headed by the existing prime minister Atanasov. The second, headed by Lukanov, was the all-communist govern-ment sworn in on Feb. 8, 1990, after the UDF had refused to participate and the former front parties had also withdrawn. Following the 1990 elections, this government resigned on Aug. 22, as the now renamed BSP sought in vain to build a coalition with the opposition parties. When it abandoned this in September, Lukanov formed his

The first non-socialist government was that headed by the unaffiliated Dimitur Popov; its composition was approved by the Assembly on Dec. 20, 1990.

The unexpected longevity of this transitional government reflected the time taken to draft a new Constitution and hold fresh elections. After the UDF's narrow election victory, it formed its first government, which took office on Nov. 8, 1991, with Filip Dimitrov as prime minister and Stoyan Ganev as deputy premier responsible for foreign affairs. Ivan Kostov was foreign minister and Yordan Sokolov interior minister, with Dimitur Ludzhev in charge of defence.

CHRONOLOGY

9 September 1944. The anti-fascist Fatherland Front, formed in 1943 by the communists, left agrarians and social democrats, takes power as the Red Army enters Bulgarian territory.

March 1946. The Fatherland Front forms a new government following the resignation of Georgiev.

May 1946. Bulgaria retains the territory of southern Dobruja, previously annexed by Romania, in the settlement agreed at the Paris peace conference.

8 September 1946. Bulgaria votes to become a republic in a referendum which overwhelmingly rejects restoration of the monarchy; the People's Republic constitution is adopted formally in December of the following year.

October 1946. Elections for the Grand National Assembly produce a victory for the ruling Fatherland Front, with the communists taking 277 out of 465 seats and the Front as a whole winning 364; the following month Georgi Dimitrov forms a new government.

23 September 1947. The Agrarian leader Nikola Petkov is executed as a traitor after a show trial.

December 1947. Soviet forces withdraw from Bulgarian territory under the terms of the peace settlement.

August 1948. The merger of the Social Democrats into the Communist Party marks a further stage in the consolidation of that party's grip on the Fatherland Front, which is completed early the following year when the smaller parties dissolve themselves, leaving only the Bulgarian Communist Party (BCP) and its compliant junior partner the Bulgarian Agrarian People's Union (BAPU).

December 1948. Dimitrov expounds his theory of people's democracy as a model for Eastern European communist regimes.

April 1949. The party is purged of "nationalist deviationists" led by Traicho Kostov, who is tried and hanged in December allegedly for plotting with Tito; he is rehabilitated in 1956 following the first criticisms of Stalinism by the Soviet leadership under Khrushchev.

2 July 1949. Death of the veteran communist leader Georgi Dimitrov.

March 1954. Todor Zhivkov becomes party first secretary, with his predecessor Vulko Chervenkov as premier; these two represent respectively the Khrushchevite and the more hardline Stalinist (and pro-Chinese) wings of the party over the succeeding years.

January 1959. Plans for full agricultural collectivization are announced, reflecting Chervenkov's admiration for the apparent achievements of the Chinese communes.

1961-62. Zhivkov confirms his supremacy in the party by ousting Chervenkov and others, and takes over as prime minister from Anton Yugov, who is accused of responsibility for the execution of Kostov in 1949. Zhivkov's long period in power is characterized by loyalty to the prevailing Soviet regime; he even put to Khrushchev the suggestion that Bulgaria might join the Soviet Union.

April 1965. Elements within the army attempt unsuccessfully to mount a coup apparently directed simply at the removal of Zhivkov from the leadership.

1971. Zhivkov takes over the state presidency (Chairman of the State Council), Stanko Todorov becomes prime minister and Petur Mladenov foreign minister.

June 1980. The first laws are introduced to permit the formation of joint ventures with foreign capitalists.

January 1982. Under the so-called New Economic Mechanism, enterprises are instructed to be guided by market pressures with the objective of becoming financially self-supporting, with a minimum of central planning (although in practice the economy remained largely directed by the centre).

July 1987. Zhivkov, who has in recent months begun to take an apparently reformist stance and to advocate liberalization and decentralization of the economy, issues the "July Conception". At least on paper, this seems more far-reaching than the Soviet programme propounded by Gorbachev, but it remains largely unimplemented rhetoric, although causing a measure of administrative confusion. By the end of the year new election rules have been approved to offer voters a choice between different candidates, but all candidates must still be approved by the Fatherland Front.

16 January 1988. The dissident Independent Society for Human Rights is formed.

February 1988. Elections allow a choice between candidates for the first time.

July 1988. Two prominent reformists, Chudomir Aleksandrov and Stoyan Mikhailov, are dismissed from the politburo and party secretariat respectively.

February 1989. *Podkrepa* (Support) is formed as the first independent trade union, initially consisting mainly of intellectuals and too cautious to advocate the use of strikes.

May-August 1989. Hundreds of thousands of ethnic Turks are effectively expelled into Turkey after troops have crushed a mass demonstration called to resist an official campaign to deny the separate ethnic identity of Bulgarian Turks in the name of assimilation.

16 October 1989. The CSCE's environmental conference in Sofia gives opposition human rights campaigners and Ecoglasnost access to international publicity, especially when 40 Ecoglasnost environmental activists are beaten up and arrested on Oct. 26; a demonstration on Nov. 3, however, passes off peacefully.

26 October 1989. The resignation of Petur Mladenov, foreign minister since 1971, is offered but rejected; it reveals, however, that the party leadership faces an internal crisis over its response to the still small but growing wave of demands for real reform.

10 November 1989. Zhivkov is persuaded to resign, following careful maneouvering by his opponents on the party central committee; he is replaced as party general secretary by Petur Mladenov. Mladenov had apparently discussed the plot to depose Zhivkov when he saw Gorbachev in Moscow en route for a trip to China earlier in November.

18 November 1989. Large crowds demonstrate in Sofia, celebrating the fall of Zhivkov and pressing for further reform.

December 1989. Formation of the United Democratic Front (UDF).

11 December 1989. The communist government puts forward proposals for free elections, ending the communist party's monopoly on power.

January 1990. There are large demonstrations of opposition to the decision to restore minority rights to ethnic Turks, announced on Dec. 29 by the government and backed by the main opposition UDF alliance.

15 January 1990. Parliament votes to repeal constitutional provisions guaranteeing a leading role to the communist party.

16 January 1990. Round table talks begin, in which the UDF delegation is led by Zhelyu Zhelev and Petur Beron.

29 January 1990. It is announced that Zhivkov is in prison awaiting trial for abuse of power, embezzlement, and inciting racial hatred.

30 January-2 February 1990. The BCP holds its first party congress since the fall of Zhivkov, and ends by affirming that the party will remain Marxist, but committing itself to a reformist programme and electing Aleksandur Lilov as its chairman, heading a new 17-member presidium.

8 February 1990. After the UDF refuses to join a broad coalition government, a new interim communist government is formed (ironically, the first ever entirely communist administration, since the junior partner of the communist years, the Bulgarian Agrarian People's Union, has now withdrawn). The government is headed by Andrei Lukanov.

25 February 1990. The biggest opposition rally in Sofia to date attracts some 200,000 participants, demanding postponement of the proposed elections at least until late 1990 to give time for the UDF to organise itself as an effective political party.

5 March 1990. A bill legalising the use of Muslim names is endorsed unanimously by the Assembly and takes effect on March 13.

3 April 1990. Mladenov is elected formally as interim President by the parliament, which then dissolves itself pending elections scheduled for June under the newly approved electoral and political parties laws.

3 April 1990. The communists adopt the new name of Bulgarian Socialist Party (BSP), intending thereby to denote a clean break with "the dictatorship of the time before 10 November 1989".

June 10 and 17, 1990. The first free multi-party elections leave the former communist BSP with 211 seats in a 400-member Grand National Assembly, while the opposition UDF alliance wins 144. Amid protests over alleged BSP intimidation, and claims that there was widespread fraud, the BSP is unable to bring the opposition into a broad alliance, and no government is formed for over three months.

6 July 1990. Mladenov, accused of urging the use of tanks against demonstrators on Dec. 14, and repudiated even by the BSP after a videotape of the event is declared authentic, is forced to resign as President.

1 August 1990. After repeated rounds of deadlocked voting in the new Assembly, Zhelyu Zhelev of the UDF is elected unanimously as a compromise candidate.

26 August 1990. Rioting in Sofia ends with the burning of the BSP party headquarters.

September 1990. Bulgaria joins the IMF; food rationing is extended to the capital.

20 September 1990. Andrei Lukanov finally forms a government, comprising BSP members and two independents, which survives for only two months in a state of near paralysis and in the face of mounting opposition protest.

22-25 September 1990. A congress of the BSP, which is dominated by controversy over the party's inability to govern effectively, ends with the re-election of Aleksandur Lilov as party leader, although he has been accused by radicals of having insufficient commitment to reform .

15 November 1990. Members of the Grand National Assembly vote overwhelmingly in favour of changing the country's official name so that it is no longer the People's Republic but simply the Republic of Bulgaria.

29 November 1990. Andrei Lukanov resigns as prime minister. The student-led protests on the streets of the capital in recent weeks, and the opposition boycott of parliament since Nov. 23, have by now been backed up by a general strike, called originally by the independent *Podkrepa* trade union organisation and then endorsed by the Confederation of Independent Trade Unions.

December 1990. A coalition government is finally formed under the non-party leadership of Dimitur Popov, pending fresh elections.

3 January 1991. An all-party agreement is reached on a peaceful transition period for the completion of a new constitution and the passage of essential reforms in the economic sphere.

1 February 1991. Subsidies are removed and prices increase dramatically for basic foodstuffs, fuel and transport, under the market economic reform programme

endorsed by the Assembly the previous day, which is subsequently backed by the IMF.

25 February 1991. Parliament passes a land reform law stipulating the return of communist-expropriated land and property to its former owners. Zhivkov's trial begins, but is adjourned in April, and again indefinitely in June, because of his poor state of health.

5 June 1991. Parliament votes out the plan to hold a referendum in July on whether to revert from a republic to a monarchy.

9 June 1991. Parliament passes legislation on financial compensation for the victims of communist rule.

13 June 1991. The unions sign an agreement undertaking not to call further general strikes, after receiving guarantees about minimum wages and the payment of unemployment benefit.

28 June 1991. The nine-member COMECON organisation is formally dissolved at a meeting in Budapest.

1 July 1991. The Warsaw Treaty Organisation or Warsaw Pact is formally dissolved by its six remaining members - the Soviet Union, Bulgaria, Hungary, Poland, Romania and Czechoslovakia.

12 July 191. A new constitution is approved by the Assembly and comes into effect the following day; it provides for direct presidential elections, which are subsequently scheduled for 12 January 1991.

July 1991. Profound domestic and international environmental concern about nuclear reactor safety in outmoded and ill-maintained Soviet-designed power stations prompts the announcement of the temporary closure from September of one of the six reactors at Kozloduy, the source of an estimated 40 per cent of Bulgaria's electricity.

13 October 1991. Legislative elections leave the UDF as the largest single group in the Grand National Assembly with 110 out of 240 seats; the BSP is narrowly beaten into second place, with 106 seats.

8 November 1981. Filip Dimitrov forms a UDF minority administration, the first government without communist representation since 1944.

14-19 December 1991. The BSP, holding its 40th congress but the first since its relegation to opposition status, disappoints its reformist wing by rejecting a social-democratic orientation and by electing a new leadership headed by Zhan Videnov, regarded as a relative hardliner despite his being, at 32, a member of the young generation. Aleksandur Lilov had withdrawn from the leadership contest in Videnov's favour after the first round.

CZECHOSLOVAKIA

The country's official name was the Czechoslovak Socialist Republic)
(*Ceskoslovenská Socialistická Republika*) from July 1960 . It was
renamed after the 1989 revolution, becoming the Czech and Slovak
Federative Republic on April 20, 1990.

Czechoslovakia is a land-locked country in central Europe comprising two republics covering a total area of 127,881 sq. km. It is rather larger than its south-eastern neighbour, Hungary; its population, of 15,600,000, is somewhat smaller than that of the former East Germany and less than half that of its northern neighbour Poland, but significantly larger than either Austria or Hungary. The Bohemian Massif in the west and the Morava valley characterize the Czech Lands (Bohemia and Moravia); Slovakia includes the Carpathian Mountains and the southern lowlands and fertile levels along the Danube. Praha (Prague), the Czech and federal capital, is by far the largest city with a population in excess of 1,200,000, about three times that of either Bratislava (the Slovak capital) or Brno. Other main towns are Ostrava, Kosice and Plzen (Pilsen); three quarters of the population is defined as urban, although Slovakia has remained to a significant extent an agrarian society.

In ethnic terms the country is divided between the majority Czechs (about 63 per cent of the total) and the Slovaks (about 31 per cent), both speaking related West Slavic languages and both using the Roman as opposed to the Cyrillic alphabet. Minority groups are principally the ethnic Hungarians, some 600,000 in number, and about half as many gypsies; there are small minorities of Germans, Poles and Ukrainians (Ruthenians). Religion is one factor in the differing identities of the Czech and Slovak republics, with the Roman Catholic Church concentrated in Slovakia (and, with about 3,700,000 members, by far the largest denomination and of growing importance). Other main Christian denominations are Hussites (400,000), the Orthodox Church claiming 200,000 members, the presbyterian Czech Brethren and the Slovak Lutherans. There are now only an estimated 6,000 Jews in Prague.

Unlike other countries in Eastern Europe, Czechoslovakia's experience of democratic government in the inter-war period was a successful one, even if it was not always quite as glorious a period as Czechs under communist rule were tempted to think, when looking back. With first the national hero Thomas Masaryk as President, then (from 1935) under Edward Benes, coalition governments generally embraced most or all principal parties, except the Communists; the proliferation of parties in parliament, however, introduced an element of instability in the coalition system. Prague was the focal point, and northern Bohemia the predominant economic power, and the expectations of autonomy which many Slovaks had cherished at the creation of the state of Czechoslovakia were to a large extent brushed aside in the early postwar years. Among Slovaks, as well as among minority Germans, there grew a sense of resentment that they were being marginalized, especially when economic depression made this more acute in the early 1930s.

The threat from Nazi Germany, expressed in Hitler's insistent demand for annexation of the Sudetenland, led directly to Czechoslovakia's dismemberment in 1938-39, the British and French governments having betrayed Benes's expectations by their appeasement policy at Munich in September 1938.

Germany, having annexed the Sudety region, carved up the rest after March 1939 (Hungary having taken part of eastern Carpathia, and Poland having annexed the Czech bit of Teschen). Slovakia, where the late 1930s had seen the growth of "clerico-fascism", was handed over to a pro-German regime which declared an independent Slovak state. In the remaining Czech lands Germany established the Protectorate of Bohemia-Moravia, whose head, Reinhard Heydrich, was assassinated in 1942, provoking brutal reprisals.

Benes, rather than embarking on what would clearly be a nationally suicidal attempt to meet the German army in battle after Munich, had fled to London, where his Czechoslovak National Committee was officially recognized by the Allies in 1941 as the country's government. The Communist leaders, meanwhile, their party banned after Munich, had gone into exile in the Soviet Union.

It was principally the Red Army which liberated Czechoslovakia, although this was preceded by an unsuccessful Slovak uprising in August-October 1944 and assisted by the Prague Uprising in May 1945, an episode which enabled the Czechs at least to feel they had liberated their own capital, even if their resistance record as a whole had been muted. The US army under Gen. Patten, driving eastwards, also entered Czechoslovakia before the end of the war, liberating Plzen.

CPCz general secretary Klement Gottwald, meeting with Benes in Moscow in March 1945, was able to drive a favourable bargain in establishing the immediate programme for a coalition National Front government. The coalition was to have six participating parties, balancing left and right groups from the pre-war party scene, but including most of the principal elements except the Agrarians and the Slovak Populists (both banned for wartime transgressions against the national interest). Its programme would include a commitment to nationalized ownership of key industries and finance (much of it, recovered from German hands, being in any case already in state rather than its pre-war private ownership), expanded welfare provision, and a Soviet-oriented foreign policy. There would be equality for Czechs and Slovaks, and the German and Hungarian minorities were to be expelled (a policy which was carried through comprehensively in 1945-46 regarding the former, whereas with Hungary there was a more limited and partial exchange of population). Postwar territorial changes involved the return of what had been stripped away in 1938-39, but the incorporation of Carpathian Ruthenia, on the eastern border, into the Ukraine (the various Soviet acquisitions in this area making it for the first time a direct neighbour of Czechoslovakia). The National Front government arrived in Prague on May 10, 1945.

At the time of the general elections in May 1946, the stock of the Communists was riding high, and they won 38 per cent of the vote (doing particularly well in the more industrialized Czech lands), making them the largest party. This was not a by-product of Soviet occupation and strong-arm tactics; the Red Army, and US forces in the west, had been withdrawn simultaneously, by agreement, the previous December, and a plan to move Red Army troops through the country towards the Elbe during the polling period was postponed after an explanation that this timing was a coincidence and an oversight. Nor was the measure of Communist success attributable to intimidation at the polls, which were entirely peaceful. Rather it reflected a sense that liberal capitalism had been shown to be costly in social terms in the 1930s, and that the Western liberal democracies had betrayed the country in 1938, whereas the Soviet Union had liberated it in 1945. It also corresponded to what Benes himself identified as a European tide running towards socialism, after the experiences of the war and the need to rebuild shattered economies. The CPCz, the strongest communist party in the world at the time apart from the Soviet party itself, also proved itself particularly well supported in what Marxist theory defined as its natural constituency, the industrial proletariat, more developed here than in other East European countries (apart from eastern Germany).

Pressure from Stalin in Moscow, rather than the undoubtedly growing frictions of the Communist-led coalition, precipitated the takeover of full power in the February 1948 "Prague coup" in response to the resignation of non-socialist ministers. This was rapidly followed by a new constitution, defining the country as a people's democracy, and the reduction of the surviving parties to mere ciphers within a subservient Front. Gottwald, President from June 1948, then turned on any possible opponents or rivals within the CPCz, using show trials, purges and executions in the early 1950s and deploying the full battery of charges of Titoism, Trotskyism, bourgeois nationalism and treason. Zionism was added to the charge sheet for dealing with Jewish intellectuals in the party leadership. Gottwald's death in March 1953 did not mark a change of direction, and indeed Antonin Novotny, under whom the collectivization of agriculture was completed in the late 1950s, would resist the winds of destalinization until well into the 1960s, even though he had repudiated the Gottwald personality cult.

It was the experience of this extreme and protracted form of Stalinism from 1948 which was to make the "Prague Spring" seem such an attractive alternative twenty years later. Under the 1960 Soviet-style Constitution the CPCz had laid claim, by the adoption of the title Socialist Republic, to be more advanced in building socialism than the rest of Eastern Europe. Economic stagnation, however, attributed to over-reliance on traditional industries, was what prompted the beginnings of reform, which accelerated in 1967 to adopt the ideas of decentralization and "a socialist market economy" as propounded by Ota Sik.

Dubcek replaced Novotny as first secretary in January 1968 partly just because he was the leading Slovak, and Slovaks had been growing increasingly dissatisfied over the centralization of power in Prague. Dubcek's receptiveness to liberal reforms, however, encouraged excitement to spread about a "third way", a market socialism in conditions of political pluralism and greater individual freedom. It was part of the tragedy of 1968 that this heady prospect inspired Czechs and Slovaks alike beyond the limits of cautious prudence. The Soviet regime and most of the Warsaw Pact allies saw the experiments not as a challenge but as an attack on socialism—or on the kind of socialism which kept them in power. To them, the risks of invasion were great, but the risks of contagion seemed worse. Their classic form of warning, "military manoeuvres", went unheeded in June, and in August the military action came.

The only significant reform which survived was the introduction of a federal system, with devolution of powers to Czech and Slovak republican governments. In April 1969 Husak succeeded Dubcek as first secretary (later general secretary), and "normalization" began in earnest. Misha Glenny has described this as "one of the most crushingly tedious and spiteful forms of Stalinism to have emerged in Eastern Europe". Its basic premise, however, was that the people's quiescence must be not only enforced (hence the harassment, and complete alienation, of intellectual dissidents), but also bought through higher living standards. The economic stagnation of the early 1980s exposed the extent to which relative consumer affluence had been achieved only by resource exploitation, with appalling costs in pollution, while little had been available for the restructuring of the country's increasingly outmoded industrial base.

A limited emulation of Gorbachev's ideas of *perestroika* was attempted from 1987, notably the increased devolution of managerial powers. At the same time, Czechoslovakia began to borrow abroad, not as heavily as countries like Poland, but with increasing urgency as trade within Comecon became more problematic. Meanwhile, there was no concession to the ideas of *glasnost*. The CPCz structure and leadership was completely defined by the "normalization" process, with its rigid orthodoxy, its massive "loyalty" purge, its vengeful pursuit and humiliation of opponents, and the central falsehood that it had all been undertaken to "save socialism". In these circumstances, any admission of criticism was bound to mean giving expression to critics of the 1968 invasion. The threat hung over the CPCz leaders in late 1989 that a Soviet recantation was imminent, as indeed it was; but the regime which the invasion had called into service in Czechoslovakia could not survive recanting thus itself.

Milos Jakes, who had taken over Husak's duties as general secretary in December 1987, represented stagnation not change in the leadership, having been as much part of "normalization" as Husak himself. Within the party, there were some figures apparently more open to reform ideas; Adamec, prime minister since October 1988, was the most prominent of these. There were also those, like Prague party chief Miroslav Stepan, who might favour resort to force to crush the opposition, as the Chinese had done at Tiananmen Square in June. The opposition, once launched on its mass defiance by the events of Nov. 17, 1989, showed undoubted courage in the face of this, not allowing the real dangers to interrupt the momentum of protest. They had, of course, been watching the drama in neighbouring East Germany, and had seen that the Soviet Union did not step in there to prop up an old guard leadership. They also showed skill, in using the network of contacts built up from the start of Charter 77, and in negotiating at the highest political level, despite having very little experience to call on in that regard.

It was suggested that Soviet intelligence might have encouraged the police brutality on Nov. 17, as a calculation to provoke a reaction which would topple Husak and Jakes, just as Gorbachev apparently connived at the "palace coup" to topple Zhivkov in Bulgaria the week before. If this was so, then it was badly miscalculated. The opposition was too tenacious to settle for minor change, as the reaction to the proposed new government on Dec. 3 proved. In this, a crucial factor was the massive support of workers, shown in the two-hour general strike on Nov. 27. For the first time, the intellectuals, students, artists and actors knew that they had the people with them, that "normalization" had truly bankrupted the regime.

The "velvet revolution" was brief, euphoric, and quite remarkably thorough in levering the communists from power. The corrupting legacy of the StB secret police state remained to haunt the first years of democracy, fuelling the proposal in the latter part of 1991 that the eradication of the system which spawned it would necessitate a ban on the communist party. Ousted from power, however, that party had appeared in 1990 to integrate itself into a pluralist system with fewer problems on either side than elsewhere. On economic change, the post-communist government moved with caution but had achieved much within two years, albeit still facing daunting problems, not least in the environmental sphere, and needing a large and sustained flow of funds for investment. The broad opposition movements of 1989 were split by 1991, it is true, by disagreement over whether to go rapidly for a free market economy, using "shock treatment", or to temper such changes with a more gradual approach and cushion their social impact through welfare. This debate, however, can be seen as a legitimate development of separate political party standpoints, and thus as a feature of the maturing process of a pluralist political system. (Much play has been made, in commentary on the state of democracy in Eastern Europe, of the advantage enjoyed by Czechoslovakia as a result of its historical experience. Not merely founded as a democratic state in 1918, it had also been governed democratically for a full 20 years thereafter. It is piquant to remember in this regard, however, the explanation sometimes offered in 1989, prior to Nov. 17, for the apparent absence of turmoil in Czechoslovakia—the obliteration of politics itself for the generation raised under the conditions of "normalization".)

For all the relative success, there remained at the end of 1991 the unanswered questions of nationalism, separatism, autonomy and the structure of the Czech and Slovak federal state. On this last issue turned Czechoslovakia's prospects of completing the revolution intact, from East European communist regime to economically viable Central European democratic state.

The principal personalities of Communist rule

Klement **Gottwald** (1896-1953). General secretary of the Communist party from 1929, he stood unsuccessfully against Masaryk in the 1934 presidential election, then led the party's switch to a popular front policy as recommended by the Comintern, supporting Benes as Mararyk's successor. He went to the Soviet Union when the party was outlawed after the 1938 Munich debacle, spending the war in exile there, and meeting Benes there to arrange the formation of the National Front, which was set up as the provisional government after liberation. With Rudolf Slansky taking on the post of general secretary, Gottwald concentrated initially on his government role. He became prime minister in 1946 when the CPCz, apparently following a parliamentary "Czech road to socialism", emerged from elections as the largest party. Ultimately, however, he showed himself a loyal follower of orders from Moscow, implementing the takeover of all government power in February 1948 and the Stalinist purges of the party thereafter. He became President under the new constitution in 1948, and after 1951, when Slansky was purged, he resumed the party leadership himself, but two years later he fell ill and died, exhausted, in a Moscow sanatorium.

Antonin **Novotny** (1904-75). The perpetuator of Stalinism in Czechoslovakia from 1953, when he succeeded Gottwald as first secretary of the CPCz, until the mid-1960s, when he accepted some hesitant steps towards reform. A domineering character, he was especially unpopular in the party with Slovaks, whose leading figures, including Husak, he had had imprisoned in the 1950s for "bourgeois nationalist" deviations. It was a Slovak, Dubcek, who replaced Novotny in early 1968.

Alexander **Dubcek** (b. 1921). The first secretary of the CPCz during the 1968 "Prague spring", Dubcek's name was to stand for the attempt to build "socialism with a human face". Replacing Novotny in January 1968, his appointment was seen initially as placating disgruntled Slovaks in the party; Dubcek, a Slovak himself, was little known nationally, although leader of the Communist Party in Slovakia. Arrested when Warsaw Pact forces invaded in August, but then released at President Svoboda's insistence, he had to sign a protocol in October effectively ending his reform policies. By April 1969 he had been ousted as first secretary, and was successively relegated under the Husak regime to the posts of chairman of the Federal Assembly, then ambassador to Turkey, then administrator in the Slovak forestry service, by which time he had also been purged from the party itself. The November 1989 revolution brought him back into the spotlight, a frail figure receiving an ecstatic welcome, urging the demonstrators on Nov. 24 to be confident that their time had come, and embraced by Havel when the news came through of Jakes's resignation. Suggested as a possible figurehead President, he ultimately stood down to leave that post to Havel, but became president of the assembly, and was re-elected to this office by the new Federal Assembly in June 1990.

Gustav **Husak** (1913-91). The man chosen to bring Czechoslovakia back into the required line after the crushing of the "Prague Spring" in August 1968, Husak had been part of the Dubcek leadership as a deputy premier, and had himself been arrested in 1951 and imprisoned in 1954-60 as a "bourgeois nationalist". He had first made his name in the Communist Party of Slovakia, a separate formation until 1949, and in particular as a leader of the 1944 Slovak uprising against the German occupation. In the post-1968 period so closely identified with his name, Husak was at first formally in charge only of the Slovak wing of the CPCz, and may be credited with helping to ensure that the devolution of government to the republics was implemented from 1969 onwards. He became CPCz first secretary in April of that year when Dubcek was finally ousted, and held that office until his replacement by Jakes in 1987, while also holding the office of head of state from 1975. His resignation on Dec. 10, 1989, marked the triumph of the "velvet revolution". For his leadership throughout the process of "normalization", and his resistance to reform in the latter part of the 1980s, he was despised by the demonstrators in equal measure with Jakes, although seen as less of a potent threat in view of his age and poor health. Expelled by a rejuvenated CPCz in February 1990, he died on Nov. 18, 1991.

Milos **Jakes** (b. 1922). A friend and contemporary of Dubcek from the time that both had spent at the Higher Party School in Moscow in the 1950s, he was a deputy interior minister from 1966, until his appointment in March 1968 to chair the CPCz central control and auditing commission. Far from becoming identified with Dubcek's "Prague Spring", however, he retained his post after the Warsaw Pact invasion and put himself comprehensively behind the vengeful purges; Husak, Vasil Bilak and he were the three key leaders of "normalization". In December 1987, having been by then a member of the presidium and secretariat for six years, and having shown himself to favour some degree of flexibility on economic if not political reform, he was chosen to succeed Husak as party general secretary. Feared for his power and his preference for threats over arguments, his departure was an early demand of the demonstrators in November 1989, and his resignation along with hardline colleagues on Nov. 24 marked the ecstatic fist triumph of the revolution. The party expelled him on Dec. 7, and he was subsequently detained for criminal investigation, but was not among the first to face charges.

Karel **Urbanek** (b. 1941). The figure put forward as CPCz general secretary when Jakes resigned on Nov. 24, 1989, he was replaced less than a month later (by Vasil Mohorita), and relegated to chair the central control commission. The party had hoped that, as a member of a younger generation, he would symbolize a credible adaptation and thus help stem the tide of opposition demands for wholesale change. He had been part of the party's central leadership in Prague only since 1988, having risen through its Moravian regional apparatus and been party chief in Brno.

Constitutional changes

The Czechoslovak Republic was redefined in May 1948 as a People's Democratic Republic, "a single state comprising two Slav nations", under a constitution which enshrined in its economic provisions the recent nationalization of industry. The National Assembly was in theory the supreme expression of the authority of the people. There was also an elected Slovak National Council and a government for Slovakia working through a board of commissioners.

The country was renamed as the Czechoslovak Socialist Republic, with a new constitution modelled on that of the Soviet Union, in July 1960. Its economic provisions recognized only state ownership and co-operative ownership as basic forms of property, removing the recognition of private property for small enterprises and small farms. The Communist Party was "the leading force in society and the State". Slovakia's board of commissioners was abolished and central powers strengthened in 1960, but the change to a more federal structure was agreed in 1968 and introduced in January 1969; one of the only developments to survive the post-1968 "normalization", it returned more autonomy to parallel Czech and Slovak National Councils.

Political power prior to 1989 was effectively in the hands of the Communist Party of Czechoslovakia (CPCz), organized in the Slovak SR as the Communist Party of

Slovakia, and which headed a National Front including four nominally separate parties.

After the 1989 revolution, the essential changes were rapidly made, as constitutional amendments passed on Nov. 29 by the Federal Assembly, to adopt a pluralist political system in time for elections in June 1990. Czechoslovakia was renamed on April 20, 1990, as the Czech and Slovak Federative Republic. The two constituent republics had been renamed in March, both dropping the adjective Socialist to become simply the Czech Republic (March 6) and the Slovak Republic (March 1).

The intention of framing a new Constitution, an issue which threatened to reduce government to a state of paralysis, remained to be resolved as of the end of 1991, although a Bill of Rights was adopted on Jan. 9, 1991. There were continuing differences about reconciling republican autonomy with the functions of a federal government, and a referendum in prospect on the question of Slovak secession, while there were growing signs from Havel that he regarded an increase in presidential powers as the only way to break the impasse. General elections were due to be held under the as yet uncompleted constitution in June 1992.

Position and status of communists

Party name

The Communist Party of Czechoslovakia (CPCz) has operated under this name since its formation from the 1921 split in the Social Democratic Party. Alone of the communist parties of Eastern Europe, it has not opted for a change of name in the post-communist period to make it more palatable to the electorate, deciding at a congress on Nov. 3-4, 1990, to retain the title CPCz.

A separate Communist Party of Slovakia (CPSl) existed clandestinely from 1938, and legally in the immediate post-war years, until 1948; it was then merged into the CPCz, but retained its identity as the party's regional organization there, with considerable autonomy especially after 1969, under the long-term leadership of Jozef Lenart. A counterpart specifically Czech body, the Communist Party of Bohemia and Moravia, was not created within the CPCz until March 1990.

The National Front, through which the party (nominally in a five-party alliance) had controlled single-list elections in 1948-89, was wound up in February 1990.

Legal status

Having surrendered its constitutionally guaranteed "leading role" at the end of 1989, the CPCz lost many of its members at rank and file as well as leadership levels; the total had fallen from some 1,700,000 to 1,200,000 by January 1990 and to 900,000 by June. Old guard leaders were expelled, notably Husak, former prime minister Lubomir Strougal and 20 others on Feb. 17, 1990, and the many younger leaders who left included federal prime minister Marian Calfa (on Jan. 18) and the then Slovak premier Milan Cik (on March 10). The party now presented itself as committed to democratic pluralism, and in May 1990 the government rejected the call that it should be banned, if it would not withdraw from the impending elections voluntarily and thereby show its acceptance of responsibility for 41 years of totalitarianism.

As the problem of eradicating the legacy of StB secret police activity proved increasingly intractable, the view gained support that the elimination of communist influence would require a ban on the party itself. A bill containing this proposal was discussed, and this element of it supported, by the Federal Assembly's defence and security committees in September 1991, while the following month legislation was passed on vetting the holders of state office to expose any involvement with the former communist regime.

Workplace organization

Organization into workplace cells, a key ingredient of communist power elsewhere, was not a characteristic of the CPCz, which used the residential branch as its basic unit, a legacy of its participation in democratic parliamentary politics in the inter-war and immediate post-war years. Party control at work under the communist regime was principally through its control of the Revolutionary Trade Union Movement, the sole legal federation. This body dissolved itself in March 1990; its successor, the Confederation of Czechoslovak Trade Unions, brought together the proliferating independent unions.

Party assets

Legislation was adopted on Nov. 16, 1990, to confiscate party assets acquired during its period in power, and thereby to remove its perceived illegitimate advantage over other parties. It was allowed to retain only what it could show to have been received by the collection of membership fees. The move provoked a walkout by the party's MPs, who regarded it as unconstitutional. In May the government had prohibited the party from making asset transfers, pending a decision on confiscation.

Ideological orientation

The extraordinary party congress on Dec. 20-21, 1989, formally abandoned (and apologised for) the hardline ideological stance of the Husak-Jakes regime, adopting an action programme "For a Democratic Socialist Society" which embraced political pluralism and democratic freedoms. The main thrust of its subsequent policy was to temper the acceptance of market economic reforms with the protection of "justified needs and rights" of the working people, and in particular the entitlement to welfare benefits and social security payments.

Vasil Mohorita, the party first secretary from December 1989 and then chairman after Adamec's retirement in August 1990, caused controversy in October 1990 by comments suggesting a more assertive stance in defending these rights. Using words uncomfortably reminiscent of 1948, he said on Oct. 7 that "national accord is over, and a hard and uncompromising struggle begins".

Electoral significance

Under the single-candidate electoral system of the communist regime the CPCz worked within the Fatherland Front structure which regularly recorded figures of practically 100 per cent of the vote in turnouts of over 99 per cent. About 80 per cent of the seats in parliament went to the CPCz under this arrangement and the remainder to its four nominally separate partners. The party's parliamentary majority was removed in January 1990 as a result of the decision of the round table talks, with 120 new members co-opted to replace party members who had resigned or been recalled.

At the multi-party election in June 1990 the CPCz won 13.7 per cent of the vote, and took 23 seats out of 150 in the Chamber of the People and 24 out of 150 in the Chamber of Nations; in the Czech parliament it held 32 seats out of 200, and in the Slovak parliament 22 out of 150. Local elections on Nov. 23-25 saw the Communists polling somewhat higher percentages, 17.2 per cent in the Czech Lands and 14 per cent in Slovakia (where the concentration of its vote in particular municipalities gave the party 24 per cent of the mayorships).

Principal parties in the post-communist period

Civic Forum was formed as a broad opposition alliance in November 1989, operating as the effective co-ordinating force of the pro-democracy groups which successfully toppled the communist regime through the weeks of massive popular protest. Its preponderant position (with its Slovak sister group People Against Violence) in the 1990 round table talks and the subsequent elections enabled the formation of a primarily Civic Forum government, and the re-election of Havel to the presidency immediately afterwards, but did not disguise the fact that it contained members with widely disparate views. Preserving its unity on issues of democratization and civil liberties, it was unable to do so on economic policy, the issue which led to the election of right-winger Vaclav Klaus as its chairman in October 1990, its ultimate split in February 1991, and the formation of separate parties. It was to continue to exist as an umbrella for co-operation pending the elections due in mid-1992. The **Civic Democratic Party**, formed in February 1991 from within Civic Forum by supporters of its chairman Vaclav Klaus, backed his right-wing liberal economic policies and the prescription of more "shock treatment" in the restructuring of the economy. At its founding congress on April 20-21, 1991, Klaus was elected as its chairman. The **Civic Movement** was constituted formally on April 27, 191, from the nucleus of the Liberal Club within Civic Forum, comprising those who, like Havel, advocated a "social market" approach. Its leading members included Dienstbier, who was elected as its first chairman, and Pithart.

The **Society for Moravia and Silesia** advocated autonomous government within the Czech lands for the territories of Moravia-Silesia, representing the complaint that their interests were otherwise subordinated to those of Bohemia; its demands further complicated the process of drawing up a constitutional settlement which would embody an acceptable federal and republican division of powers.In the Czech parliament it controlled 22 seats out of 200, while in the Federal Assembly it was also represented, having campaigned in the June 1990 elections with the Movement for Self-governing Democracy (abbreviated as MSD-SMS).

The **Christian Democratic Movement** was the junior partner at federal level in the government formed in June 1990, represented by Jozef Miklosko as a deputy premier with human rights responsibilities. It was a particular force in Slovakia, where it was a partner in the republic's government from June 1990; as of September 1991 it held the largest number of seats (31 out of 150) in the republic's parliament. Its roots lay in the long tradition of Catholic involvement with Slovak national issues and identity, and its strength in 1990 reflected the rapid resurgence of the power of the church. Its leader Jan Carnogursky became premier of Slovakia in April 1991; on the separatism issue the party was relatively moderate, believing in the advantages of a loose confederation and seeing independence as a longer-term objective fraught with difficulty. In the Czech lands smaller groups, the **Christian Democratic Party** and the **Christian Democrat Union**, held respectively seven and 14 seats out of 200 in the republic's parliament, but clericalism has much less historical and current significance. The Christian Democrat Union incorporated the **People's Party**, formerly a junior partner in the communist-dominated Front, which in the 1989 revolution under its leader Josef Bartoncik had rapidly distanced itself from the CPCz from Nov. 17 onwards. In the June 1990 elections it was hit by the allegation that Bartoncik had been a police informer, but it came third in local elections in the Czech lands in November 1990.

Public Against Violence, the sister movement in Slovakia of the Civic Forum, was likewise a broad alliance formed in November 1989 within the opposition movement which was successfully confronting the communist regime. It performed unexpectedly well in outpolling the Christian Democrats in the June 1990 elections. The issue of Slovak secessionism, espoused with increasing assertiveness by Vladimir Meciar from the end of 1990, ultimately split the movement. Meciar, expelled from the PAV and replaced as Slovak premier by Jan Carnogursky in April 1991, formed the separate **Movement for a Democratic Slovakia**, of which he was elected chairman on June 22, some two months after his expulsion from People Against Violence and his replacement by Jan Carnogursky as Slovak Premier. The new formation claimed the support of 19 members of the Slovak parliament, leaving 24 still backing the rump of People Against Violence, led by Marian Calfa (the federal prime minister who resigned from the communist party in January 1990).

The **Slovak National Party**, which performed strongly in the June 1990 elections and held 19 seats in the Slovak parliament, subsequently saw the support for its militant nationalism fall off quite sharply, as shown in the local elections in November 1990. To a considerable extent its supporters were attracted instead to back Meciar's Movement for a Democratic Slovakia as a more powerful political vehicle for their secessionist aims. In March 1991 the party elected Jozef Prokes as its leader in place of Vitazoslav Moric, and adopted new party statutes, stressing its Christian principles as well as its commitment to independence for Slovakia.

Among the ethnic minorities, there was strong support in the ethnic Hungarian community in Slovakia for the **Hungarian Christian Democratic Movement** and the **Hungarian Independent Initiative**, while Romany and other smaller ethnic minorities found some representation for their interests through alliances in the **Civic Initiative** (in the Czech Lands) and the **Coexistence** movement (in Slovakia).

The post-communist political leaders

Vaclav **Havel** (b. 1936). A self-described reluctant President, the former leading dissident and playwright was twice elected on an interim basis, first in December 1989 and again, for two years, in July 1990. The difficulties of framing a new constitutional arrangement, taking account of the increasing Slovak insistence on autonomous powers, contributed to his continuing strong influence as a President prepared to develop his own initiatives. His known concern about preserving social justice also acted as a brake on the more zealous free marketeers within the government, while in the foreign policy area he enjoyed a high profile and international esteem. The son of a wealthy family, Havel had been excluded from higher education by "anti-bourgeois" regulations in the 1950s. He was attracted to the theatre (and especially Prague's Theatre on the Balustrade), working first as a stage hand but then gaining fame as a playwright. His political involvement under the Prague spring resulted in his being afterwards banned from public life and, supporting himself by working in a brewery, he became a prominent and frequently-detained dissident. A leading founder of Charter 77, and of the Committee for the Defence of the Unjustly Persecuted (VONS) in 1978, his most recent arrest, in February 1989 for "incitement and obstruction", helped attract great international attention to the opposition's grievances against the hardline regime. Released in May, he was one of Civic Forum's founders and its unofficial leader through the November 1989 revolution, although as President he has been nominally non-partisan.

Marian **Calfa** (b. 1946). Calfa was the head of the first cabinet without a communist majority, as the interim federal prime minister from December 1989. He formally left the CPCz a month later, joining Public Against Violence and winning a seat in the June 1990 elections, and being asked to continue as prime minister at the head of a mainly Civic Forum/Public Against Violence administration—a Slovak balancing the choice of the Czech, Havel, as President. The son of a railway worker, he had been a legal official and had held a government post (as minister without portfolio) for only 18 months before becoming prime minister.

Vaclav **Klaus** (b. 1941). Finance Minister since Dec. 10, 1989, a Civic Forum leader and subsequently chairman of the Civic Democratic Party, Klaus has consistently been the most convinced advocate of a rapid privatization programme and the untrammelled adoption of liberal free market economic policies. A Czech born in Prague, he had identified with the 1968 reformists as a young economist, but had to take a lower profile, working in the state bank, under the Husak regime.

Jiri **Dienstbier** (b. 1937). The foreign minister from Dec. 10, 1989, and also a deputy premier after June 1990, Dienstbier was a friend, ally and fellow Chartist with Havel, and a co-founder of Civic Forum in November 1989. His foreign experience dated from his days as a radio correspondent, but he had been dismissed in 1970 and relegated to working as a stoker, the classic dissident experience under "normalization", with a bout of three years in prison from 1979.

Lubos **Dobrovsky** (b. 1932). A founder member of Charter 77, and prominent in Civic Forum in November 1989, he was brought into the government in June 1990, and became Defence Minister in October. He had been a fellow radio journalist with Dienstbier in the 1960s and, like him, did manual work as a stoker under the Husak regime.

Vasil **Mohorita** (b. 1952). The principal new face of the CPCz in the post-1989 era, initially as first secretary (from December 1989) and then taking over the chairmanship when Ladislav Adamec retired in August 1990. A Czech born in Prague, and educated in Moscow, he had already been a party member for 18 years when he was first elected to the central committee at the age of 36 in 1988. He was young enough, and unknown enough, to be free of the taint of personal responsibility for "normalization".

Petr **Pithart** (b. 1941). Premier of the Czech republic. A signatory of Charter 77, Pithart had been a law lecturer and Oxford scholar but was relegated to labouring and clerical work under "normalization" from 1970. He was prominent in co-ordinating Civic Forum's activities in the "velvet revolution", became Czech premier in February 1990, and was reappointed after the June elections.

Jan **Carnogursky** (b. 1944). Premier of the Slovak Republic since April 1991. A lawyer with a reputation for defending dissidents, he was arrested himself in August 1989 for dissident activity, and released only on Nov. 25. He was brought into Calfa's interim federal government on Dec. 10, as a deputy premier, but after the June 1990 elections he devoted himself to politics within the Slovak context, his recently-founded Christian Democratic Movement having come second in the elections in the republic. In alliance with Public Against Violence, he was initially Slovak deputy premier, taking on the leadership of the republican government (and trying to steer a moderate course on autonomy amid the increasing populist clamour for secession) when Public Against Violence split and former premier Meciar was ousted from government.

Vladimir **Meciar** (b. 1942). The premier of Slovakia from June 1990 to April 1991, Meciar had by that time embarked on a populist Slovak nationalist course which split the Public Against Violence movement; his supporters in the Movement for Democratic Socialism followed him into opposition and Carnogursky replaced him as premier. He had worked in the communist youth movement but was expelled from the party under "normalization"; he then worked as a welder while training to become a lawyer. From late 1989 until the June 1990 elections he was Slovakia's interior minister.

Elections

Legislature

The highest organ of state authority under the Communist regime was the bicameral Federal Assembly, comprising a 200-seat Chamber of the People and 150-seat Chamber of Nations. From 1954 onwards, both were elected in single-member constituencies; the only candidates were those approved by the National Front, which from 1954 onwards, put forward only one candidate in each constituency. Voting was compulsory for adults (18 and above). The frequency of these elections was set under the 1971 electoral law as five-yearly. The Czech and Slovak republics each had a National Council or parliament, elected in the same way.

The legislatures elected on June 8-9, 1990, under interim arrangements pending completion of the constitution-making process, were (i) a bicameral Federal Assembly, 150 seats in each chamber, the numbers divided between the Czech and Slovak republics 101-49 in the Chamber of the People and 75-75 in the Chamber of Nations; and (ii) separate Czech and Slovak National Councils, of 200 and 150 seats respectively. The system adopted for all these chambers was proportional representation, but with different minimum thresholds for representation; in the federal chambers, a party needed to win at least 5 per cent in either the Czech Lands or Slovakia; for the Czech National Council the 5 per cent hurdle applied, but for Slovakia it was 3 per cent.

General election results

The June 1990 general election resulted in a victory for Civic Forum and People Against Violence, but with unexpectedly strong residual support for the communists.

June 8-9, 1990 election of Federal Assembly				
	Chamber of the People		Chamber of Nations	
	percentage	seats	percentage	seats
Civic Forum & PAV	46.6	87	45.9	83
CPCz	13.6	23	13.7	24
CDU/CDM	12.0	20	11.3	20
MSD-SMS	5.4	9	3.6	9
Slovak National Party	3.5	6	6.2	7
Coexistence	2.8	5	2.7	7
Others	16.1	0	16.6	0

Presidency

Under the communist regime from 1948 there were elections at five-yearly intervals in which the Federal Assembly elected the President of the Republic (Gottwald in 1948, Antonin Zapotocky succeeding him in 1953, Novotny in 1957, Ludvik Svoboda from early 1968 until 1975, and thereafter Husak until Dec. 10, 1989).

Havel became interim President on Dec. 30, 1989, his election having been declared unanimous by the Federal Assembly after other candidates had all stood down. Re-elected for a further interim period of two years on July 5, 1990, he was again the sole candidate (after others had been disqualified as not properly nominated). Requiring a three-fifths majority in each 150-member chamber of the Federal Assembly, he received 114 to 25 in the Chamber of the People, and 120 to 25 (nine of the Czech section and 16 of the Slovak section) in the Chamber of Nations.

Local elections

The local government system under the communist regime had involved district committees closely controlled from the centre, which were replaced in November 1990 by district bureaus elected on Nov. 23-25 in Slovakia, along with the direct election of mayors, and on Nov. 24 in the Czech Lands. In Slovakia, where the turnout was nearly 64 per cent, the Christian Democratic Movement won 27 per cent, Public Against Violence 20 per cent, the Communist Party 14 per cent, and the Slovak National Party barely 3 per cent. In the Czech Lands, where the turnout was nearer 75 per cent, Civic Forum won 36 per cent, the Communist Party 17.2 per cent and the Czechoslovak People's Party 11.5 per cent.

Governments in the post-communist period

The resignation of the communist government was promised by prime minister Adamec on Nov. 28, 1989, but his new cabinet as put forward on Dec. 3 still contained an overwhelming communist majority, and was rejected by the opposition. Adamec's resignation on Dec. 7 opened the way for the first government without a communist majority, that formed by Marian Calfa on Dec. 10, including notably Dienstbier, Klaus and Vladimir Dlouhy from Civic Forum. These three, and Calfa, were all among those who retained their posts in the government formed after the June 1990 elections.

Principal government members, June 1990 to December 1991

Federal prime minister: Marian Calfa (PAV)

Deputy premiers: Vaclav Vales (indep) until September 1991, Pavel Rychetsky (indep), Jozef Miklosko (CDM), Pavel Hoffmann(indep) from October 1991

Deputy premier and foreign minister: Jiri Dienstbier (Civic Forum / Civic Movement)

Defence: Miroslav Vacek (indep.) until October 1990, then Lubos Dobrovsky (Civic Forum / CM)

Interior: Jan Langos (PAV)

Finance (and from October 1991 also Deputy Premier): Vaclav Klaus (Civic Forum / CDP)

Economy: Vladimir Dlouhy (Civic Forum / CM)

Premiers of the Republics:

Czech Lands—Petr Pithart (Civic Forum / CM),

Slovakia—Vladimir Meciar (PAV / MDS) until April 1991; Jan Carnogursky (CDM)

Security and human rights issues

Links with the former state security services

The Statni Bezpecnost (StB, the security police) was abolished in February 1990, after rumours that it might be involved in preparing a counter-revolutionary coup, but there was a succession of revelations, and allegations, about individuals' former StB links or their activity as informers. A bill on screening all state office-holders for such links was put forward by the government in June 1991 and signed in October by Havel, who retained reservations, however, about the danger of infringing the civil rights of those being screened. He had sought a limit of two years on the period for such screening, and limitations on the definition of collaboration to prevent its potentially vengeful application to anyone who had passed on information.

Among those who resigned from government office amid allegations that they had StB links were two deputy interior ministers in April 1990, and two federal cabinet ministers (citing health reasons) in May. The most controversial case, however, arose when a parliamentary commission in March 1991 named ten deputies as alleged collaborators, including former People's Party leader Jan Bartoncik and the noted dissident and former long-term exile Jan Kavan. Angry debate followed in which several of those named threatened legal action, claiming that their names were on such lists by mistake or as a result of attempts to frame or blackmail them.

Bill of rights

The basic constitutional document guaranteeing individual rights and freedoms in a pluralist society was approved by the federal Assembly on Jan. 9, 1991, as a bill of rights, pending completion of the framing of the constitution itself. Laws on freedom of association and freedom of the press had been passed the previous May.

Amnesty and abolition of death penalty

A comprehensive amnesty and release of prisoners, declared by Havel in a New Year's Day speech in 1990 as one of his first acts as President, had the unintended side-effects of depriving several major industries including Skoda motors of the prison labour on which they had depended, and precipitating a wave of common crime. The death penalty was abolished in May 1990.

Nationalities and minorities issues

Apart from the Czech-Slovak divide there remained the issue of the status and treatment of minority nationalities. Proposals in 1960 to grant recognized minority status to the Hungarians, Ukrainians and Poles were dropped because of resistance to granting equivalent rights to those Germans who had remained; the great majority of ethnic Germans (some 2,000,000) had been expelled immediately after World War II and only about 50,000 remained. All four of these minorities were recognized, however, under the October 1969 nationalities law (framed in the liberal climate under Dubcek although actually passed after the crushing of this "Prague spring" in August 1968), which gave their languages official protection and stipulated minority representation on elected bodies. After the 1989 revolution, there were repeated Slovak nationalist protests over the October 1990 Slovak language law which, while designating Slovak as the official language in the republic, also allowed official use of minority languages in towns with significant non-Slovak populations. The Hungarians, much the largest group at nearly 600,000 and living mainly in Slovakia, have their own political parties represented in the Slovak parliament, and feel threatened by the hostility of Slovak nationalists, although few would identify with the territorial claims raised by some in Hungary itself to the southern Slovakian uplands or *Feldivek*.

The Coexistence coalition of Hungarian and other minority nationalities won representation in the Federal Assembly in June 1990, and the Romany gypsy / Civic Initiative group holds five seats in the Czech parliament. There have been violent racist attacks by Czech skinhead groups since the 1989 revolution, on gypsies and also, particularly in Moravia, on Vietnamese, who represented some three quarters of the 46,000 foreign workers employed under contracts during the communist period.

The trend of increasing assertiveness of republican autonomy since 1989 has been compounded by the articulation of similar demands in Moravia and Silesia within the Czech Lands (which officially comprise Bohemia and Moravia). The Society for Bohemia and Silesia, which won 22 seats out of 200 in the Czech parliament in 1990 and was also represented in the Federal Assembly, launched in February 1991 a boycott of the Czech parliament to press its demands for a "tri-federal" rather than "bi-federal" constitution. This was effectively excluded in Havel's proposals for resolving the constitutional debate, but the demand was reiterated in November.

CHRONOLOGY

March 1945. Edward Benes, the pre-war President who has maintained a government-in-exile in London, reaches agreement in Moscow with the exiled communist leader Klement Gottwald on the formation of a National Front in which all pre-war political groups will be included in a six-party coalition.

April-May 1945. The liberation of the country by the Red Army (and by the US forces in the far west) allows the National Front to establish itself on Czechoslovak territory, first in Slovakia and then (after the May 5 Prague uprising) in the capital. Its programme includes nationalization of industry, a Soviet-oriented foreign policy, and the expulsion of Germans (which is carried out comprehensively) and Hungarians (which is not).

May 1946. General elections are held in which the Communist Party wins 38 per cent of the vote; Gottwald, as leader of the largest party, is thus invited to head the all-party coalition government.

July 1947. An initial decision to accept Marshall Plan assistance is rescinded under pressure from the Soviet Union.

25 February 1948. Gottwald's new communist-dominated cabinet is sworn in reluctantly by President Benes after an effective coup in Prague; the intimidatory tactics of the Communist Party have driven non-communists in the previous coalition to resign over the nationalization of industry.

March 1948. Jan Masaryk's death, officially described as suicide, removes the last leading opponent of communist power, and in the following month the social democrats are merged into the Communist Party.

9 May 1948. Under a new constitution, Czechoslovakia is declared a people's democracy.

30 May-2 June 1948. After the election victory of the communist-dominated National Front in single-list elections, Gottwald becomes President on the resignation of Benes.

October 1949. The arrests of "bourgeois elements" begin on a large scale.

March 1950. Religious leaders are put on trial for treason.

October 1950-March 1951. Political show trials reach their height.

September 1951. Gottwald becomes general secretary of the party.

November 1952. The trial of fourteen (mostly Jewish) senior communist officials ends with eleven being executed, including Rudolf Slansky, former CPCz general secretary.

14 March 1953. Death of Gottwald; a reorganization of the government and party, in September, makes Antonin Zapotocky the President while the party leadership goes to Antonin Novotny. The emphasis in industrial planning shifts from heavy industry towards consumer goods, but repressive measures are the standard response to any political "deviation" and to a workers' protest in June 1953 over price rises and currency reform.

April 1954. Gustav Husak, one of a group within the party charged with Slovak separatism, receives a life prison sentence.

November 1957. Novotny becomes President, combining this post once again with the party leadership, after the death of Zapotocky.

June-September 1963. Novotny ousts the leading pro-Stalinists in the party following the rehabilitation of Klemetis, Slansky and other victims of the show trials of the early 1950s. His subsequent modest reforms are insufficient to placate the proponents of change, who also resent his autocratic style.

January 1968. The so-called "Prague Spring" begins when Alexander Dubcek, a Slovak, takes over the party leadership from Novotny. Novotny is also replaced as President, in March, by Ludvik Svoboda.

April 1968. The "Prague Spring" leadership puts forward the action programme proposing comprehensive political reforms and measures to liberalize the economy.

June 1968. Intellectuals publish the "2000 words" statement advocating greater liberalization.

June 1968. Warsaw Pact manoeuvres in Czechoslovakia in June underline the threat to the reform leadership.

21 August 1968. Tanks roll into Prague in a massive invasion by Warsaw Pact forces, crushing the "Prague Spring" without mass armed resistance, but meeting large numbers of demonstrators who leave no doubt of the unwelcome nature of such "fraternal assistance".

27 August 1968. Dubcek and other leading reformers, held for a week in Moscow, are allowed to return on the insistence of President Svoboda, but their reform movement is forced into reverse.

November 1968. The Soviet party leader Leonid Brezhnev, speaking at the PUWP congress in Warsaw, supports the theory that socialist states have limited sovereignty and that other socialist countries may have an "internationalist obligation" to intervene in the defence of socialism. This "Brezhnev doctrine", essentially presenting the theoretical justification for the military clampdown on the Prague Spring, is presumed to have wider applicability, and overhangs Eastern Europe for twenty years. Already set out in a *Pravda* article in September, it is further elaborated by Brezhnev at the Soviet party congress on March 30, 1971.

January 1969. Jan Palach sets fire to himself in Wenceslas Square, providing by his death a potent symbol of refusal to accept the Warsaw Pact invasion; there are anti-Soviet riots in March.

April 1969. Dubcek is ousted and replaced by Husak, under whose control the party in May reasserts democratic centralism.

September 1969. The purge of reformers from the party begins, accompanied by cabinet changes; Husak reports in December 1970 that 326,817 people have been expelled from the party in the "loyalty drive", including Dubcek in June 1970.

July 1972. Trials begin of former supporters of Dubcek in the party.

December 1973. Relations with West Germany are formalized under a treaty signed in Prague by Chancellor Brandt.

1976. Members of the rock music group "Plastic People of the Universe" and other figures in the "alternative" youth culture are sent to prison,

1 January 1977. Opponents of the Husak regime publish Charter 77, the intellectuals' document on the regime's failure to meet human rights criteria. Drafted in large part by the dissident playwright Vaclav Havel, it brings together the "Chartists" who will provide a focus for dissident intellectual activity in the remaining years of the communist regime.

June 1983. Police break up an anti-government demonstration in Prague, continuing to deal with dissidents through surveillance, harassment and frequent imprisonment.

March 1986. The party congress in Prague is marked by the extremely cautious approach of the leadership to the idea of Gorbachev's new proposals for radical reforms in the Soviet Union.

February-April 1987. Public disagreement emerges within the party over the relevance of Gorbachev's programme of reform, which is supported in statements by Husak in March; Gorbachev himself, visiting Prague in April, is given an enthusiastic public reception.

May 1987. Prison sentences are imposed on members of the Jazz Section for unauthorized publications.

17 December 1987. Husak is replaced as general secretary by Milos Jakes, his hardline colleague; Husak retains the post of state President.

21 August 1988. Demonstrations in Prague, on the anniversary of the Warsaw Pact invasion in 1968, usher in a period of increasingly overt public protest activity by students and others inspired by the intellectual-led dissident movement.

October 1988. Ladislav Adamec is appointed as prime minister and soon announces an acceleration of the process of economic reform, bringing forward to January 1990 the proposed date for the introduction of a New Economic Mechanism to reduce over-dependence on traditional heavy industries.

January 1989. Protests over human rights abuses are followed by the arrest of over 800 dissidents, including the frequently-detained Havel, who is sent to prison again, receiving this time a nine-month prison sentence; Havel is released on parole in May.

Adamec, returning from a visit to Moscow, speaks of a desire for dialogue.

Travel restrictions are relaxed for those wanting to visit the West.

October 1989. Inspiration and hope is offered to the pro-democracy movement by the dramatic example of the successful challenge to the regime in East Germany on the streets of its major cities. In Czechoslovakia, however, the authorities provide further confirmation of their readiness to repress dissent, as riot police attack an anti-government demonstration, using clubs to break up a crowd estimated at over 10,000.

17 November 1989. The rapid sequence of events which become the "velvet revolution" begins with a student march to the Vysehrad national cemetery in Prague. Officially sanctioned, it commemorates the 50th anniversary of the funeral of a student killed by the Nazis, but the crowd swells as a large-scale pro-democracy demonstration develops. Afterwards, riot police block the access to Wenceslas Square, preventing a hard core of students from marching there, then trapping them and finally attacking them with clubs, injuring 140 and making many arrests. The outrage over this brutality is magnified by reports that one demonstrator, Martin Smid, has been killed. Police denials are widely dismissed as lies, and Smid becomes a martyr figure. His supposed death, which actually never happened, helps to rally huge demonstrations in the succeeding days.

19 November 1989. The opposition organizes itself around the Civic Forum coalition in Prague and the parallel Public Against Violence movement in Slovakia. A joint resolution by Civic Forum and the Socialist Party and People's Party, hitherto both part of the CPCz-dominated front organization, urges dialogue and demands the resignation of communist hardliners.

21 November 1989. Adamec opens discussions with the protestors.

24 November 1989. Dubcek, having emerged from oblivion and spoken out in Bratislava the previous day, joins Havel to address over 250,000 cheering demonstrators in Prague. Jakes resigns, and there are major changes in the party presidium, with Karel Urbanek becoming general secretary.

25 November 1989. The hardliner Miroslav Stepan resigns as Prague party leader.

26 November 1989. Adamec leads a party and government delegation in discussions with Civic Forum, and tells a crowd of nearly 500,000 that he will put forward the protestors' demands to the party central committee, but urges cancellation of a planned general strike.

27 November 1989. Workers show massive support for what has hitherto been a movement of intellectuals, artists and students, mobilizing 60 per cent support nationwide for a two-hour general strike.

28-30 November 1989. Adamec effectively capitulates and agrees to put forward a new government; the party concedes the abolition of its "leading role" and the Federal Assembly approves amendments to the constitution.

1 December 1989. The party's reassessment of the 1968 Warsaw Pact invasion, now recognized as "unjustified and mistaken", is made known.

3 December 1989. Huge protests resume when a government with a large Communist majority is put forward by Adamec. Civic Forum and People Against Violence demand further changes.

7 December 1989. Adamec resigns, and the new party leadership expels Jakes and Stepan (who is arrested on Dec. 23 over the police action of Nov. 17).

10 December 1989. A government with a non-communist majority is formed under Marian Calfa, and President Husak resigns.

17 December 1989. The border with Austria is opened ceremonially by the cutting of the wire fence.

20-21 December 1989. The CPCz congress apologises for "unjustified reprisals" and for "gross disrespect" for dissident opinion; Adamec becomes party chairman and Vasil Mohorita is elected to the new post of first secretary, while the hardliner Vasil Bilak is expelled and Husak and others suspended from party membership.

30 December 1989. Havel is elected unanimously by the Federal Assembly as Federal President, with Dubcek, who has stood down in his favour, becoming president of the assembly.

January-February 1990. The political parties hold round-table talks, agreeing on arrangements for the forthcoming elections, and on reducing the Communist presence in the existing parliament and co-opting replacements.

1 February 1990. The Statni Bezpecnost (StB, the security police) is abolished.

17 February 1990. Husak and 21 others are expelled from the Communist Party for erroneous decisions.

26-27 February 1990. Havel visits the Soviet Union (having already been to East and West Germany, Poland, Hungary, Iceland, the USA and Canada, and with visits to France and the UK to follow on March 19-23). During talks with Gorbachev, the latter expresses regret over the "unfounded invasion" in 1968, and an agreement is signed on a complete Soviet troop withdrawal by July 1991.

27-28 March 1990. New laws are approved on freedom of association, assembly and the press, together with a new citizenship law.

20 April 1990. A compromise formula comes into effect under which the name of the country becomes the Czech and Slovak Federative Republic.

8-9 June 1990. The first free multi-party elections since 1946 end in victory for Civic Forum and Public Against Violence, with a combined overall majority in both chambers of the Federal Assembly; the parliaments of the Czech and Slovak republics are elected at the same time. The Communists do unexpectedly well, emphasising their role in a pluralist democracy, and beating the Christian Democrats to finish second.

27 June 1990. A new government is formed, again with Calfa (now a member of Public Against Violence) as prime minister, and consisting of PAV, Civic Forum, the Christian Democrats and unaffiliated experts. PAV heads a coalition government in Slovakia led by Vladimir Meciar, and Petr Pithart, already premier of the Czech republic since February, forms a new coalition dominated by Civic Forum.

5 July 1990. Havel is re-elected by the Federal Assembly for another two years as president.

20 September 1990. Czechoslovakia joins the IMF.

2 October 1990. Parliament passes legislation on the return of an estimated 70,000 houses, shops and small businesses confiscated between 1955 and 1962.

17-18 October 1990. Defence minister Gen. Miroslav Vacek is replaced by the civilian and former dissident Lubos Dobrovsky. According to a presidential commission on the security forces, Vacek had been implicated in preparations for army action against the demonstrators in November 1990.

25 October 1990. The Slovak language law, adopted by the republic's parliament and making Slovak the official language there, sparks off protest by nationalists who want less scope for the use of other languages.

16 November 1990. The law on confiscation of Communist Party assets is passed by the Federal Assembly.

17 November 1990. A visit by US President Bush, who has approved earlier in the month the granting of most-favoured-nation trading status to Czechoslovakia, coincides with the first anniversary of the start of the revolution in Prague.

23-25 November 1990. Local elections for new district bureaus confirm Civic Forum as the leading force in the Czech Republic, but with a reduced share of the vote, and with the Communists second. In the Slovak Republic the Christian Democratic Movement overtakes People Against Violence as the most popular party, with the Communists third and the specifically nationalist vote declining as compared with its June general election showing.

12 December 1990. The Federal Assembly passes the power-sharing law, increasing the devolution of authority to the parliaments of the Czech and Slovak republics.

1 January 1991. A programme of economic reforms includes lifting price controls on most goods (which results in prices doubling on average in January), allowing firms to buy foreign currency freely for foreign trade, and privatizing small businesses (under legislation passed on Oct. 25, 1990); the first auction sale of state-owned shops, on Jan. 26, is highly successful.

9 January 1991. A Bill of Rights is passed by the Federal Assembly, to be incorporated into the future constitution, guaranteeing individual freedoms and political pluralism.

10 February 1991. An "amicable divorce" between rival factions in Civic Forum is agreed at a meeting at Havel's presidential residence, and approved by the Civic Forum extraordinary congress in Prague two weeks later. The two factions agree to remain in coalition until the 1992 elections. Vaclav Klaus, the Civic Forum chairman for the last four months, has emerged as leader of a Democratic Right Club committed to rapid economic liberalization, while a rival Liberal Club, known to be closer to Havel's viewpoint, places more emphasis on civil liberties and a more gradual economic reform supported by social security measures.

21 February 1991. Legislation is finally passed on the return of property seized after the 1948 coup; the debate on the return of farm land continues until May, however.

25 February 1991. The Warsaw Treaty Organization or Warsaw Pact is disbanded as a military alliance (and formally dissolved on July 1), a process in which Czechoslovakia has been a prime mover.

4 March 1991. The framework for a new constitution, linking the two republics voluntarily in a federative state, is agreed by the leaders of the principal parties,

but there is growing support among Slovak politicians for Jan Carnogursky's view that the linking mechanism should be a treaty as between sovereign states, rather than a political declaration as advocated by Havel, most Czechs, and pro-federation Slovaks.

22 March 1991. The controversy about links between politicians and the former state security service (StB), which leads to the passage of a screening law in October, is fuelled when a special commission names as collaborators ten current members of parliament, among them the prominent former exiled dissident Jan Kavan.

9 April 1991. The Bratislava summit meeting between Czechoslovakia, Poland and Hungary resolves to plan for "entering Europe".

23 April 1991. Vladimir Meciar, who since early March has led a minority faction within Public Against Violence, is dismissed by the presidium of the Slovak parliament and is succeeded as Slovak premier by Jan Carnogursky. Accused of incompetence and of abusing access to police files, Meciar has alienated many former colleagues in Public Against Violence by his strident adoption of Slovak nationalist demands.

April 1991. Splits are formalized both in Civic Forum (Klaus's Civic Democratic Party and Dienstbier's Civic Movement hold their founding congresses on April 20-21 and April 27) and in Public Against Violence, which holds an extraordinary congress in Kosice on April 27 and sees Meciar's Platform for a Democratic Slovakia formally split away (to become the Movement for Democratic Slovakia on June 22).

21 May 1991. The former owners of land confiscated in 1948 are offered the return of "fixed assets", under legislation passed by the Federal Assembly. Until arrangements have been worked out to break up or transform agricultural co-ops, those whose former land the co-ops are using will be given an ownership stake.

13 June 1991. A privatization programme is launched for large nationalized industries—the first so-called "large-scale privatizations" under legislation approved on Feb. 26 and effective from April.

17 June 1991. At the end of meetings between Havel and federal and republican leaders, it is agreed that under its proposed new constitution the country should be a "voluntary union" of republics.

19 June 1991. The Soviet troop withdrawal, agreed in February 1990, is completed (Gen. Vorobyov leaves on June 30); the Soviet Union is to pay compensation worth $160 million for damage done since the 1968 invasion.

28 June 1991. Comecon is formally dissolved after its 46th session in Budapest, leaving a liquidation committee charged with winding up its business and making decisions on remaining assets.

1 July 1991. Prague hosts the final meeting at which the Warsaw Treaty Organization or Warsaw Pact is formally dissolved by its six remaining members - the Soviet Union, Bulgaria, Hungary, Poland, Romania and Czechoslovakia.

18 July 1991. The Referendum Law is passed, allowing either a republican parliament or the Federal Assembly to propose (subject to presidential veto) a referendum on

secession, but the Assembly does not pass until Nov. 6 the necessary legislation on procedures, and on Nov. 13 it fails to agree on wording the question; the government ends by pledging that it will submit draft proposals to both the republican and the federal parliaments.

25 July 1991. Giving the go-ahead for the Gabcikovo hydroelectric project on the Danube to start operation in October, the Federal Assembly is in effect bowing to Slovak intransigence, despite Hungarian opposition to what had once been a joint project, and in the face of sustained protests by environmentalists.

3 October 1991. Dienstbier initials a friendship treaty with the Soviet Union.

6 October 1991. President Havel, President Walesa of Poland and Hungarian prime minister Jozsef Antall adopt the Krakow Declaration, on acting together for European union and integration with NATO.

17 October 1991. Havel signs, but states that he will seek amendments to, a law on screening state office-holders for connections with the former security services. In its strict version as passed by the Federal Assembly on Oct. 4, the law (originally put forward by the federal government on June 27) will ban not only former StB members but also those found to have collaborated.

3 November 1991. Havel elaborates his proposals for simultaneous enactment of new federal, Czech and Slovak constitutions, to take effect by May 1, 1992.

17 November 1991. In a television broadcast Havel puts forward ideas for constitutional changes, with the republican parliaments linked into the federal legislature through a second chamber (a federal council). His intention is to avoid the recurrence of the current deadlock between federal and republican parliaments, which has reduced the legislature to paralysis over the constitutional issue. He also suggests dissolving the present Federal Assembly and governing by presidential rule until fresh elections in June 1992, as well as incorporating in the referendum law a provision for the President to call a referendum.

21 December 1991. The Federal Assembly passes the federal budget for 1992. Finance minister Klaus comments on "satisfactory" progress in transforming the economy, with inflation now under control (and predicted at 13-15 per cent in 1992) and only a small increase in total foreign debt over the last year. Gross domestic product has fallen by 12-14 per cent in 1991 but is expected to fall much less steeply, by only 3-6 per cent, in 1992. Earlier in December, agreement has been reached on a one-off subsidy from the federal to the republican budgets. Federal revenues are to be distributed in 1992 in the proportions 35 per cent federal expenditure, 41.5 per cent to the Czech republican budget and 23.5 per cent to Slovakia.

EAST GERMANY

The eastern part of Germany used as its official title the German Democratic Republic — GDR (*Deutsche Demokratische Republik*, *DDR*) until the unification of Germany on Oct. 2-3, 1990.

The former GDR, which ceased to exist upon the reunification of Germany, had occupied a total area of 108,333 sq. km excluding West Berlin (480 sq. km), mainly in the North German plain. The Elbe river crossed the country from south-east to north-west, the Harz mountains rose in the south-west and the Erzgebirge in the south. The GDR's longest border was the "inner German border" which separated it from West Germany. The northern border was the Baltic coast; to the south-east lay Czechoslovakia, and, to the east, Poland, whose border with the GDR followed the line of the Oder and Neisse rivers.

The 1990 population of 16,434,000 was only just above a quarter that of West Germany. The GDR had slightly more inhabitants than Czechoslovakia, but less than half as many as Poland, and the combination of emigration and a low birthrate meant that the population fell during its 41-year history (having been calculated at

17,314,000 in the 1946 census for the Soviet zone excluding Berlin). Three quarters of its people lived in urban areas. East Berlin, i.e. the Soviet sector of divided Berlin, was by far the largest city and also the GDR's capital; the second city was Leipzig, south of Berlin in Saxony, and the most urbanized (and polluted) part of the country was the southern industrial belt around Leipzig, Dresden and Karl-Marx-Stadt (the GDR name for Chemnitz). The main Baltic port was Rostock.

Ethnically, the GDR was homogeneous; 99.7% of the population (excluding Gastarbeiter from Vietnam and elsewhere) were German, and the only surviving indigenous ethnic minority of any numerical significance were the Sorbs, a Slavic people, some 110,000 of whom lived mainly around Cottbus. There were estimated to be 5,000 Jews in the GDR. The predominant religious faith was Christianity (mainly Lutheran Protestant, but with a significant Roman Catholic presence in the south-west); rather under one-third of the total population belonged to one or other of the Christian churches as of the late 1980s.

The existence of German minorities elsewhere in Eastern Europe, notably in Poland, Czechoslovakia, Hungary, and the Soviet Union, was of little real political significance for the GDR, with affluent West Germany a more obvious magnet for emigration.

The year of the formal creation of separate German states was 1949; the German Democratic Republic was proclaimed on Oct. 7 in the Soviet-occupied zone of Germany, some four months after the creation of the Federal Republic of Germany (FRG) in the three Western zones. The effective separation dated from the wartime decisions of the allies, at Yalta and Potsdam, that a defeated Germany should be placed under an occupation regime consisting of Soviet, US, British and French zones. (To add a French zone, the US and British reallocated some territory from their zones.) In a 'partition within a partition', Berlin, an enclave 150 km inside the Soviet zone, was divided into a Soviet and three Western sectors under joint four-power control.

The eastern boundaries of what was to become East Germany were regarded as definitive by the Soviet side, but seen by the Western Allies as provisional pending a formal peace treaty with Germany. They entailed a major redrawing of the map and the enforced migration westwards of millions of ethnic Germans. All formerly German territory to the east of the Oder-Neisse line was given to Poland, while the Soviet Union itself took northern East Prussia (as well as pre-war eastern Poland and part of Czechoslovakia) and exacted heavy reparations from the area of Germany under its own control.

As the Soviet side resisted Western plans for economic integration and self-government in Germany, their application in Berlin proved to be a particular flashpoint. The Western powers included West Berlin in their 1948 West German currency reform, but the Soviet authorities responded by blockading road and rail access. The massive airlift by which the West kept West Berlin supplied (July 1948 to May 1949) provided a potent symbol of the Cold War, and hastened the political division of Germany into two states, one a free-market democracy aligned with the West and the other a Communist-ruled state within the Soviet bloc, which was admitted to membership of the Council for Mutual Economic Assistance (Comecon) in October 1950. The GDR was regarded by the West as having no legal basis.

In April 1946 the Socialist Unity Party (SED) had been formed by a merger of the Communist Party of Germany (KPD) and the Social Democrats (SPD) in the Soviet zone (a fate which the socialists of Berlin resisted). The initial idea of each party being jointly represented in the SED leadership (the social democrat Otto Grotewohl and the communist Wilhelm Pieck were its joint chairmen) survived only until 1947 when it was declared that the Russian road to socialism was the only model. Backed by the Soviet administration, the SED dominated the political scene and the communists dominated the SED. In September 1946 the SED topped the poll in all five provincial (*Land*) elections; thereafter, elections were conducted on a single-list basis, as used for the People's Council election in May 1949 (when two-thirds were recorded as approving and one-third as opposing the single list) and for elections to the unicameral parliament, the *Volkskammer*, commencing with that of 1950. When the GDR was declared in October 1949, the SED took half the ministerial portfolios in its first coalition government, with Grotewohl as prime minister while Pieck became President. The SED's partners (Christian Democratic Union—CDU, Liberal Democratic Party—LDP, National Democratic Party—NDPD and the Democratic Peasants' Party—DBD) were progressively reduced in significance within the National Front, the umbrella organization formed in 1950.

Walter Ulbricht, a KPD leader who had been in exile in the Soviet Union since 1933, was the dominant figure in the first two decades of the GDR's history, SED general secretary from 1950 (the post was restyled first secretary in 1963), and head of state as well from 1960. He imposed policies of rigid Stalinism within the party, which he systematically purged of his opponents (after the breach with Yugoslavia, in 1953-54, and again after liberal hopes inspired in Hungary had been crushed by Soviet tanks in 1956). This party machine was in turn harnessed to the central planning of the economy, in an effort to match the "economic miracle" of the capitalist West, with an emphasis on the heavy industrial base, and a determination to extract maximum effort from the workforce. When the workers of East Berlin and other cities came out on the streets in protest in 1953 they were ruthlessly suppressed with assistance from the Soviet occupation forces. A temporary "new course", a relaxation in the drive for socialization of the economy, gave way to a further push to fully centralized planning, nationalization of industry, and collectivization of farming by 1960. From the 1960s, however, the GDR's economic planners placed a continuing emphasis on consumer goods, attempting to satisfy the demand for improved living standards, and on social policy, education and welfare provision. They could (and did) claim partial success. The GDR reached by some way the highest standard of living in Eastern Europe, but no propaganda could obliterate the message which could be drawn from measurements on the other yardstick, the comparison with a much more affluent West Germany. This comparison was all too glaring when it could be seen on television, as was possible almost everywhere in the East except in the area around Dresden.

Throughout the 1950s there had been a continuing exodus of East Germans to the West. This serious drain of manpower (and stain on the pride of the regime) was one of the factors which provoked the building in August 1961 of the ultimate symbol of divided Germany, the Berlin Wall (later extended along the whole length of the border with West Germany, ostensibly to prevent Western subversion). The decision to build the wall was taken by the Warsaw Pact (of which the GDR was a founder member in May 1955, the month in which West Germany joined NATO), and also reflected the growth of tension over Berlin between the Soviet and the three Western administering powers, after the Soviet side had in 1958 begun moves to integrate the whole of Berlin into the GDR.

When Warsaw Pact forces moved in to crush the reform communist experiment in Czechoslovakia in August 1968, German troops were among them. The "Prague Spring" ideas of political pluralism had found no echo within the SED, but the Soviet ideological justification for intervening, the Brezhnev doctrine of "internationalism" for the defence of socialism, was clearly full of import for the future of the GDR. Its 1968 constitution, describing itself as 'a socialist state of the German nation', had referred to the goal of unification 'on the basis of democracy and socialism', was significantly amended by 1974, dropping the words 'of the German nation' to leave simply the description "a socialist state", and replacing wholesale the article about eventual unification. Henceforth, the GDR proclaimed itself 'an inseparable part of the socialist community' linked 'irrevocably and for ever' to the Soviet Union.

An East-West German treaty which guaranteed the inviolability of the intra-German border (December 1972) enabled both states to become members of the UN the following September 1973. Meanwhile, tensions in Berlin had been eased by a new Quadripartite Agreement (September 1971) specifying that the status quo could not be changed unilaterally. In 1975 both the GDR and the FRG signed the Final Act of the Conference on Security and Co-operation in Europe (CSCE), in which the existing borders of all European states were declared to be inviolable. These international developments were pursued under the leadership of Erich Honecker, who had succeeded Ulbricht on the latter's resignation in 1971. This was, however, apparently the measure of his experimentation, a limited openness to change in external policy, until the advent of Mikhail Gorbachev's reformist regime in the Soviet Union in 1985 put him under added pressure to find an East German response. Relations between the two Germanies also suffered in the 1970s and 1980s from high-profile political scandals which accompanied the uncovering of evidence of the extensive spy networks which each side was using against the other.

Internally, the Honecker regime was in tune with the Brezhnev conservative line, and quite unprepared for the challenge of reform. By 1985, the East German economy had been in serious trouble for at least five years, although the systematic falsification of statistics under economy secretary Günter Mittag concealed some of the extent of this problem. Industry was in need of large-scale investment, in technology which could make it possible to increase productivity. The response was, in part, large-scale foreign borrowing (running up a hard currency debt of over $20 billion by the end of 1989); there were also cuts in spending on housing and social welfare programmes. Honecker and his associates maintained, however, that the example of the *perestroika* reform programme in the Soviet Union was not applicable in the GDR. The Soviet leader's visit for the SED's 11th congress in April 1986, and the embarrassment caused by his references to the Soviet party's spirit of self-criticism and efforts to overcome stagnation, set the tone of his difficult relationship with Honecker.

The East German response was essentially two-fold; to censor, if possible, the information on policy changes in the Soviet Union, and to seek to divert attention (and get more Western money) by arranging the first-ever visit to Bonn by an East German leader. Honecker's visit to West Germany eventually took place in September 1987, but not before it had been made abundantly clear that Gorbachev would not welcome such a visit giving another lease of life to the GDR's elderly hardline leadership.

The coming of *glasnost* would ultimately expose the luxury in which Honecker, official trade union leader Harry Tisch and his associates had isolated themselves from the realities of East German life; these revelations, however, were to follow rather than to precede the collapse of the regime. That collapse, when it came in 1989, was spectacularly rapid and, within a year, quite unexpectedly complete.

One precipitating factor was the sudden wave of refugee emigration. Most of those who abandoned East Germany in this way were the young, often the well-educated, people whom the GDR could least afford to lose. They left at first legally, on visa-free trips to Czechoslovakia, and then took refuge in Western embassies across Eastern Europe. Many began going through Hungary, escaping into Austria. There was a marked absence of decisive action from Berlin to stop the departures, and on Sept. 11 the Hungarians opened the border to Austria, letting the East Germans out. A breach of Eastern European solidarity which had previously seemed unthinkable, this decision brought down no Soviet retribution or condemnation; and the floodgates opened. More people poured into Western embassies in Prague and Warsaw, then across the border from Czechoslovakia to West Germany after Nov. 4, and finally through Berlin when the Wall itself was breached five days later.

A third of a million East Germans left for West Germany in 1989, compared with under 40,000 the previous year. Even larger numbers became demonstrators on the streets of Leipzig, Dresden, East Berlin and other cities. The first signs of public protest came in May 1989, when church-based pro-democracy groups arranged to observe the local election process and then denounced the cynical fraud of the officially-announced near-unanimous vote for the approved National Front list. The protest demonstrations centred on Leipzig, and were firmly suppressed. Leipzig's Catholic church of St Nicholas, however, became a centre for Monday meetings of pro-democracy and civil rights groups, and it was from this initial nucleus that the massive-scale demonstrations of October developed and spread across the country. When the crowds reached many tens of thousands, the security forces could no longer disperse them, without recourse to army action on the scale of China's Tiananmen Square massacre in June. Honecker drew this parallel himself on Oct. 10 (and indeed his regime had been one of the few to congratulate the Chinese leadership, whom Egon Krenz had visited in June). The demonstrations, however, continued to grow, demanding reform, demanding dialogue.

Within the SED leadership, Honecker's position had been weakened both by his chronic ill health and by the pressure for reform which was coming from the Soviet leadership. Gorbachev had visited Berlin as recently as Oct. 6-7, for the GDR's 40th anniversary celebrations, and warned Honecker that leaders who failed to respond to popular pressures "put themselves in danger". Demonstrators in Leipzig, clearly identifying the Gorbachev line as offering positive hope for reform in the GDR, had chanted "Gorby, Gorby" and "we want to stay"; but, within hours of his departure, the East German police had broken up demonstrations in Berlin and Dresden. On that anniversary day, for those who looked back over the history of the GDR, there was a striking contrast with 1953, when it had been Soviet troops who put down the country's previous large-scale popular protests.

As in Hungary, and as would soon be the case in Bulgaria and Czechoslovakia, the fall of the old leadership in the GDR (Honecker resigned on Oct. 18 and was replaced by Egon Krenz) apparently offered a brief moment for reformists within the ruling party to regain the initiative. In this respect, however, East Germany was to be like Czechoslovakia, in that the initiative had already passed to the democratic opposition.

New Forum, the first of the opposition groups to apply for recognized association status (unsuccessfully, in September 1989), had grown by mid-October to a membership of over 25,000, drawn mainly from among the artists, students and intellectuals who dominated the demonstrations early on. Groups of the leftist "citizens' movement", like New Forum, Democracy Now, the Peace and Human Rights Initiative and the Greens, had been associated closely with the churches, particularly the St Nicholas church in Leipzig. They were joined, as the SED's hardline grip was loosened, by rejuvenated non-communist parties which for 40 years had disappeared or been subservient within the National Front. The Social Democrats, the Liberal Democrats and (more cautiously) the Christian Democrats took up critical positions; in this they were sustained by the renewal of links with their West German counterparts, a factor which later contributed to the impetus towards unification.

For all Krenz's concessions (and they were many and major; it was Krenz who opened the Wall, who agreed to open elections, and who conceded on ending the SED's "leading role"), he cut an implausible figure in his new reformist garb, and was swept aside within seven weeks. Few believed his claim that he had prevented violence in early October, by countermanding Honecker's orders for the use of force. As Honecker's own chosen successor, and as the former head of the hated *Stasi* security police, Krenz could not win support as a leader capable of setting the SED on a genuinely new and democratic course. The most credible candidate for such a task, Hans Modrow, the reform-minded SED leader from Dresden, now took over the government from Honecker's long-serving prime minister Willy Stoph. With free elections promised, Modrow formed a new government in mid-November. The formerly subservient National Front parties (in particular the Christian Democrats) were given a real role, and by February 1990 Modrow had broadened the spectrum, bringing in eight opposition party representatives to give the GDR its first-ever government without a communist majority. But, by then, the important policy decisions were being made not in the government, but in the round-table talks under way between the SED and opposition groups since early December; and the elections had been brought forward from May to March.

The unification of Germany, scarcely on the agenda when the Wall was first opened on Nov. 9, had become the dominant issue by the time of these elections. Indeed, so far had the picture changed that the main arguments concerned when and how, not whether, to unite. Relegated to the fringe (as the results confirmed) were those, perhaps expressing a majority view only three months before, who stressed positive aspects in the old GDR, distinguishing it from capitalist West Germany, and seeking the continuation of a distinct East German state, which should be democratic, certainly, and respectful of civil rights, but egalitarian, preserving the best achievements of the East's social and welfare system.

The election left the CDU and its Alliance for Germany partners in a position of unexpected strength. The figure who loomed largest in its campaign, not an East German at all but the West German CDU leader and Federal Chancellor Helmut Kohl, was in effect the dominant character in the last year of the GDR. The Social Democrats, also reliant on their Western sister party for weight in their campaign, trailed behind in second place; and third, with a solid core of support even now, were the communists, restyled now as the Party of Democratic Socialism (PDS).

It took four weeks to form the first fully post-communist government in East Germany, a "grand coalition", but excluding the PDS, with the Christian Democrat Lothar de Maizière as prime minister. The process was complicated by an issue which was to become a recurring feature of the political scene; allegations against leading figures (now focusing on SPD leader Ibrahim Böhme) about working for, or at least informing to, the hated *Stasi*. It had already been decided, in December, to disband the *Stasi*, and its East Berlin headquarters building had been ransacked on Jan. 15. The compromising entries in its files, kept on more than one East German in three, went on leaching out for the next two years, even after unification, ultimately ruining the political career of de Maizière himself and prompting the government to propose (but then abandon) the idea of an amnesty.

Once formed, the first and last East German democratic government was heavily preoccupied with the economic, political and external dimensions of the unification issue (this last, however, being worked out principally between the Soviet Union on the one side and the NATO allies including West Germany on the other).

First to be decided were the terms of economic union (which took effect on July 1). This agreement, and the accompanying programme of privatization administered by the Treuhand, in effect defined the nature and the speed of the transition to free market economics. The package was costly for the West in immediate terms. Only gradually did it also become apparent how severe the dislocation would be in the East, in a society where the inefficiencies of outmoded industrial production had been concealed behind state ownership, guaranteed employment and public subsidy.

More debated at the time than economic union was the form and timing of political union (which took effect at midnight on Oct. 2-3). In effect it involved the disappearance of the East German state, its merger into the existing structure of the Federal Republic, and the holding of all-German elections on Dec. 2, 1990. These elections returned to power the CDU-led coalition under Helmut Kohl, who could claim them as his triumph. More than anyone, he had identified and ridden the tide of German unification in the past twelve months.

For many Germans, however (and for non-Germans too), the celebrations of unification were clouded with concern, in a way that had not been the case on the euphoric day the Wall came down. In rebuilding the economy, large-scale unemployment had already emerged as a heavy price, even though the East started from a higher point, and had far better chances of attracting investment, than the post-communist regimes elsewhere in the region. Many individuals found themselves paying the price of involvement with the old system; not just the corrupt top party officials and the secret police informers, but others such as the border guard imprisoned in January 1992 for shooting to kill a would-be escaper, and many thousands of teachers, debarred from teaching if they were too heavily implicated in the indoctrination of the "*Stabu*" lessons in "citizenship studies". The emergence of racism and crude Nazi-style violence among skinhead gangs, hitting the headlines with attacks on immigrant workers, was the response of a fringe minority, but a warning sign nevertheless, of what could grow up among those left discarded by the dismantling of the GDR.

The principal personalities of Communist rule

Walter **Ulbricht** (1893-1973), a Weimar Republic Communist from Leipzig who had fled to Moscow in 1933, became an SED politburo member in January 1949 and general secretary in July 1950, and over the next two decades (from 1960 as head of state as well as party leader) imposed rigid Stalinism, both in terms of party terror and in terms of economic nationalization and the collectivization of agriculture. Ousted from the party leadership by his former protégé Honecker in 1971 (although still head of state until his death), his dominance was subsequently played down.

Willi **Stoph** (b. 1914). A Communist in his youth, and a prominent SED member with a politburo seat from 1953 onwards, he was prime minister for nine years under Ulbricht, then his successor as President, then again prime minister from 1976 to 1989, as a loyal number two to Honecker. He resigned on Nov. 7, 1989, and was arrested in May 1991 to face charges of responsibility for murder over the GDR's "shoot to kill" policy against would-be escapers.

Erich **Honecker** (b. 1912). A communist organizer from the Saar, he was imprisoned in 1935-45 by the Nazi regime, then rose rapidly within the SED, and joined the politburo in 1958. It was on his initiative that the Berlin Wall was built in 1961. He was regarded as Ulbricht's chosen successor, but ousted him early, with Soviet support, in 1971, and was the dominant figure of GDR politics for the next two decades (adding to the party leadership, in 1976, the role of head of state). Keen to promote his own and his country's international image, he found himself quite out of step with the changes of the late 1980s. The growing perception of his inadequacy was compounded by his serious illness, and he was ousted from power in October 1989 in what was in effect a bid by the SED to give itself a new lease of life in power. The discovery of his corruption and use of funds for personal luxury helped inflame the public against him and his regime, but he was found to be too ill to stand trial. Arraigned again, in 1990, this time for responsibility for the "shoot-to-kill" policy against would-be escapers from the GDR, he was moved in March 1991 from a Soviet military hospital to Moscow, from where the German government sought to extradite him, but without success as of end-1991.

Günter **Mittag** (b. 1926). A politburo member from 1966 and SED secretary for the economy, Mittag was principally responsible for the mismanagement, under-investment and corruption of the latter years of the GDR. He was also blamed by his own colleagues in the SED old-guard leadership for his failure to deputize effectively in the summer of 1989, when Honecker was ill and a firm line was needed over the exodus of young East Germans. After Honecker's resignation, the fate of his hardline associate Mittag provided an index of the party's efforts to show a genuine commitment to change. Dropped from the politburo on Oct. 18, he was expelled from the central committee on Nov. 10 and from the party itself on Nov. 23, and arrested for abuse of office on Dec. 3.

Egon **Krenz** (b. 1937). Rising through the SED youth movement, with a seat in the party politburo from 1983 and responsibility for security policy, Krenz was often seen as Honecker's chosen successor. He followed the hard line of his mentor's regime until mid-1989, making it unlikely that reformists would subsequently dissociate him from the rigging of the local elections in May, and the congratulations which he offered to the Chinese party leadership for dealing with their pro-democracy demonstrators in Tiananmen Square. Ultimately, convinced of the need for changes by the attitude of Gorbachev, the exodus of asylum-seekers and the size and tenacity of the demonstrations of early October, he engineered the ousting of Honecker. Taking over himself as SED general secretary and then head of state, but lasted only seven weeks at the top. Unable to present himself as a credible reformer (although he put through such crucial changes as allowing freedom of travel, opening the Wall, and renouncing the party's leading role), he disappeared from the stage almost as soon as he had resigned his party and state posts (on Dec. 3 and 6 respectively); in the following month the party expelled him, as part of the process of making its break with the Honecker regime.

Hans **Modrow** (b. 1928). Brought into full membership of the SED politburo as an indication of its commitment to change on Nov. 8, 1989, Modrow, the party secretary from Dresden with a good name for personal honesty, had managed to sustain a real dialogue with the pro-democracy demonstrators. He was charged later the same month with heading what would be the GDR's last communist-led government, in which capacity he put forward his own plan for a unified but neutral Germany. At the March 1990 elections his reputation as a genuine reform leader was credited with helping his party (now renamed the PDS) retain a significant vote and finish third. He remained as caretaker prime minister until the new government was formed, and then stood, unsuccessfully, as the PDS candidate for the post of *Volkskammer* speaker.

Constitutional changes

A key phrase in Article 1 of the Constitution, which specified that the GDR was led by "the working class and its Marxist-Leninist party", was deleted on Dec. 1, 1989, with the almost unanimous support of the *Volkskammer*. Thereafter, there were a series of changes necessary for the holding of free elections, and the round table discussed a draft for a new constitution for East Germany, agreeing at its final session on March 12 that this should be discussed by the new parliament and then put to a referendum. This never took place, as the general consensus for unification made it irrelevant. However, changes were made in April 1990 by the new *Volkskammer*, removing the description of the GDR as "a socialist state of workers and peasants" and abolishing the State Council (whose chairman had been head of state), with the speaker of the *Volkskammer* becoming head of state in an acting capacity.

The state treaty on unification, signed on Aug. 31, determined that the two Germanies would be united, on Oct. 3, by means of the GDR ceasing to exist, and five *Länder*, recreated on the territory of the GDR, joining the Federal Republic under the provisions of Article 23 of its Basic Law. It was agreed that any further matters arising from unification, which required settlement by amendment of the constitution, should if possible be regulated within two years from that date. This would apply in particular on the issue of abortion, where West German law had been much more restrictive than that of East Germany, and where both sets of legislation would remain operative pending a compromise.

Position and status of communists

Party name

The name Socialist Unity Party of Germany (SED) was used from 1946, denoting the merger of the Social Democrats in the Soviet zone with the German Communist Party (DKP, founded in 1918 by left-wing Social Democrats from the underground wartime Spartacus League, and revived in 1945 after having been banned and persecuted under the Hitler regime). The SED was the dominant partner in the National Front umbrella organization.

The emergency party congress in December 1989 adopted the half-new name Socialist Unity Party-Party of Democratic Socialism (SED-PDS), and the decision to drop the first half was announced the following February, the name PDS being confirmed at an election congress on Feb. 24-25.

Membership

A mass membership party with 2,400,000 members in 1989, the SED lost members very rapidly from October 1989 onwards. As of early 1991 its PDS successor had a membership of 280,000, falling to 180,000 by end-year.

Legal status

The SED's "leading role" having been abolished as of Dec. 1, 1989, and many of its leaders having been expelled (and in some cases subsequently prosecuted), the party under its new name PDS remained a legal political formation in East Germany, contesting the March 1990 elections and the December 1990 all-German elections.

The *Land* government of Bavaria took the decision (not followed by other *Land* governments) in 1991 to put the PDS under surveillance as a possible danger to the constitution. The exclusion of civil servants (including teachers) from employment under federal regulations, if they had been too closely associated with promoting communist ideology in the GDR, involved a massive screening exercise which remained controversial as of the end of 1991.

Workplace organization

The fundamental units of organization of the SED were residential and grouped by district. Control in the workplace was exercised principally through the communist-dominated unions, the Confederation of German Free Trade Unions (FDGB) being the sole legal formation under the communist regime; its chairman, Harry Tisch, was an influential politburo member. His replacement and subsequent disgrace in late

1989, and the further leadership changes at a congress on Jan. 31, 1990, were not sufficient to give the FDGB a new face or role in the post-communist period, and it was dissolved on May 9, 1990. Trade union independence had been accepted in the SED's November 1989 programme.

Party militia

The SED-controlled workers' militia groups in factories throughout the GDR were abolished by a decision of the interim government on Dec. 15, 1989, under pressure from opposition parties in the round table talks.

Party assets

Legislation introduced by the East German government on May 31, 1990, allowed it to investigate and establish the value of party assets, and provided for expropriations of funds and property acquired by parties by the misuse of their position under the communist regime. As of October 1990 the PDS declared its assets to be worth DM4,000 million. Allegations that the PDS was transferring funds abroad illegally in that month led to police raids on the party headquarters, and charges against its treasurer and other officials.

The Treuhand agency, set up to handle privatization, took control of all PDS property and froze its bank accounts in June 1991, preventing it from spending money without permission. This followed the problems experienced by an independent commission which had been set up by the federal government to audit the funds and property of all the former GDR's ruling parties, to establish how it had been acquired and what parts of it could be retained by the parties concerned.

Ideological orientation.

The party, formerly considering itself the "Marxist-Leninist party of the working people in town and country", redefined itself as a socialist party committed to democratic pluralism, at the emergency congress on Dec. 8-9, 1989, at which it changed its name and leadership. That congress endorsed key decisions of the "action programme" agreed by the central committee on Nov. 8-10, with regard to pluralism, civil liberties and internal party democracy. The "action programme" had also called for the restructuring of the economy as "a socialist planned economy guided by market conditions". The main plank of the PDS election campaign in March 1990, however, and its subsequent principal concern as an opposition party, was the effort to preserve as far as possible within a free market context the level of social welfare and employment protection which had been built up under the communist regime. The PDS deputies in the *Volkskammer* voted against the terms of both the treaty on economic and monetary union, and the unification treaty.

Electoral significance

The single-list parliamentary elections under the communist regime allowed the division of seats between the SED, other National Front parties, and mass organizations, to be predetermined. In comparison with other such Front arrangements elsewhere in Eastern Europe, the National Front formula in the GDR allocated only a modest proportion of the parliamentary seats to the SED (127 out of 500 in the *Volkskammer* in 1986), but nonetheless gave it complete dominance in policy terms.

Competing under its new name in the multi-party East German legislative elections in March 1990, the PDS did unexpectedly well, finishing third with 16.4 per cent (30 per cent in East Berlin) and 66 out of 400 *Volkskammer* seats. It scored 14.6 per cent in local elections on May 6, and between 9.7 and 15.7 per cent in the elections for the five reconstituted *Land* parliaments in the East on Oct. 14. In the all-German elections in December 1990 the PDS, clearly disadvantaged in comparison with the other major parties in that it had no powerful counterpart organization in the West, nevertheless still won 17 seats in the *Bundestag*, on the basis of its 11.1 per cent of the poll in the East; in the elections for a unified Berlin parliament at the same time the PDS won nearly a quarter of the votes in what had been East Berlin.

Principal parties in the post-communist period

The **Christian Democratic Union** (CDU) in East Germany, which had been for over 40 years a subordinate part of the communist-dominated National Front, became the dominant element in the **Alliance for Germany** which won nearly half the total vote in the March 1990 elections. Its campaign and pro-unification programme were dominated by the influence of its West German counterpart led by Federal Chancellor Helmut Kohl, under whose leadership the CDUs of West and East merged on Oct. 1, 1990. The East German CDU leader Lothar de Maizière was prime minister of the last East German government, from April 1990 until unification in October. The post-unification disillusionment caused by economic problems in the East led to a marked falling-off in CDU popularity there in 1991, as did the conviction of its 1966-89 leader Gerard Götting in July 1991 for diverting party funds into his own holiday home, and the discrediting, over alleged *Stasi* connections, of de Maizière himself. He had taken over the CDU leadership on Nov. 10, 1989, as the party distanced itself from the SED (although participating in the Modrow government), and he led its participation in the subsequent round-table talks. The CDU's programme of pluralism, democracy based on Christian values, and the creation of a market economy with encouragement for Western investment, was set out at an extraordinary conference on Dec. 15-16, 1989.

Also part of the Alliance for Germany (set up on Feb. 5, 1990) were the **German Social Union** (DSU) and the centre-right **Democratic Awakening** (DA). The DSU had been founded on Jan. 20, 1990, with a right-wing former Christian Social Party leader, the Leipzig pastor Hans-Wilhelm Ebeling, as its first chairman. Both Ebeling and Peter-Michael Diestel, who became de Maizière's deputy premier, left the DSU on July 2, 1990, after which the party retained no real significance. The DA was formally constituted as a party in Leipzig on Dec. 16, 1989, led first by the lawyer Wolfgang Schnur and, after his disgrace over *Stasi* connections, by pastor Rainer Eppelmann.

The **Free Democrats / Liberals** in the East consisted of (i) the Liberal Democratic Party (LDPD), one of the four non-communist parties in the ruling National Front, which had begun to take a much more independent and pro-democracy line after Honecker's departure in October 1989, under the leadership of Manfred Gerlach and Rainer Ortleb, and which on Nov. 3 joined the calls for the resignation of the government of prime minister Willy Stoph; (ii) a separate Free Democratic Party, critical of the LDPD for its history of collaboration with the communists, and set up later in November; (iii) the German Forum, and (iv) the National Democratic Party (NDPD), which like the LDPD had been one of the parties which existed under the communist-dominated National Front umbrella and then tried to reassert its separate identity. The Free Democrats / Liberals came together on Feb. 12, 1990 (with the NDPD joining in March), as the League of Free Democrats (BfD) to avoid splitting the centre vote in the March elections. This was the first group to merge formally with its West German counterpart, on Aug. 11, 1990; the FDP leader in the West, Otto Graf Lambsdorff, continued as party chairman and the BfD and Eastern FDP leaders were added as deputy chairmen.

The **Social Democratic Party** was reformed as a separate entity illegally on Oct. 8, 1989. It sought to symbolize its return to its pre-1946 independence by adopting at its first national conference on Jan. 12-14 the name Social Democratic Party of Germany (i.e. SPD, like its counterpart in the West) rather than Social Democratic Party of the GDR (SDP). The same conference confirmed its conversion to the objective of German reunification. The allegation of *Stasi* connections made against Ibrahim Böhme, who was elected as party chair at the Feb. 22-25 party congress, affected its performance in the March 1990 elections, and he resigned thereafter, giving way initially to Markus Meckel. Meckel then took on the role of foreign minister in the coalition government, until the SPD left the government in the crisis over economic policy management in September. The party merged in late September 1990 with its Western counterpart, and its then current chairman Wolfgang Thierse became a deputy chairman of the all-German party.

Alliance 90 was the electoral alliance formed on Feb. 7, 1990, for the March 1990 East German elections by the left-wing citizens' movements which had first emerged as authentic voices of the democratic opposition in 1989—-Democracy Now, whose leading figure was the documentary film-maker Konrad Weiss; New Forum, co-founded in September by the Berlin painter and activist Bärbel Bohley and the biologist Jens Reich, and legalized on Nov. 8; and the Peace and Human Rights Initiative. The revival of mainstream parties linked closely to their respective West German counterparts, and the rapid change of focus on to the issue of unification rather than that of changing East Germany, meant that the Alliance 90 platform (although it did accept, in the face of some dissent, the idea of gradual reunification, leading to a demilitarized Germany) won only 2.9 per cent of the vote and 12 *Volkskammer* seats in March 1990. Its deputies subsequently agreed to form a joint parliamentary group with the **Greens** (formed on Nov. 24, 1989). In the December 1990 all-German elections, campaigning jointly with the Greens in the East, they increased their joint vote and narrowly passed the 5 per cent minimum threshold now applicable there, securing six Alliance 90 and two Green seats in the Bundestag; they did better in former East Berlin, winning nearly 10 per cent there in the December 1990 election of a unified city government. In September 1991 at a meeting in Potsdam the three movements within the Alliance 90 merged formally into a single organization of that name, with statutes in line with federal party laws; part of New Forum opposed this merger.

The post-communist political leaders

Ibrahim **Böhme** (b. 1944). Elected as SPD party chairman in late February 1990 as a figure whose dissident credentials apparently represented a clear break with the party's role within the SED (from which he had himself resigned, as a young historian in his early 30s, and been imprisoned and then banned from teaching history), Böhme came under attack immediately after the March elections as an alleged *Stasi* informer; he denied any such connection, but nevertheless stood down and then formally resigned the party leadership on April 1.

Gregor **Gysi** (b. 1948). A lawyer, long-standing SED party member and son of one of Honecker's government ministers, Gysi was not himself in tune with the hardline stance of the Honecker regime, and was known for defending dissidents; the party brought him in as its new leader in December 1989 to signify the break with the past, and, under its new name of PDS, he led it to respectable performances in the multi-party elections of 1990. The PDS re-elected Gysi as its leader in January 1991 and again in December.

Pastor Rainer **Eppelmann**. The leading figure, after the disgrace of Wolfgang Schnur, in the Democratic Awakening group which campaigned within the centre-right Alliance for Germany coalition. An East Berlin pastor known as sympathetic with dissidents and pacifists under the communist regime, he had himself been imprisoned for refusing military service, and it was at his insistence that the cabinet post which he took up in April 1990 had the unusual title "defence and disarmament".

Joachim **Gauck** (b. 1940). A member of the *Volkskammer* for Alliance 90, the former dissident pastor Gauck was chosen to oversee the administration of files compiled by the *Stasi*, and was thus at the centre of one of the hottest political legacies of the defunct GDR.

Lothar **de Maizière** (b. 1940). Once a professional viola player, he was a lawyer with no real political experience when the CDU chose him as its new leader in November 1989. Associated with the pro-unification drive of West German Chancellor Kohl, the CDU and its allies won a strong enough position in the March 1990 to make its leader the obvious choice as the prime minister who would lead the GDR out of existence. De Maizière became a deputy chairman of the merged all-German CDU in October 1990, and a minister without portfolio in Kohl's government, but was then exposed to allegations that he had been a *Stasi* informer. He resigned, resumed his party post after the announcement in February 1991 that an inquiry had exonerated him, but resigned again in September, and gave up his parliamentary seat, as the allegation persisted.

Markus **Meckel**. The SPD's deputy leader in East Germany from February 1990 and then chairman following Böhme's resignation in April, Meckel was the foreign minister (and one of the three pastors) in de Maizière's government until his party left the coalition in August 1990. He was replaced as SPD chair in the East on June 9, 1990, by Wolfgang Thierse.

Elections

Legislature

Under Communist rule, the legislature, the 500-member unicameral *Volkskammer* (People's Chamber), designated as the highest state authority and nominally responsible for electing the Council of Ministers, was itself elected by universal suffrage from a single list of candidates for a term of five years, most recently in 1986.

A new unicameral *Volkskammer* of 400 members was elected on March 8, 1990 (and dissolved on Oct. 2 immediately prior to the unification of Germany; 144 of its members were then delegated to sit in the *Bundestag* pending all-German elections). The system used in March 1990 was proportional representation with no minimum threshold for representation; the turnout was given as 93.4 per cent.

Electoral regulations for the first all-German elections (on Dec. 2), as approved by the *Volkskammer* on Aug. 22, would have adopted the West German system—i.e. proportional representation in the 662-member *Bundestag* within the unit of the *Land*, and with 5 per cent of the overall national vote as the minimum threshold for party representation. Its only real concession to the smaller Eastern groups would have been to allow for "piggy-back" arrangements, in which parties of similar outlook might aggregate their votes for the purpose of calculating the 5 per cent, provided that they had not put up lists in competition with each other. After unification, however, the rules were changed because the Federal Constitutional Court had found this system to be unfair to smaller parties in the East with no counterpart in the West. For the 1990 elections only, the minimum threshold was 5 per cent in either the former West or the former East. The turnout on Dec. 2 was given as 74.7 per cent in the East and 77.8 per cent overall.

The allocation of seats in the *Bundesrat*, the upper house, was reorganized to allow each *Land* to send between three and eight members.

General election results

March 18, 1990: elections to *Volkskammer* in East Germany

	percentage	seats
CDU	40.82	163
DSU	6.31	25
Democratic Awakening	0.99	4
Free Democrats	5.28	21
SPD	21.88	88
PDS	16.40	66
Alliance 90	2.91	12
Others		21
Total		400

Dec. 2, 1990: elections to *Bundestag* in united Germany			
	% in West	% in East	seats
CDU	35.5	41.8	268
CSU	8.8	-	51
Free Democrats	10.6	12.9	79
SPD	35.7	24.3	239
PDS	0.3	11.1	17
Alliance 90/Greens	4.8	6.1	8
Others			0
Total			662

Presidency

Under communist rule the head of state was the Chairman of the 25-member Council of State, elected by the *Volkskammer* (Honecker until Oct. 18, 1989, then Egon Krenz briefly on Oct. 26-Dec. 6, then Manfred Gerlach pending election of a new *Volkskammer*.

On April 9 the new *Volkskammer* abolished the Council of State, provided that the state presidency should be a directly elected post, and meanwhile approved the appointment of its new speaker, Sabine Bergmann-Pohl, as acting head of state. She discharged the duties of this office until unification on Oct. 2-3, when East Germany became part of the Federal Republic with federal President Richard von Weizsäcker as its head of state.

Local elections

Local elections were held throughout East Germany on May 6, 1990 (when the CDU won some 35 per cent, the SPD 21 per cent, the PDS 14.6 per cent and the Free Democrats 6.7 per cent; the SPD came first in East Berlin and the PDS second).

Elections for five reconstituted *Land* parliaments took place on Oct. 14, giving the CDU control in Mecklenburg-Western Pomerania, in Saxony, in Saxony-Anhalt and in Thuringia, while the SPD emerged as the leading party in Brandenburg and second everywhere else. The PDS was third in four *Länder* but fourth behind the FDP in Saxony-Anhalt.

Berlin held its first elections for a unified city parliament at the same time as the all-German legislative elections on Dec. 2, 1990. The CDU emerged in first place overall, although behind the SPD (and only narrowly ahead of the PDS) in the former East Berlin.

Governments in the post-communist period

The interim government formed under the leadership of the reform-minded communist Hans Modrow in November 1989, as approved on Nov. 17, consisted of the SED and the four other parties of the National Front which had previously been subservient to it, but which were now given much greater participation (the CDU, the Liberal Democratic Party—LDPD, the National Democratic party—NDPD and the Democratic Farmers' Party (DBD). From January 1990 Modrow sought to broaden the basis of this government, and a "government of national responsibility" was formed with the addition of eight opposition party representatives on Feb. 5. This put the SED into a minority, for the first time, in the brief period before the elections now brought forward from May 6 to March 18.

The first, and only, post-communist government was formed under the leadership of Lothar de Maizière of the CDU after the March 1990 elections, and after a lengthy period of consultations among the different political parties. Sworn in on April 12, it was initially a coalition of the CDU-dominated Alliance for Germany with the Free Democrats and Social Democrats; the former left in July and the latter in August, and the government itself ceased to exist with German unification on Oct. 2-3.

Principal members of the de Maizière government, April-October 1990

Prime minister: Lothar de Maizière (CDU)
Deputy premier, internal affairs: Peter-Michael Diestel (initially DSU, joined CDU in July 1990)
Foreign affairs: Markus Meckel (SPD) until Aug. 20 when the SPD left the coalition
Finance: Walter Romberg (SPD) until his dismissal on Aug. 15
Economics: Gerhard Pohl (CDU) until his resignation on Aug. 15
Defence and Disarmament: Rainer Eppelmann (Democratic Awakening)

Government crises

The uneasy relationship between the parties in the broad coalition government broke down first in July 1991, over a question of essential interest for future party political advantage; de Maizière's proposal that unification should follow, rather than precede, all-German elections, which would avoid the application of existing West German rules in those elections. The Free Democrats (who left the coalition in protest on July 24), and the Social Democrats, saw this as favouring the CDU's ally the DSU, which could be eliminated from parliament if the West German 5 per cent minimum threshold were applied.

The SPD left the coalition the following month (raising the question of whether the government would still be able to get a two-thirds majority for a unification treaty), protesting over the dismissal of SPD finance minister Romberg and other cabinet members whom de Maizière held responsible for poor economic management.

Security and human rights issues

Freedom of travel was a major issue in the period leading up to the fall of the communist regime, with thousands defying the strict rules preventing them going to the West. Restrictions on travel to Czechoslovakia were lifted on Nov. 1, 1989, and two days later it was made clear that those wishing to leave would not have to renounce their East German citizenship. The dramatic change came on Nov. 9 with the announcement that East Germans were free to travel abroad as they wished, requiring only to have their identity documents stamped with an exit visa (which could readily be obtained). This allowed them to cross the Berlin Wall, and the intra-German border, which they did in huge numbers in the ensuing days, to the extent that the exit visa requirement was waived because it was impossible to administer. Television carried footage of people who, crossing the open checkpoints in the Wall, embraced security guards who had hitherto been under orders to shoot to kill at anyone trying to escape. A new law on the right to foreign travel, removing the threat of the deprivation of citizenship, was approved by parliament in December 1989 to take effect in February.

A social charter, the product of the work of the round table, was approved by the East German parliament on March 7, 1990, guaranteeing the right to work and the right to strike.

The *Stasi*

The decision to disband the *Stasi*, the Ministry of State Security, was taken by the Modrow government on Dec. 14, 1989, but it was not until Jan. 12, and as a result of much pressure, that Modrow agreed not to set up any replacement, pending the holding of elections and formation of a democratically-elected government. It was revealed at this time that there had been 85,000 *Stasi* personnel, of whom 25,000 had already been dismissed, and on Jan. 15 Modrow promised that disbanding would be completed within 10 days. Meanwhile direct action in a number of cities gave protestors a degree of temporary control over the huge number of files, which the *Stasi* had kept on one GDR citizen in three. The Leipzig offices of the *Stasi* were occupied on Dec. 4 and the East Berlin *Stasi* headquarterswas ransacked on Jan. 15.

The state treaty on unification stipulated that the files would remain for the time being in East Germany, where a commission under pastor Joachim Gauck was set up on Sept. 28 by parliament to supervise them, following further occupations of the Berlin headquarters in that month by demonstrators demanding access to their files. In November 1991 the federal parliament approved legislation allowing people the right of access to their own files, but leaving Gauck's commission to decide on the publication of any records, thereby seeking to control the spread of rumours and allegations about politicians having been informers. A suggestion to screen all members of parliament was rejected in March 1990. Those who resigned over the issue of *Stasi* connections, while in many cases denying that allegations about them had any substance, included: Democratic Awakening's first leader Wolfgang Schnur and the SPD leader Ibrahim Böhme in March 1990; the Free Democrat construction minister Axel Viehweger in September 1990 (after the publication of a list of 68 government members and parliamentarians with alleged *Stasi* links); Lothar de Maizière, by now minister without portfolio in the all-German government and CDU deputy chairman, in December 1990, and again in September 1991, after he had resumed the post of CDU deputy chair on the strength of having been exonerated by a government inquiry in February; and the Saxony *Land* interior minister Rudolf Krause, also in September 1991. In the neighbouring *Land* of Saxony-Anhalt, the minister-president, Gerd Gies, resigned in July 1991 amid accusations that he was using against others the tactic of allegation of *Stasi* involvement.

CHRONOLOGY

8 May 1945. Nazi Germany surrenders to the Allies, and the areas liberated by the Red Army in the eastern part of the country become the Soviet-occupied zone.

1 July 1945. The Western allied forces arrive in Berlin, which, like Germany as a whole, is divided into zones occupied and administered by the USA, Britain and the Soviet Union. (The French zones are subsequently carved out of the US and British zones.)

1946. Elections are held.

April 1946. The Social Democrats and the Communists are merged to form the Socialist Unity Party (SED) led by Walter Ulbricht.

January 1949. Poland officially incorporates the territories formerly part of Germany; mass expulsions of Germans to the west follow in March 1950.

May 1949. The end of the Berlin blockade.

7 October 1949. The German Democratic Republic is proclaimed officially.

February 1950. Creation of the Ministry of State Security, the *Stasi*.

June 1950. East Germany formally accepts the Oder-Neisse line as its border with Poland.

July 1950. A new constitution is adopted by the Socialist Unity Party.

17 June 1953. Riots begin in Berlin and spread to other cities but are then suppressed by Soviet forces.

September 1955. A treaty is signed with the Soviet Union, which formally recognizes the sovereignty of the GDR.

13 August 1961. The Berlin Wall goes up.

November 1968. Soviet party leader Leonid Brezhnev articulates the doctrine that socialist states have limited sovereignty and that other socialist countries may have an "internationalist obligation" to intervene in the defence of socialism.

March-May 1970. Meetings between Premier Willi Stoph and West German Chancellor Brandt lead to recognition of the GDR by West Germany, and an agreement on access to Berlin from the West.

August 1970. West Germany signs a treaty with the Soviet Union recognizing postwar border arrangements.

May 1971. Erich Honecker takes over from Ulbricht as party leader.

September 1971. The Four-Power Agreement is signed on the status of Berlin; the final protocol to this treaty is signed in June 1972.

December 1972. A treaty is signed with West Germany to normalize relations, although it falls short of full diplomatic recognition.

February 1973. The GDR is recognized by Britain and France.

September 1974. Diplomatic relations are established with the USA.

January 1982. As part of a sustained peace campaign primarily focused around the Lutheran and Evangelical churches, the so-called Berlin Appeal is launched by 35 activists including Pastor Rainer Eppelmann. It calls for a pacific alternative to military service and, in its wider aims, for the removal of all foreign troops from Germany as a whole and the creation of a nuclear-free zone.

April 1986. Gorbachev visits East Germany during the SED congress, but Honecker fails to get Soviet backing for his already-postponed plan to be the first East German leader to visit West Germany.

September 1987. Honecker finally visits West Germany.

May 1989. Local elections are held. The usual declaration of almost unanimous support for the National Front's sole list is challenged by church organizations who have observed the count; demonstrations against widespread rigging are suppressed by police in Leipzig.

11 September 1989. East Germans who have left the country in large numbers in recent weeks effectively as refugees, are allowed to cross the border from Hungary into Austria, marking a critical breach in the solidarity of the East European regimes against the free movement of their citizens.

9 September. Opposition groups come together to form a broad alliance known as New Forum.

7 October 1989. The 40th anniversary of the founding of the GDR is marked by official celebrations at which Gorbachev, the principal guest, makes no secret of having pressed the East German leadership to implement a programme of reforms.

7 October 1989. A meeting at Schwante near Potsdam decides on the refounding of a separate SPD, with Ibrahim Böhme as its first leader.

9 October 1989. Some 70,000 people attend the largest yet of Leipzig's regular Monday demonstrations at the St Nicholas Church, focus of opposition protest. Whereas these demonstrations have hitherto been countered violently by the security forces, on this occasion the police do not attack, local SED party leaders having joined in an appeal for a "free exchange of views about the further development of socialism in our country". The SED politburo holds an emergency meeting on Oct. 10-11 to discuss its response, with a split evident between hardliners and the more liberal-minded leaders from Leipzig and Dresden. By the following Monday the demonstration in Leipzig has swollen to some 120,000 and there have been large-scale demonstrations elsewhere, notably in Dresden and Halle.

18 October 1989. Honecker resigns and is succeeded as party leader by Egon Krenz, who becomes head of state on 24 October. Others leaving the politburo include Honecker's hardline lieutenant, Günter Mittag.

23 October 1989. Mass demonstrations call for free elections; Leipzig again witnesses by far the largest protest, numbering some 300,000.

27 October 1989. The Council of State announces an amnesty for those who have gone abroad illegally, and those accused of criminal acts during demonstrations, in

an attempt by the Krenz regime to recover some control over the situation. Plans
to liberalize travel laws are announced in the succeeding days.

4 November 1989. More than half a million people demonstrate in East Berlin, while
in Dresden a pro-democracy demonstration is joined by the reform-minded local
SED leader Hans Modrow.

7 November 1989. The government headed by long-serving prime minister Willy
Stoph resigns.

8 November 1989. The entire SED politburo resigns at a plenum of the central
committee; its short-lived successor includes Hans Modrow. New Forum is
legalized.

9 November 1989. The decision to open the Berlin Wall is announced, and the night
ends in popular euphoria.

10 November 1989. The SED under Krenz's leadership produces an "action programme" which includes a commitment to free elections. Mittag, blamed for the
regime's failure to respond to the growing emigration exodus in August while he
was deputizing for the ailing Honecker, is expelled from the SED central committee. Lothar de Maizière is elected chairman of the CDU.

17 November 1989. Modrow forms a new government, with an SED majority
membership, and announces the reorganization and renaming of the *Stasi* (Ministry of State Security), the hated secret police.

18 November 1989. The first legal meeting of Neues Forum, in Leipzig, is attended
by over 50,000 people.

28 November 1989. Proposals for a German confederation are put forward by West
German Federal Chancellor Helmut Kohl.

3 December 1989. Krenz, who has been unable to contain the demand for the abolition
of the communist regime, resigns the SED leadership, and the whole SED
politburo and central committee also resign, on the day that some two million
people form a human chain across the country, demanding democracy and the
punishment of corrupt former leaders. *Stasi* offices are stormed in Leipzig the
following day, and then in several other cities, and pro-democracy activists begin
searching their files.

6 December 1989. Krenz resigns as head of state.

7 December 1989. The first meeting is held of the Round Table, effectively an
alternative government embracing groups across the political spectrum, from the
SED, its former National Front partners and the "mass organizations", to the
churches, newly-founded independent parties and pro-democracy citizens' movements. The first meeting agrees on holding democratic elections, initially scheduled for May 6, 1990.

7-17 December 1989. The SED extraordinary congress is held, electing Gysi as its
leader (on Dec. 8) at the head of a ten-member presidium, and ending by deciding
to adopt the name SED-Party of Democratic Socialism (further changed, to just
the PDS, on Feb. 4).

14 December 1989. The government decides to disband the *Stasi* altogether, replacing it with a smaller intelligence service and a special body for the protection of the constitution.

15 January 1990. The *Stasi* headquarters in Berlin is occupied and ransacked by protestors denouncing the police state system.

21 January 1990. Krenz and 13 other former SED politburo members are expelled from the party; Honecker, leaving hospital eight days later, is considered too ill to be arrested.

1 February 1990. The conservative Alliance for Germany is formed for the forthcoming elections, bringing together the CDU, the German Social Union and Democratic Awakening.

1 February 1990. Modrow puts forward proposals of his own for the unification of Germany, but with a precondition of military neutrality, reflecting the Soviet concern that the strategic balance would be upset if a united Germany were part of NATO.

5 February 1990. Modrow's temporary "government of national responsibility", whose formation has been agreed on Jan. 28 pending elections now scheduled for March 18, brings in eight opposition leaders to place the communists in a minority for the first time.

6 February 1990. West German Chancellor Helmut Kohl calls for immediate negotiations on economic and monetary union.

13 February 1990. Agreement is reached that the "external aspects" of German unification, including wider military and security issues, will be negotiated under the "two-plus-four" formula by the two Germanies and the four World War II allies, Britain, France, the USA and the Soviet Union.

18 March 1990. Elections result in an unexpectedly convincing victory for the right-wing Alliance for Germany.

9 April 1990. Lothar de Maizière becomes prime minister at the head of a "grand coalition" sworn in on April 12.

23 April 1990. The West German government announces that the East German Mark will be exchanged at parity with the Deutschmark upon monetary union for personal wages and savings up to 4,000 marks.

5 May 1990. The first round of "two-plus-four" talks takes place in Bonn; subsequent rounds are in Berlin (June 22), Paris (July 17) and Moscow (Sept. 7).

18 May 1990. The state treaty on economic and monetary union is signed by the finance ministers of the two Germanies; it is approved by both parliaments on June 21-23.

1 July 1990. German economic and monetary union is declared and East Germany is brought within the European Communities customs union, becoming subject to EC agricultural regulations one month later.

16 July 1990. Soviet President Mikhail Gorbachev, at a meeting in Stavropol with West German Federal Chancellor Kohl, concedes that a united Germany can decide freely whether to join NATO.

24 July and Aug. 20, 1990. Free Democrats and Social Democrats pull out of de Maizière's government, the former opposing his proposal that German unification should not take place until immediately after the all-German elections on Dec. 2, and the latter objecting to his making cabinet changes against their wishes.

23 August 1990. The *Volkskammer* reaches a compromise over the date for unification, which is brought forward to Oct. 3. The CDU has abandoned (on Aug. 9) a plan to bring forward the all-German elections from Dec. 2, and the *Volkskammer* has agreed (on Aug. 22) to use the West German electoral system almost unchanged.

31 August 1990. The second state treaty, on unification, is signed in East Berlin; it is approved by both parliaments on Sept. 20-21.

12 September 1990. The "Treaty on the Final Settlement on Germany", the outcome of the "two plus four" talks, is signed in Moscow (its ratification being concluded on March 4, 1991). It confirms the existing German borders (providing for a further bilateral treaty between Germany and Poland to confirm their Oder-Neisse border), stipulates the withdrawal of the 370,000 Soviet troops currently in East Germany by the end of 1994 (with Germany paying for their upkeep, as accepted by Kohl to resolve the last obstacle outstanding after the final round of two-plus-four talks on Sept. 7), accepts Germany's right to decide on its alliances (and thus to join NATO) while debarring alliance forces from the territory of former East Germany, and ends the "rights and responsibilities" of the wartime allies with respect to Germany and Berlin.

13 September 1990. Bilateral treaties are initialled (with ratification being completed on April 2, 1991) under which Germany and the Soviet Union pledge good-neighbourliness, partnership and co-operation; agree that neither will assist in aggression against the other; and agree on the stationing, upkeep and withdrawal by 1994 of Soviet troops.

24 September 1990. East Germany leaves the Warsaw Pact.

3 October 1990. German unity, effective from midnight on Oct. 2-3 and taking the form of the merger of the former East Germany into the Federal Republic, is celebrated nationwide, although some protests are recorded over the rising unemployment in the East.

14 October 1990. Elections are held for the five *Land* parliaments in the East; the CDU wins control of four, with the SPD heading the poll only in Brandenburg.

14 November 1990. The border treaty with Poland is signed by the German and Polish foreign ministers in Warsaw, formally abandoning German territorial claims dating from the end of World War II, a position which the GDR had already accepted in 1950.

26 November 1990. the (East German) Deutsche Reichsbahn railway network is effectively brought to a standstill in a two-day strike over pay and the prospect of

massive redundancies arising from the proposed 1991 merger of the Reichsbahn with the (West German) Bundesbahn.

2 December 1990. The all-German elections, for the chancellorship and an enlarged *Bundestag*, produce a victory for Kohl and his CDU-led governing coalition; the CDU also wins elections for a unified city parliament in Berlin.

10 December 1990. The latest in a line of former East German politicians affected by allegations of having been a *Stasi* informer, de Maizière denies giving any information except that which, as a lawyer, he felt might have assisted his clients; he nevertheless resigns his government post (as minister without portfolio) and the CDU deputy leadership which he has held since the merging of the eastern and western parties in October. He is exonerated by a government inquiry in February, and resumes the CDU deputy leadership, but the allegations persist and in September 1991 he resigns and also gives up his seat in parliament.

January 1991. Departments of Marxism-Leninism are closed in universities and institutes across the East, as are many other history, philosophy and social science departments.

11 January 1991. The separate constitutions of West and East Berlin are suspended at the first meeting of Berlin's new unified parliament.

27 January 1991. The PDS holds a congress in Berlin and re-elects Gysi as its chairman.

29 January 1991. In the first case of an East German leader to come to trial, former trade union leader Harry Tisch is charged in Berlin with diverting funds for holidays, a holiday home and a hunting lodge; convicted and sentenced on June 6 to 18 months' imprisonment, he is then released, having served nearly a year in detention already and with the benefit of a reduction of sentence for good behaviour.

9 March 1991. Plans for an amnesty for former *Stasi* agents are dropped by the government.

13 March 1991. Erich Honecker, still wanted on charges over the GDR's "shoot to kill" policy against those attempting to escape to the West (although treason charges against him and others have been dropped), is moved to Moscow with his wife, from a Soviet military hospital near Berlin.

25 March 1991. A demonstration in Leipzig, with 60,000 participants, is the largest in a series of protests over unemployment.

1 April 1991. Detlev Rohwedder, the head of the Treuhand, the agency which has become increasingly unpopular in the East as it implements its responsibilities for privatizing industries formerly in GDR state ownership, is assassinated in Düsseldorf in a shooting for which the Red Army Faction claims responsibility.

8 April 1991. The growth of racism among "skinhead" gangs in the East, raising the spectre of a rebirth of Nazism, is highlighted by attacks on Poles, who can now enter the country without visas.

20 May 1991. Four former GDR leaders including former premier Willi Stoph are arrested over the GDR's "shoot-to-kill" policy; former state security minister Erich Mielke, already in prison since July 1990, is charged on May 22 with incitement to murder, but in August he is pronounced psychiatrically unfit to stand trial.

20 June 1991. The *Bundestag* votes to move the seat of government from Bonn to Berlin; the *Bundesrat*, however, votes on July 5 to stay in Bonn.

July 1991. An OECD report on the German economy describes the East as going through "a period of severe adjustment, involving it its early stages heavy output and employment losses".

14 November 1991. The *Bundesrat* approves legislation allowing individuals to have access to files which had been kept on them by the *Stasi* (and which are now administered by a special commission set up under pastor Joachim Gauck), but restricting press publication without authorization.

12 December 1991. Honecker, whom the German government is seeking to extradite from Moscow (amidst considerable uncertainty over whether the Russian or the fast-disappearing Soviet government has jurisdiction), seeks asylum in the Chilean embassy after the Russian government has promised to extradite him. It is subsequently confirmed that Chile will not offer him asylum, but reports suggest that North Korea or Cuba might.

HUNGARY

The country's official name was the Hungarian People's Republic (*Magyar Nepköztársaság*) until Oct. 23, 1989, and thereafter the Republic of Hungary (*Magyar Köztársaság*).

Hungary is a landlocked country, with a total area of 93,030 sq. km and a population of 10,375,000 (two-thirds that of Czechoslovakia, and less than half that of Yugoslavia or Romania). Over 50 per cent of Hungarians live in

urban areas, and a quarter within metropolitan Budapest, the capital city.

The Danube flows from the north-western corner, forming for some 150 km the country's northern border with Czechoslovakia; it then flows south, through Budapest to the southern border with Yugoslavia, with Lake Balaton to the west and the fertile Alföld plains to the east. Apart from Budapest the principal towns are Debrecen and Miskolc in the north-east, Szeged and Pecs in the south, and the industrial centre of Gyor on the Danube in the north-west.

Ethnically Hungary is relatively homogeneous. 96.6% of the population are classified as Hungarian Magyars, whose ancestors reached the area in the successive waves of invasion from the east by Huns, Avars and Magyars between the 4th and 10th centuries AD. It is a predominantly Christian country, since the time of King Stephen (crowned in 1000 AD), and two-thirds of the population profess the Catholic faith, while one fifth are Lutherans. Magyar is the language of over 98 per cent of the population; there are, however, significant minorities identifiable as of German extraction (1.6 per cent) or as Slovaks 1.1 per cent), smaller Romanian and southern Slav minorities, and a gypsy population of some 320,000, many of whom are Romany speakers. Alone of the countries of Eastern Europe, Hungary still has a sizeable Jewish community, numbering some 88,000. [See under Czechoslovakia, Romania, and Yugoslavia, for the existence of ethnic Hungarian minorities in those countries.]

The Hungarian Republic, created in November 1918 as one of the successor states to the defeated and much reduced dual monarchy of Austria-Hungary, faced an early revolutionary challenge when the communist Béla Kún set up a short-lived Soviet Republic (March-August 1919). Romanian troops, marching on Budapest, entered the city on Aug. 4, and handed over power to the conservative, church-backed and increasingly authoritarian regime of Adml. Horthy (regent from 1920 to 1944).

Horthy identified Hungary in the 1930s with the Nazi German desire to redraw boundaries imposed on the defeated powers after World War I. This policy claimed its vindication in territorial gains secured in 1938-41 at the expense of Czechoslovakia, Yugoslavia and Romania, but drew Hungary into the Second World War on the German side after Hitler launched his attack on the Soviet Union in 1941. When the tide turned against the Axis powers on the eastern front, and the Red Army advance began to inflict heavy losses on Hungarian armies, the Germans pre-empted the wavering of their ally, occupying Hungary in March 1944. A campaign of "deport-ation" and subsequently of extermination was launched, with active German encouragement, against Hungary's Jewish population, then numbering approximately one million, and against the gypsies.

The Red Army invaded Hungary in October 1944, swiftly taking Szeged and Debrecen. Horthy on October 15 called for an armistice, but the Germans immediately forced him to resign, and the overtly fascist puppet regime of Ferenc Szálasi was set up. Two months later Szálasi fled the capital as the Red Army advance continued; Budapest was liberated in February 1945, albeit only after a protracted battle, and by April 4 the last German troops had been driven out of the country.

The victory of the Red Army placed all of Hungary under the administration of a broad-based anti-fascist provisional government first formed in Debrecen in December 1944, and which had signed in the following month an armistice with the Soviet Union, Great Britain and the USA, whereby the annexations of Czechoslovak, Romanian and Yugoslav territory were formally renounced. Its other most far-reaching action was the passage of a radical land reform act in March 1945 (under the then agriculture minister Imre Nagy), expropriating the feudal estates which had hitherto accounted for the greater part of the nation's land.

Prior to general elections in November 1945, municipal elections in Budapest in October indicated overwhelming popular backing for the predominantly agrarian Smallholders' Party, which obtained a clear majority vis-à-vis its Communist and Socialist partners in the provisional government. Soviet Marshal Voroshilov responded by directing that, to prevent "anarchy and civil war", the general elections should be based on a single government list. This was strongly opposed by Britain and the USA, and an eventual compromise allowed for separate lists, but a commit-ment to form a broad coalition government, which was headed by Smallholder leader Ferenc Nagy.

In mid-1947 Ferenc Nagy was ousted from power and left the country; by mid-1948 the Socialists too had fallen victim to the intimidatory 'salami tactics' of the Soviet-backed communists; and by mid-1949 a single-list general election had been held, returning to office a communist-dominated bloc whose single-party rule was enshrined in the 1949 Constitution of the People's Republic of Hungary.

There followed seven years of a brutal Stalinist dictatorship under Mátyás Rákosi, forcing through an increasingly unpopular drive for industrialization and agricultural collectivization. The "Muscovite" communists in the central leadership eliminated their rivals in factional disputes, show trials and purges. Stalin's death in 1953 brought a let-up, with Imre Nagy becoming prime minister, until he in turn was deposed in 1955.

The 1956 Hungarian uprising, or Hungarian revolution, developed with astonishing speed following student protests in Budapest in October of that year. The political bankruptcy of the regime, and the apparent (but illusory) unwillingness of Soviet troops to clamp down forcibly, left a power vacuum in which, briefly, the unthinkable appeared possible. Imre Nagy returned as prime minister, declaring that multi-party democracy would be restored and that Hungary would leave the Warsaw Pact. On Nov. 4, however, the Red Army's tanks crushed the illusion, and the resistance.

The Kádár years began with the rooting out of resistance, the execution of Nagy and others and the reassertion of monolithic communist power. From the 1960s onwards, however, the regime introduced its New Economic Mechanism (NEM); Hungarians enjoyed a period of relative prosperity, and Hungary took on characteristics which marked it out as a peculiarity in the communist bloc. In its obedience to Soviet foreign policy, Hungary would be orthodox to the point of slavishness. But in domestic policy there could be scope for different attitudes. The party would not demand the total allegiance of all, in the classic totalitarian model; there could be non-party contributions to national life, since "whoever is not against us is with us".

From the mid-1970s the economic basis of this strategy of "depoliticized" communism began to come seriously apart. The NEM had moved away from the classic command economy, using market mechanisms as a vehicle, but the regime was unwilling to allow for the harsher consequences of an unfettered freeing of the markets. It became dependent on heavy foreign borrowing to sustain the illusion of prosperity. Critics called for more radical "reform of the reform", but the regime retreated into conservatism, in turn converting its intellectual critics into opponents.

Gorbachev's accession to power in the Soviet Union and his espousal of the policies of *perestroika* (restructuring) provided a changed international context. It encouraged Hungary's own reformist communists, who had themselves been allowed more leeway in the Kádárist system than was the case elsewhere in Eastern Europe. They believed that their own future lay not in confronting the growing opposition but in changing the system from within. 1988-89 marked the success of these reformists in the peaceful takeover of the party leadership, ousting first Kádár and then Grósz in successive years. The flexibility of the party, and its involvement in a serious dialogue with opposition forces, was a key factor in the Hungarian experience of the fall of Communism. The reformed party was to be heavily defeated in multi-party elections, but this outcome would not have been predicted at the time the party took that road.

The abandonment of communist power in Hungary was thus, in one sense, the result of a political gamble which did not pay off. In this respect it was atypical in Eastern Europe, and cannot be symbolized in the dramatic images of popular defiance which swept across the region in late 1989. However, in Hungary too the demonstrations did play an important role, putting public pressure on the regime as early as March 1986, and pressing the opposition view over two key issues; the joint hydroelectric power scheme with Czechoslovakia and Austria which threatened extensive environmental damage along the Danube river, and the harsh mistreatment of the ethnic Hungarian minority in neighbouring Romania. In June 1989, a quarter of a million people attended the reburial of Imre Nagy, the martyr of 1956, as witnesses to the regime's belated recognition of the lie on which it had been based.

Under democratic rule, the Antall government had by the end of 1991 provided relative stability for 20 months. A conservative coalition, it was initially slow in adopting reforms which would transform its financial and economic structure. The Democratic Forum managed, however, to placate its ally the Smallholders with a property restitution measure which was not so comprehensive as to obstruct the broader policy of privatization. This compromise, eventually embodied in legislation in 1991, contained the threat of a split in the ruling coalition. To some extent it took the impetus out of a challenge from opposition parties, spearheaded by the Young Democrats, who nevertheless sustained their argument that greater democratization and participation in public life was necessary for a healthy political future. Low electoral turnouts even in 1990 were a warning sign, and surveys in 1991 revealed widespread disillusion about politics in general.

On the economic front, the resolution of the Smallholders' main demands helped to open the way for the full implementation of the privatization programme, involving large state-owned concerns, which had been under preparation for many months, and which had the support of foreign capital and lending institutions. This programme, under the administration of the specially-formed State Property Agency, accelerated rapidly in mid-1991. Small businesses had already been established in their tens of thousands by this time, and it was anticipated that the economy as a whole would move from contraction to growth in 1992. Particular characteristics of the Hungarian economy included the rapid development of the banking industry, and a highly productive agricultural sector. The level of foreign debt was officially given as having fallen below $14 billion by the end of 1991, a year in which new borrowing had been reduced from $4.6 billion to $3.6 billion. The expected debt servicing cost of $3.6 billion in 1992 was forecast as falling below "the crucial proportion of 30 per cent" of total foreign exchange earnings.

The broadly optimistic economic picture was clouded, however, by the problems of heavy industry, in particular in engineering and metallurgy, where few enterprises (with the likely exception of the Ikarus bus manufacturers) were able to survive the transition to a market economy intact. Almost all were badly disadvantaged by outmoded and polluting plant and low levels of labour productivity, and there were a number of instances where Western companies backed away from possible joint venture arrangements. In human terms, a measure of Hungary's problems with industrial restructuring was the rapid growth of unemployment; negligible in official figures in 1989, it was over 80,000 by the end of 1990 and quadrupled again in 1991. Steps taken in late 1991, to limit the number of non-nationals (mainly ethnic Hungarians) coming to work in Hungary, showed how far the country's successes to date had failed to dispel the less positive, inward-looking side of its strong sense of national identity.

The principal personalities of Communist rule

Mátyás **Rákosi** (1892-1971), party leader 1945-56, closely identified with Stalinism and with Hungary's show trials and brutal purges of this period. A communist activist in 1918 and part of the soviet set up under Bela Kun, he was imprisoned in 1925-40 by the Horthy regime, then exiled. He spent the war in Moscow, returning with the Red Army to lead the communists, who dominated "coalition" governments even before the single-party regime was formalized in the 1949 Constitution. Identified with the "Muscovites", he conducted a series of purges of rival party factions, condemning the "home" former resistance leader Laszlo Rajk in 1949 and ousting "revisionist" prime minister Imre Nagy in 1955. In July 1956, his position totally undermined by the discrediting of Stalin, he himself resigned the party leadership, which was taken on briefly by Ernö Gerö in the months prior to the return of Nagy and the Hungarian uprising.

Imre **Nagy** (1896-1958). A Russian prisoner at the time of the 1917 revolution, Nagy fought in the Russian civil war as a communist party member, returning to Hungary in the 1920s but then going back to the Soviet Union, and working there until the Red Army liberated his native country in 1944. He was briefly agriculture minister, then interior minister (until February 1946), but became a critic of the agricultural collectivization programme, and was expelled from the politburo in 1949. Nagy escaped further punishment in the purges, however; he returned to government in 1951, and was made prime minister in July 1953 at the urging of the Soviet leadership, charged with improving living standards in an attempt to modify the unpopularity of the Rákosi regime. Ousted in April 1955, he retired to write and then advocate a "revisionist" alternative to the Stalinism of Rákosi. In the dramatic conditions of October 1956 he was recalled to office, called for free elections and declared neutrality, becoming the reluctant leader of the uprising when Soviet tanks rolled into Budapest. With his arrest, secret trial and June 1958 execution, Nagy became and remained the most potent of martyr figures. His posthumous rehabilitation and ceremonial reburial in June 1989 thus marked the end of the great lie of the Kádár regime, which had tried to brand him a counter-revolutionary.

Janos **Kádár** (1912-1989), party first secretary for over three decades (1956-88) and dominant figure of what became known as the "Kádár era". A youthful communist opponent of the Horthy regime and an active wartime resistance leader, he emerged after the liberation as party secretary in Budapest, then (1948-50) as minister of the interior. In the party's factional disputes he turned against his close friend László Rajk, who was executed in 1949, but was himself purged in turn in 1950, and then imprisoned from 1951 to 1954 under Rákosi. Rehabilitated in 1954, he was soon identified with Imre Nagy and the brave new policies of 1956, but swiftly changed horses when Soviet troops moved to crush the Hungarian uprising. The Soviet authorities left Kádár in charge, as prime minister (1956-58) as well as party leader, of pursuing the repressive process of "normalization", in which process Nagy was executed in 1958. However, once the lesson had firmly been driven home that challenges to Soviet hegemony were no part of the Hungarian agenda, Kádár launched a new experiment; "whoever is not against us is with us" on the ideological front, and the "new economic mechanism" (introduced in 1968) which encouraged a "regulated market" to deliver material benefits which would win public support. It was only in the 1980s, when Hungary's external debt crisis exposed the full extent of the structural weakness of the economy, that Kádár came seriously under challenge, and he became entrenched in a sterile defensiveness against calls for "reform of the reform". The May 1988 party conference provided the occasion for the reformers to oust him, designating him as party president but without a politburo seat. Seriously ill, he died in hospital on July 6, 1989.

Károly **Grósz** (b. 1930), short-term successor to Kádár as party leader (May 1988 to October 1989). A lifelong party activist, he made Budapest a power base as party first secretary there from 1984. The ageing Kádár made him prime minister in July 1987 and he used this office adroitly, appearing as a champion of economic reform. However, having reached the high point of his career when he took over the party leadership from Kádár in May 1988, he proved unable or unwilling to pursue the increasingly vertiginous road of reformism, recognizing that it would mean the abandonment of party power. He refused to join the HSP as a "newly created party" at the 1989 party congress, and was left marginalized with the HSWP "old guard".

Rezsö **Nyers** (b. 1923). The reformist leader with the longest track record, dating back to his appointment as finance minister in 1960, he was later to be the first president of the HSP (October 1989 to May 1990). Nyers had first emerged in post-war Hungarian politics as a member of the social democratic party, then joined the central committee of the HSWP which was created by the 1948 "merger" of the social democrats into the communist party. A politburo member from 1966 to 1975, he directed the introduction of Hungary's new economic mechanism in the 1960s, but lost influence in the mid-1970s as power tilted back towards the party's conservatives, and Kádár accepted modifications which undermined the coherence of the economic reform process. The renewed reform movement in the 1980s benefited from Nyers' authority, and he returned both to the HSWP top leadership (politburo May 1988, party president and inner presidium member in June 1989) and to the government. Seen as less radical than the ambitious Imre Pozsgay, he was a good compromise choice to continue as party president in the reconstituted and renamed HSP; by May 1990, however, after the chastening experience of electoral defeat, he was ready to cede this role to Gyüla Horn.

Miklós **Németh** (b. 1948), the last communist prime minister (November 1988 to May 1990), and one of the principal party reform leaders together with Rezsö Nyers and Imre Pozsgay. From a peasant background, Németh joined the party in 1968. He studied and worked as an economist, in academia, in government and, from 1981, within the party apparatus. In 1988, coinciding with the fall of Kádár, he emerged quite suddenly as a key figure, promoted to the politburo in May and appointed to succeed the new party leader Károly Grósz as prime minister in November. His attention was devoted primarily to the management of the rapid programme of economic change and to piloting through an IMF-backed austerity package. The party, reconstituted as the Hungarian Socialist Party, refused to back this programme and Németh, who had originally been part of the HSP presidium in October 1989, left this party post only two months later. His endorsement of the transition to multi-party democracy, and his consequent replacement as prime minister by Jozsef Antall in May 1990, was summed up in his memorable assessment: "The revolution happened not only because people did not want to live in that way, but also because the government did not want to govern in that way." In early 1991 he was appointed to the new European Bank for Reconstruction and Development (EBDR), as a vice-president in charge of personnel and administration, and vacated his seat in the Hungarian parliament.

Imre **Pozsgay** (b. 1933), one of the four-member party presidium in June-October 1989, and politically pre-eminent among the reform communists in the transition to multi-party democracy. A career party official in the HSWP, he first marked out his reformist credentials as minister of culture in 1975-82. Out of favour with Kádár thereafter, he commissioned the influential 1987 "Change and Reform" document, which helped open the floodgates with its advocacy of fundamental political as well as economic change. After Kádár's departure, he set up the round table talks of 1989 and supported the reappraisal of 1956, then worked to make the new HSP a contender for office in a multi-party democracy, but was disappointed in his hopes of winning the presidency, when in November 1989 a referendum rejected the constitutional proposal for early direct presidential elections, in favour of letting a new parliament choose. His popularity as the midwife of change waned rapidly thereafter: he finished only third in his Budapest constituency in the March 1990 general election, but obtained a seat in parliament on the HSP national list. In November 1990 he left the party, sitting as an independent, and in May 1991 he was instrumental in forming, with Zoltan Biro, a new National Democratic Federation, an apparently unsuccessful attempt to launch a national centrist movement.

Constitutional changes

The 1949 Constitution, establishing the People's Republic, was subjected to fundamental amendment in 1989, including the change in the country's name, with effect from Oct. 23 (the anniversary of the 1956 uprising), to simply the Republic of Hungary. In all nearly 100 constitutional changes, the product of the round table talks, were approved by the parliament on Oct. 17-20, 1989, to introduce a multi-party democratic system.

The preamble to what was effectively a new transitional constitution stipulated that Hungary was a "democratic legal state in which the values of bourgeois democracy and democratic socialism prevail in equal measures". A constitutional court was established. The Presidential Council was abolished but the method of election of the President was left for subsequent resolution [see under Elections below]; laws on parliamentary elections and on political parties were passed. Authority was vested in the National Assembly (*Országgyülés*) which was responsible for electing the Council of Ministers.

Position and status of communists

Party name

Hungary's ruling communist party operated under the name Hungarian Socialist Workers' Party (HSWP) from 1956 to 1989. Its predecessor, the Hungarian Workers' Party, had come into being in June 1948 (when the Social Democrats were merged into what had been the Hungarian Communist Party), but had collapsed in October 1956, to the extent that Kádár, after becoming party leader on Oct. 25, announced within a week its abolition and the formation of the HSWP as its successor.

The special HSWP congress, on Oct. 6-10, 1989, secured majority agreement for recreating the party as the Hungarian Socialist Party (HSP) under reformist leadership.

A rival "14th congress of the HSWP" was convened on Dec. 17, 1989, by those who rejected the reformist line. Delegates committed themselves to revive and reorganize a rump party, which regarded itself as the continuation of the HSWP and which retained the HSWP name.

The Patriotic People's Front (PPF), an umbrella grouping under the communist regime dominated by the HSWP, and including the union federation and other social organizations, contested the 1990 general election as the Patriotic Election Coalition but decided to dissolve itself in May 1990.

Legal status

The political parties law of October 1989 allowed parties of all political persuasions to apply for registration, subject only to the provision that they recognize and observe the constitution. No attempt was made at this time (with the government still in the hands of the "transitional" regime of former communists) to debar communists from political activity, nor has any such ban been introduced in the subsequent period (as of the end of 1991). A bill passed by the parliament in late November 1991, but then referred to the constitutional court, would allow prosecutions for murder and acts of treason committed under communist rule, a feature of the post-communist period elsewhere in the region but as yet unknown in Hungary.

Workplace organization

The umbrella Central Council of Trade Unions (SZOT) ended its affiliation to the HSWP in early 1989, independent unions having begun to proliferate in the course of the preceding year. The issue of HSWP party cells in the workplace, the key to its power, then became the principal focus of the round-table talks. The opposition parties were united in demanding that workplace cells be disbanded and banned. Within the party, Pozsgay argued for accepting such a ban; the HSWP, at a crisis meeting in September 1989, refused. The Sept. 18 round-table compromise left this unresolved. At the Oct. 6-10 party congress, Pozsgay was defeated in a vote which decided that what was now the HSP should continue to support party cells in the workplace. However, the Oct. 17-20 session of parliament, which adopted the transitional constitution and the political parties and electoral laws, also voted on Oct. 19, 1989, by 279 to 44, to prohibit party organization in the workplace. HSP cells were to be disbanded within 90 days of the elections (or by end-1990 in the armed forces and police).

Party militia

The HSWP had run an armed voluntary Workers' Guard, which numbered some 60,000 as of 1988. Under the September 1989 round-table agreement the party accepted the transfer of control over this militia to the army, and a reduction in numbers to 40,000. The HSP in October supported the transfer to government and parliamentary control, but parliament voted on Oct. 20, 1989, by 274 to 6, to approve the immediate disbanding of the Workers' Guard.

Party assets

The majority of HSWP assets worth some $166 million in 1989, consisting principally of real estate, were renounced on Oct. 10, 1989, by the HSP, with the exception of assets required for the operation of the party. Parliament decided on Oct. 20 that the government should make proposals on whether these former party assets should be used for political parties or for community purposes.

In July 1991 parliament passed a controversial bill (which trade unions sought to refer to the constitutional court) on the redistribution of trade union property in proportion to the current level of support for different union federations.

Ideological orientation

The HSP, on its foundation, invited all former HSWP members to apply to join. Effectively, however, its name change, and its commitment to a multi-party system and free market economy, were designed to mark its transformation into what Pozsgay called a new democratic socialist party in the European tradition. (This process of redefinition was continued at the May 1990 HSP conference following its poor showing in the general elections.) The HSP described itself as a people's party, rather than a class party, and repudiated the doctrine of the dictatorship of the proletariat.

The rump of the HSWP continued to define itself as a Marxist party, representing above all the interests of the industrial worker.

Electoral significance

In the 1990 general election the HSP won 10.89% of the vote on the first round (coming fourth), and finished with 33 members in the National Assembly. The HSWP won only 3.68% (coming seventh) and no seats; a communist-oriented Agrarian Alliance won one seat.

Principal parties in the post-communist period

The **Hungarian Democratic Forum** (HDF), founded in September 1987 and officially constituted as a political party one year later, was the principal representative of the "populist" strand of opposition. It drew its support principally from provincial and rural areas, and tapped into a powerful Hungarian nationalist cultural tradition. Its policies were broadly described as "centre-right", embracing liberal democratic elements (including the eventual party leader Jozsef Antall) and more radical populist nationalists. In 1988-89 its opposition rivals, the "urbanist" Free Democrats, feared the manipulation of the transition process by means of "deals" between the Forum and the reform communist leaders. The 1990 election proved the extent of support for the HDF, which became the dominant party in Antall's governing coalition. Antall was re-elected as party president at the December 1990 congress, with Balazs Horváth as acting vice-president.

The **Alliance of Free Democrats** (SzDSz) was founded in November 1988, bringing together liberal urban intellectuals like eventual party leader Kiss, who had been active as a critic and opponent of the Kádár regime since the mid-1970s. Its first assembly of delegates, in April 1989, adopted a radical programme for the implementation of liberal and free market principles. The growing confidence of the Free

Democrats, as they sensed a groundswell of popular support in mid-1989, underlay their assertiveness in the latter stages of the 1989 round-table talks. The decisions of the dramatic October 1989 parliamentary session, and the party's success in getting a referendum to reject direct presidential elections, marked a high-point after which the 1990 general election result came as a disappointment. However, the party recovered ground vis-à-vis the government coalition at the September-October 1990 local elections. Figures such as Demszky added youthful appeal, but in 1991 the party's effectiveness was badly damaged by a divisive leadership dispute.

The **League of Young Democrats** (FIDESZ), closely linked with the Free Democrats, was formed by radical students in March 1988, contested the general elections in 1990 with an unexpected level of success, and reached agreements with the Free Democrats to present an effective alliance at the local elections later that year; its leadership is collegiate. Victor Orban, its most prominent individual, was a major factor in the sustained increase in the party's popularity in 1991, making it a force much more significant than its parliamentary representation might suggest.

The **Independent Smallholders' Party** (FKgP) was reactivated in February 1988, claiming direct descent from the party of the same name which had been forced out of power in the immediate postwar period despite its pre-eminent position in terms of seats in the 1945 elections. Effectively a single-issue party, it campaigned for the restoration of property to its pre-1947 owners. It suffered a split with the formation of a breakaway National Smallholders' Party in December 1989, and has been affected by subsequent intra-party disputes, passing a vote of no confidence in its parliamentary group leader Jozsef Torgyan in March 1991. At the 1990 general election it emerged as the third largest party and obtained four cabinet posts as part of its price for joining Antall's coalition government. By the time of the October local elections its support had fallen off dramatically, as legal setbacks impeded the implementation of the government's compromise property restitution scheme, which was eventually enacted in the first half of 1991. Torgyan subsequently won the support of the party's national board for a move in November 1991, to withdraw the party whip from two ministers and two state secretaries, accusing the party's labour minister Gyula Kiss of concealing his alleged past membership in the communist party.

The **Christian Democratic People's Party**, formed in September 1989 and regarding itself as the continuation of the pre-communist Christian Democrats, became the third and smallest party in the Antall governing coalition after the 1990 general election, with one cabinet post.

The post-communist political leaders

Jozsef **Antall** (b. 1932), prime minister since May 1990. The son of a founding leader of the original Independent Smallholders' Party. Banned from teaching history because he had been active in youth organizations supporting the 1956 uprising, he became an archivist and, by 1974, director of the Semmelweis museum. He was a founder member of the Hungarian Democratic Forum in September 1987, on the liberal democratic rather than the populist nationalist wing. As HDF president from October 1989, he was charged with forming a coalition after the party's success in the 1990 elections, and has been the dominant figure in the post-communist government, despite a serious illness in late 1990 and early 1991. His style is serious and reserved rather than charismatic, and his political objective has been to oversee fundamental changes with minimum upheaval.

Arpad **Göncz** (b. 1922). President. A lawyer, and personal secretary to one of the Smallholders' Party leaders before 1947, he worked as a welder under Communist rule, and served six years of a life sentence for his involvement in the 1956 uprising. He then became a literary translator, playwright and dissident intellectual in the Budapest "democratic opposition" from which the Alliance of Free Democrats ultimately emerged in late 1988. He became president of the writers' union in 1989. At the 1990 general election he entered parliament, and was elected as its Speaker and thus as interim President, with the approval of the HDF. On Aug. 3 the parliament re-endorsed the choice of Göncz as President in an unopposed election.

Janos **Kis** (b. 1943). Free Democrat leader. A leading dissident philosopher, formally expelled from the HSWP in 1973 for his outspoken opposition to the Kádár regime, he was the most prominent member of the radical Free Democrats through the upheavals of 1988-89 and in the 1990 election campaign, and was confirmed as party chairman in April 1990. Compared with some Free Democrat advocates of unfettered market economics, Kis represented a strand of opinion identifiable as on the social democratic wing of his party. His leadership came under criticism as the party became preoccupied with internal disputes.

Gabor **Demszky** (b. 1952). Prominent among the younger generation of Free Democrats, he became Mayor of Budapest in late 1990, as a result of his party's successful alliance with the Young Democrats at the municipal elections.

Gyüla **Horn** (b. 1932). Leader of the Socialist Party, Horn was a figure closely associated with the transition from communism, having been a party foreign affairs expert before becoming state secretary for foreign affairs in 1985. Promoted to be foreign minister in 1989, he was part of the reform group in the Hungarian party, and one of the founders of the HSP in October; abroad, he stood out as a key figure in the changing politics of the rapidly disintegrating Soviet bloc. In the spring 1990 elections he was defeated in his constituency but won a seat on the national HSP list, and became HSP chairman in May 1990. He has retained a position of some influence through the parliamentary foreign affairs committee.

Elections

Legislature

Under the communist regime candidates for the National Assembly were required to accept the programme of the official mass movement, the Patriotic People's Front (PPF), which was completely dominated by the HSWP. The last such elections, in June 1985, took place under a 1983 electoral law which stipulated that voters should have a choice of candidates. After the legalization of opposition parties, four by-elections in July-September 1989 were won by opposition candidates, and a fifth, held in January 1990 with the Assembly about to be dissolved, went to prominent former dissident Gaspar Miklós Tamas.

The multi-party electoral system introduced under the law of Oct. 20, 1989, contained highly complicated arrangements for electing the National Assembly. 176

members were elected in single-member constituencies, by overall majority in the first round (provided the turnout exceeded 50 per cent) or by simple majority in a second round run-off of the top three candidates (when the turnout could be as low as 25 per cent). The election of a further 210 members, by proportional representation, used two mechanisms; (i) 152 members were elected on the basis of votes cast for party lists in the country's 19 counties, with a minimum national threshhold of 4% for representation, and (ii) 58 members were elected from the "national lists" of parties which had contested seven or more counties. The distribution of "national list" seats among the parties was determined in proportion to each party's total number of "scrap votes", i.e. votes cast in individual constituencies for the party's candidates who did not win election, plus votes cast for the party's list in the various counties which fell short of the number required for the return of a member.

General election results

The electoral system was first used for the general election of March 25 and April 8, 1990, for which 43 parties were registered and 28 took part, 12 of them at national level.

General election results

March 25 and April 25, 1990: election of National Assembly (*Országgyülés*)		
Party name	1st round vote	seats
Hungarian Democratic Forum (HDF or MDF)	24.71%	164
Alliance of Free Democrats (SzDSz)	21.38%	92
Independent Smallholders' Party	11.76%	44
Hungarian Socialist Party (HSP or MSZP)	10.89%	33
League of Young Democrats (FIDESZ)	8.94%	21
Christian Democratic People's Party	6.46%	21
Agrarian Alliance	3.15%	1
Independents and others		10
Total (not including eight seats for minorities)		386

Presidency

Under the communist regime the Assembly elected a figurehead national President. The proposal to change to direct presidential elections was overturned by a referendum on Nov. 26, 1989, when there was a narrow majority in favour of having the president elected by the new Assembly. This was an interim arrangement, and could be changed by decision of the new Assembly. In the event Arpad Göncz was elected overwhelmingly by the Assembly on May, 2, 1990, as interim President; a referendum on a proposal to change to direct election failed on July 29 because of the inadequate turnout (of only 13.8 per cent); and Göncz was confirmed in office by an election in the Assembly on Aug. 3, 1990.

Local elections

The communist-dominated local councils were replaced by a local government structure for which elections were first held on Sept. 30 and Oct. 14, 1990. Widespread voter apathy, with an average turnout of 36 per cent, meant that only 20 per cent of seats could be decided on the first round (when a 40 per cent minimum turnout was required; no such minimum applied in the second round). The eventual results reflected the falling popularity of Antall's governing coalition; the opposition coalition of Free Democrats and Young Democrats won in Budapest (where Gabor Demszky became mayor) and in most municipal councils, with 42 per cent of the vote, while independents dominated the rural council elections.

Governments in the post-communist period

Hungary has experienced a degree of stability in its post-communist government which contrasts strongly with other states in Eastern Europe. The coalition cabinet formed by Antall in May 1990 had undergone only two minor reshuffles as of late 1991, in December 1990 and January 1991, occasioned in both cases by disagreements among ministers over the pace of economic reform.

Principal members of the Antall government, 1990-91

Prime minister: Jozsef Antall

Justice: Istvan Balsai

Industry and Commerce: Peter Akos Bod

Defence: Lajos Für

Interior: Balazs Horváth (until Dec. 1990); Peter Boross

Foreign Affairs: Geza Jeszenszky

Finance: Ferenc Rabar (until Dec. 1990); Mihaly Kupa

International Economic Relations: Bela Kádár

Agriculture: Ferenc Jozsef Nagy (until Jan. 1991); Elemer Gergatz

Labour Affairs: Sandor Györivanyi (until Jan. 1991); Gyula Kiss

Government crises

The only serious domestic crisis which the government faced during this period was over the strike and blockade of city streets, main roads and border crossings by taxi and lorry drivers in October 1990. Their action was occasioned by sharp fuel price increases, announced because of reduced Soviet oil deliveries and the consequent need to buy supplies at high world market prices. With Antall ill in hospital, Horváth initially directed an uncompromising government response to the strikers, but then had to back down and offer to halve the price increase.

Nationalities and minorities issues

As a relatively ethnically homogeneous country, Hungary has not faced any threat of fragmentation such as has split the Soviet Union, torn apart Yugoslavia, or challenged the unity of Czechoslovakia. Its small ethnic minorities pressed successfully for each to be represented with one seat in the National Assembly; in January 1991 they set up a round table forum to seek guaranteed protection of their minority rights, and the government announced in May 1991 that it would introduce legislation on these issues.

More significant in Hungarian politics, indeed a matter on which national feeling runs high, is the desire to ensure the protection of Hungarian national minorities abroad. Prior to mid-1991, the principal concern was over Hungarian-speakers in Transylvania in Romania, a traditional bone of contention in relations between the two neighbours [see Romania chapter]. Within Hungary the attitude to this population was ambivalent, in that there was a high level of resentment over their ill-treatment at Romanian hands, but defensiveness, particularly over jobs, when their arrival in Hungary threatened to be an economic burden. Restrictive legislation was passed in October 1991, and border controls tightened, to prevent the inflow of foreign nationals without work permits; the majority of the estimated 50,000 foreigners in Hungary without the proper papers at this time were ethnic Hungarians of Romanian nationality.

The civil war in Yugoslavia, following the Slovene and Croat independence declarations in June 1991, turned the attention of the Hungarian government with great urgency towards the threat posed to the safety and future of Hungarians living in hotly contested areas of Croatia [see Yugoslavia chapter]. Many had fled their homes as refugees (an estimated 20,000 of them to Hungary) to escape attack by Serbian groups and the predominantly Serbian Yugoslav federal army.

CHRONOLOGY

December 1944. Formation in Soviet-liberated Debrecen of a broad-based anti-fascist provisional government

February 1945. Liberation of Budapest by the Red Army, which by April 4 has driven the last German troops out of the country.

March 1945. Land reform act (introduced by the then agriculture minister Imre Nagy), expropriating the feudal estates which had hitherto accounted for the greater part of the nation's land.

November 1945. General elections, in which the Smallholders emerge as by far the largest party in the parliament, with 245 out of 409 elective seats, and head a broad coalition government.

June 1947. Smallholder prime minister Ferenc Nagy leaves the country, one of a succession of non-communist politicians to fall victim to communist intimidation; the party's 'salami tactics' progressively eliminate any real competition from its notional coalition partners.

August 1947. The Communists emerge as the largest single party in Hungary's second post-war general election.

June 1948. The Social Democrats are forcibly merged with the Communists to form the Hungarian Workers' Party (HWP).

January 1949. Roman Catholic Primate Cardinal Jószef Mindszenty is sentenced to life imprisonment.

May 1949. The third post-war general election, in which a single list is put forward by the People's Independence Front, a communist-dominated bloc with four smaller participating parties. The minor parties in the Front are effectively eliminated by 1954, when the Front is renamed the People's Patriotic Front (PPF).

1949. Hungary becomes a People's Republic under its new Constitution.

1949. With the HWP split into a 'Muscovite' and a 'native' faction, the ('Muscovite') party general secretary Mátyás Rákosi purges Lászlo Rajk from the top leadership as a 'Titoist', replacing him as interior minister by János Kádár.

1950-51. Kádár in turn is dismissed, then purged and imprisoned. Rákosi's dictatorship supervises the collectivization of agriculture and the rapid creation of a heavy industrial base.

July 1953. Following Stalin's death, Rákosi's rival Imre Nagy becomes premier with the support of the new Soviet leadership; Nagy's 'New Course' allows a reduction of political terror and the release of political prisoners, while peasants may gain permission to leave collective farms, and workers' conditions are improved.

1955 Rákosi condemns Nagy as a 'right deviationist' and deposes him, reinstituting an increasingly unpopular hardline regime.

February 1956. Following Khrushchev's denunciation of Stalin, the prominent 1949 purge victim Rajk is rehabilitated.

18 July 1956. Rákosi surrenders the party leadership to Ernö Gerö.

23 October 1956. A student-led demonstration in Budapest, inspired by the loosening of Soviet control over Polish affairs, demands the reinstatement of Imre Nagy and the withdrawal of Russian forces. The demonstration becomes a popular uprising, overwhelming the militia's vain attempts to control the protests. A revolution appears briefly to be succeeding as Soviet forces withdraw the tanks initially sent in to back the militia.

24-25 October 1956. Nagy becomes prime minister again, with Kádár as first secretary of the party, which is soon reformed as the Hungarian Socialist Workers' Party (HSWP). Nagy announces the disbanding of the hated secret police, authorises the restoration of multi-party democracy and announces on Nov. 1 that Hungary is to leave the Warsaw Pact.

4 November 1956. The Soviet Army crushes the Hungarian uprising, launching a massive tank offensive against violent resistance particularly in Budapest, where an estimated 25,000 people are killed in the fighting. Nagy is arrested, but Kádár is chosen by the Soviet leadership to re-establish firm communist control and to consolidate the repression of political opposition.

16 June 1958. Imre Nagy is executed for treason, along with his defence minister Pal Maleter and two others, after a major show trial; another of the accused, Gèza Losonczy, died in prison before the end of the trial.

1961. After the post-1956 years of repression and consolidation Kádár moves towards policies of national reconciliation, on the basis of his 1959 statement to the party congress that 'whoever is not against us is with us'.

January 1968. The Kadar regime introduces the 'New Economic Mechanism' (NEM), an attempt to combine elements of a market economy with central planning.

August 1968. Hungarian forces participate in the suppression of Czechoslovakia's 'Prague Spring'.

12 November 1968. The Soviet party leader Leonid Brezhnev, speaking at the PUWP congress in Warsaw, presents what is intended as the vindication of the armed intervention in Hungary in 1956 and in Czechoslovakia in 1968—the doctrine that socialist states have limited sovereignty, insofar as a threat to socialism in one country is "a common problem and concern of all socialist countries" and that, as "an extraordinary step dictated by necessity", other socialist countries may have an "internationalist obligation" to intervene. This "Brezhnev doctrine", already set out in a *Pravda* article in September, is later elaborated by Brezhnev at the Soviet party congress on March 30, 1971.

November 1972. Beginning a process of retreat from the market economy experiments of the NEM, the party central committee introduces restrictions which within two years amount to an effective change of course, back to a policy of subsidising uneconomic enterprises. The ensuing increase in central support is so rapid that the regime recognises in 1979 the necessity of some efforts to control it.

1983. Kádár declares that there will be "no reform of the reform".

15 March 1986. Several thousand people in Budapest mark the anniversary of the 1956 uprising, in what will become annual student-led pro-democracy marches; that evening, police break up a demonstration on a bridge over the Danube.

November 1986. The Writers' Union Congress repudiates party control and asserts that the state of deterioration in Hungary is of concern to all responsible intellectuals.

November 1986. Influential economists issue a call for radical change in the document *Turning point and reform*.

1986. The *Social Contract* document, most significant of the *samizdat* publications circulated by democratic opposition groups, calls for Kádár's departure as the precondition for real change.

September 1987. Reformers within the party, led by Imre Pozsgay, participate in a meeting at Lakitelek near Budapest organized by one of the proliferating discussion groups. The Lakitelek meeting is dominated by a 'populist' current, distinct from the predominantly urban and intellectual 'democratic opposition'. The populists hold a series of such discussion meetings over the next twelve months, effectively taking the political initiative, and formally constitute the

Hungarian Democratic Forum (HDF) as a political movement at Lakitelek on Sept. 3, 1988.

30 March 1988. The Federation of Young Democrats (Fidesz) is formed as a student group independent of the official Communist Youth Union.

May 1988. Kádár is replaced as general secretary of the HSWP by Premier Károly Grósz; the special party conference also replaces the majority of the politburo.

12 September 1988. Environmentalists led by the Danube Circle group mount a demonstration of some 30,000 people in Budapest against the planned diversion of the Danube along the border with Czechoslovakia for the Gabcikovo-Nagymáros power scheme. (The Hungarians suspend work on the Nagymáros dam in May 1989.)

13 November 1988. The radical Alliance of Free Democrats (SzDSz) formally constitutes itself as a political party, six months after its foundation (as the Network of Free Initiatives).

11 January 1989. Parliament passes a law allowing the formation of independent political parties; the justice minister, introducing the legislation, states that "the modernization of Hungarian society cannot develop in the framework of an authoritarian political system". The HSWP on 11 February votes in favour of the establishment of a multi-party system.

28 January 1989. Pozsgay leaks the controversial finding of a party historical commission under his chairmanship, rejecting the official line that the 1956 uprising constituted a 'counter-revolution', and describing it instead as a "popular uprising . . . against an oligarchic system of power which had humiliated the nation".

2 May 1989. Hungary begins the symbolic dismantling of the fences along its Austrian border, the first step in tearing down the 'Iron Curtain'.

16 June 1989. The remains of Imre Nagy and other leaders of the 1956 uprising are given a state funeral.

6 July 1989. The death of Kádár (whose funeral on July 14 was attended by over 100,000 people) coincides with the completion of the rehabilitation of Nagy, as the Supreme Court declares null and void the 1958 verdicts of treason against him and eight associates.

22 July 1989. A joint opposition candidate wins a parliamentary by-election, the first time an opposition deputy has been elected since 1947.

22 August 1989. Effectively acknowledging the power struggle within the party, Károly Grósz announces his intention to step down as HSWP general secretary.

11 September 1989. Hungary lifts the restrictions on travel by East Germans enforceable under a 20-year-old bilateral East German-Hungarian treaty, thereby allowing thousands to pass through the country as an escape route to the West. This action, effectively breaking ranks with the rest of Eastern Europe over freedom of travel, is denounced by East Germany but, significantly, the Soviet Union describes it only as "a very unusual step".

18 September 1989. Round table talks between the HSWP, the opposition groups and the "third side" of communist-led social organizations, end in agreement on the framework for introducing multi-party democracy. The agreement represents a deal in which Democratic Forum accepts the HSWP formula of holding direct presidential elections before a parliamentary poll; the more radical opposition SzDSz and Fidesz refuse to sign.

6-10 October 1989. The HSWP holds its historic 14th extraordinary congress, ending by reconstituting itself as the Hungarian Socialist Party (HSP), electing moderate reformer Reszö Nyers as party president, and backing Pozsgay as its candidate for the state presidency.

17-20 October 1989. Parliament approves the introduction of a multi-party democratic system under a transitional constitution, as proposed in the round table agreement, and also passes a law prohibiting political party cells in the workplace.

20-22 October 1989. Joszef Antall is elected as Democratic Forum chairman.

23 October 1989. Hungary is declared a republic, rather than a people's republic.

26 November 1989. A referendum narrowly endorses the view of radical opposition parties that the president should be chosen by a democratically elected parliament, rather than elected directly as soon as possible as under the Sept. 18 round table formula. The latter course had been favoured by Pozsgay, currently thought to be at the height of his personal popularity as the man who had led the former communist party down the path of democratic reform.

21 December 1989. Parliament votes to dissolve itself in March 1990 to make way for multi-party elections.

21 January 1990. The government orders the disbanding of the State Security Service after opposition parties reveal evidence that it has been continuing its covert surveillance of their activities.

9 February 1990. Diplomatic relations are re-established with the Vatican, as the visiting Cardinal Casaroli attends a service in Esztergom commemorating the posthumous rehabilitation of Cardinal Mindszenty. (The 1949 life sentence on Mindszenty had been revoked in November 1989.)

10 March 1990. An agreement is signed with the Soviet Union on the withdrawal of the 52,000 Soviet troops in Hungary by July 1991.

14 March 1990. The IMF announces approval of a standby credit agreement to support Hungary's emergency economic plan for 1990.

25 March and 8 April 1990. Multi-party elections are held.

2-3 May 1990. The new National Assembly holds its constituent session, elects the Free Democrat Arpad Göncz as its speaker and thus interim national president, and invites Democratic Forum leader Jozsef Antall to form a government.

16 May 1990. Antall announces the formation of a cabinet based on his Democratic Forum's electoral victory, bringing the Independent Smallholders and the Christian Democratic People's Party into coalition to assure an overall parliamentary majority, and naming non-party technocrats to several key posts.

23 May 1990. Antall's government is sworn in.

29 June 1990. Privatization plans are announced, together with price rises and a social policy plan to take effect in August.

3 August 1990. Parliament elects Göncz, the interim president and the only candidate, as national President, after a negligible turnout in a July 29 referendum for which the HSP had campaigned in an effort to institute a system of direct presidential elections.

18 September 1990. Parliament approves the government's privatization plans.

25 September 1990. The government publishes its "White Book", a three-year national economic renewal programme.

30 September and 14 October 1990. Local elections, marked by voter apathy and low turnouts of 36% (first round) and 27% (second round), represent a reverse for the governing parties which is attributed to scepticism about the handling of the economic crisis.

3 October 1990. The Supreme Court rules that the government's plans to return confiscated land to its pre-1947 owners, as demanded by the Smallholders' Party, are unconstitutional without full compensation to present owners, mainly farm co-operatives.

26-28 October 1990. A strike and blockade of Budapest streets by taxi drivers forces the government to back down and halve an announced 65% fuel price increase.

20 December 1990. Cabinet changes reflect government disagreements about the speed of economic change to a free-market economy.

30 December 1990. The budget for 1991 is finally passed after prolonged controversy; it seeks deep cuts in subsidies, removal of many price controls, and continuing privatization measures, while striving to avoid the "shock therapy" approach by expanding social services and welfare provision.

15 February 1991. Antall hosts a meeting with the Czechoslovak and Polish presidents which declares the three countries' "total integration into the European political, economic, security and legislative order". The three countries had already agreed in Budapest on Jan. 21 to withdraw all co-operation with the Warsaw Pact from July.

25 February 1991. Agreement is reached to disband the Warsaw Pact as a military alliance.

24 April 1991. The National Assembly approves the legislation on compensation for land and property expropriated under the communist regime since June 1949; former owners are to be given vouchers to buy into the government's privatization programme.

4 May 1991. The remains of Cardinal Jozsef Mindszenty are returned to Hungary from Mariazell in Austria and reinterred at Esztergom.

29 May and 26 June 1991. The Constitutional Court rules that the legislation on compensation for expropriated property is unconstitutional; the Assembly then

passes a modified law, lowering the ceiling for compensation but extending its applicability to expropriations dating back to May 1939.

9 June 1991. The last Soviet soldier leaves Hungary, but disputes continue about the cost of environmental damage caused by Soviet troops since the 1956 uprising.

28 June 1991. The nine-member COMECON organization is formally dissolved at a meeting in Budapest.

1 July 1991. The Warsaw Treaty Organization or Warsaw Pact is formally dissolved by its six remaining members - the Soviet Union, Bulgaria, Hungary, Poland, Romania and Czechoslovakia.

10 July 1991. Parliament passes legislation on the return of expropriated church property.

4 October 1991. Border controls are tightened as concern grows about the economic effects of an influx mainly of ethnic Hungarians with Romanian nationality; their entry is to be linked to the issue of work permits.

5-6 October 1991. Antall signs with Presidents Havel and Walesa in Krakow a treaty of co-operation and a "Krakow declaration" in which Hungary, Czechoslovakia and Poland (the "Visegrad Three" agree to work together for union with a united Europe and for integration within NATO's security framework.

31 October 1991. A law is passed to compensate those imprisoned or deported for political reasons between 1939 and 1989, and to compensate the families of those executed.

4 November 1991. Parliament passes legislation to allow for the prosecution, for murder and treason, of those responsible for crimes under the communist regime.

1 December 1991. National Bank governor Gyorgy Suranyi is effectively dismissed (and is succeeded by former commerce minister Peter Akos Bod) as a new banking law comes into effect. His strict IMF-endorsed approach to monetary policy has been criticized on economic grounds, but the principal controversy over his departure is a political one; a non-party technocrat, he had joined with opposition groups in calling for increased democracy, and was strongly attacked by right-wing groups for so doing.

6-7 December 1991. Antall visits Moscow and Kiev, signing a treaty of co-operation and good neighbourliness with the Soviet Union (including a clause specifically describing the 1956 invasion as unacceptable and unlawful) only weeks before the Soviet Union goes formally out of existence. Antall also signs a co-operation treaty and establishes diplomatic relations with Russia, before travelling on to Kiev. Hungary becomes the first country to have full diplomatic relations with the Ukraine, which has common borders with Hungary, and which (aside from Russia itself) is now by some way the largest country in eastern Europe.

16 December 1991. Hungary, together with Czechoslovakia and Poland, signs association agreements with the European Community, as agreed in November, allowing for possible future Community membership, and providing for the introduction of free trade over a ten-year period.

POLAND

The country was officially known as the Polish People's Republic (*Polska Rzeczpospolita Ludowa*) until Dec. 30, 1989, and thereafter simply as the Polish Republic (*Polska Rzeczpospolita*).

Poland is the largest country in Eastern Europe, except for the Ukraine and Russia itself. It has a land area of 312,680 sq. km and a population of 38,400,000 in 1990 (just under half that of united Germany). It is mostly low-lying land, part of the North European plain, and there are many lakes in the northern

lowlands and in hillier Mazuria to the north-east. Along the Czechoslovak border in the south are the only significant mountains, the Carpathians and (in the south-west) the Sudety mountains. The river Vistula (Wista) rises near Lublin and flows north and slightly west, through Warsaw (Warszawa); it is then joined by its main eastern tributary, the Bug, flowing on to the Baltic near Gdansk. The Oder (Odra), Poland's other major river, originates in Moravia, flowing thence north-east into Poland and then north-west through Wroclaw before its confluence with the Neisse at the German border; it then delimits the border for much of its length, before reaching the Baltic near Szczecin. South of the Oder-Neisse confluence the Neisse, rising in the Sudety mountains, forms the border with Germany.

Although Poland has a large peasant population, its experience of rapid industrialization under communist rule changed the balance significantly. Over 60 per cent of its inhabitants are now classified as living in urban areas. Warszawa or Warsaw, the capital, is the largest city with a population of 1,660,000. The second city, about half the size of Warsaw, is the old-established industrial centre of Lodz. The main centres of the highly industrialized (and horribly polluted) upper Silesia mining region are Krakow (population 750,000) and its surrounding steelworks, and the smaller city of Katowice. Other cities of comparable size are the two major regional centres of western Poland, both with populations of well over half a million, namely Wroclaw (known under German rule as Breslau) and Poznan, and the two main Baltic ports, Gdansk (Danzig) and Szczecin (Stettin).

The Polish language (Jezyk Polski) is part of the West Slavic group (which also includes Czech and Slovak). The killing during World War II of a fifth of Poland's inhabitants, including the Nazi extermination of 3.5 million Jews, and the large-scale postwar territorial changes and population movements, left Poland ethnically 98.7% Polish, with small minorities of Ukrainians and Byelorussians, less than 0.05% Jews, and a residual minority also of German speakers. About half a million Poles live in what is now Byelorussia and a substantial number also in the Baltic states, particularly Lithuania; there are small Polish minorities in Czechoslovakia and in Yugoslavia, and an emigré population, particularly in North America.

In religious terms Poland is more strongly Catholic than any country in Europe, with the possible exception of Ireland; Catholicism claims the allegiance of 95 per cent of the population, three quarters of whom attend services on a regular basis. There is also a Polish Autocephalous Orthodox Church and other smaller Christian denominations (mainly Ukrainian Uniates, and Lutherans and other Protestants), and only an estimated 12,000 remaining Jews. The Catholic Church under the communist regime lost its formal privileges and could have no explicit political involvement, but retained its position in the eyes of the people as an institution with a moral status beyond the narrowly religious sphere. The election of the "Polish pope" in 1978, and the history of the involvement of Polish clergy in human rights issues, enhanced the importance of the stance taken by the church during the upheavals of the 1980s [see below]. A new statute on church-state relations in May 1989 restored its full status and freedoms as a social institution, capable of exerting a powerful influence on politics in a multi-party system.

Poland was recreated in the latter half of 1918 by the military collapse of Austria and Germany (which had annexed western Poland in the eighteenth century partitions, and, in 1917-18, had overrun and added to their own territory Russia's Polish provinces). Marshal Jozef Pilsudski was proclaimed Chief-of-State of the Second Polish Republic on Nov. 14, bringing together the provisional governments from the various regions. The borders were fixed at Versailles in 1919, except with Russia. Defeated Germany ceded to the new state the provinces of Posen and West Prussia (but not East Prussia, which was thus separated from Germany by a corridor of territory giving Poland access to the Baltic). Danzig became a "free city"; the southern parts of East Prussia, and Upper Silesia, reverted to Germany after plebiscites in 1920-21. Poland, however, was by this time expanding its territory by military action in the east, at the expense of Russia, and using the pretext of supporting the Whites against the Bolsheviks. At one point the Red Army fought back as far as Warsaw itself, but was decisively defeated there in August 1920. Under the Treaty of Riga in March 1921 Lenin got peace, but Poland got land, including half of what is now Byelorussia and a great swathe of the western Ukraine.

Poland had five years of parliamentary democracy under its March 1921 constitution, but Pilsudski, its dominant figure, lost patience in May 1926 with the fractious politicking of a series of weak coalition governments. His military coup was followed by nine years of his personal and authoritarian rule (with democratic trappings; there were even multi-party elections, at which the Communist Party won 7 per cent in 1928, their pre-war high point). The Pilsudski period was marked by the breakdown of the racial and religious tolerance which was specifically guaranteed in the constitution (Ukrainians, Jews and other minorities made up over 30% of Poland's population at this time). There was also growing friction with an irredentist Germany over Danzig and the Polish corridor. Pilsudski, no longer holding a formal office of state but nonetheless the effective dictator, died in May 1935, and power was thereafter exercised by a military council.

After the Western appeasement of Hitler at Munich in 1938, and the dismembering of Czechoslovakia, the Nazi threat was turned into devastating military action as soon as Hitler had reached a deal with Stalin. The Molotov-Ribbentrop pact of August 1939 included secret protocols on the partition of Poland (and Eastern Europe as a whole). British and French guarantees to Poland were now insufficient to deter Germany from invasion in September, the blitzkrieg war, and the incorporation of much of western Poland as lebensraum for the German Reich. All that remained (the east being annexed to the Soviet Union) was the so-called *General Gouvernement* area, under a ferocious Nazi regime. This was to be the SS state, in which were constructed in 1941 the extermination camps for the genocide of Jews. Poles were conscripted to forced labour in Germany, or deported to the General Gouvernement area, or deported eastwards, over one million of them, from the areas annexed by the Soviet Union, before the Nazis overran that area too in 1941. No country in Europe had a more terrible experience of World War II.

A Polish government-in-exile in London was led first by the pre-war leader Gen. Wladyslaw Sikorski, and, after his death in 1943, by Stanislaw Mikolajczyk. It was this regime which ordered the Warsaw uprising of August-October 1944. Some 200,000 inhabitants died in a heroic but desperate struggle. The Red Army, although not far short of Warsaw in its advance, declined to assist the uprising. Soviet policy involved supporting a rival, communist-dominated, Polish Committee of National Liberation, which set up a provisional government at Lublin in December 1944, the month before the Red Army finally liberated Warsaw.

The Polish Workers' Party had been revived in 1941-42, and was active in anti-German resistance. (Its predecessor, the Communist Party of Poland, had been dissolved on Comintern orders in 1938 and its leaders purged, many of them accused of having secret police contacts.) In early July 1945 a Polish Government of National Unity, dominated by the Polish Workers' Party and led by the communist Boleslaw Bierut as acting President, was established in Warsaw and recognized by the Allied powers.

The postwar territorial settlement for Poland, reached between the victorious powers at the Potsdam conference in August 1945, involved meeting the promises made by the western allies to the Soviet Union in 1943 and reiterated at Yalta. Eastern Poland was thus incorporated into the Soviet Union. German-held territory, however, was transferred to Poland. In the west this meant moving the 1919 boundary some 250 km westwards to the Oder-Neisse line, and in the north-east it meant that the southern part of East Prussia became Polish (while the Soviet Union took the north around Königsberg/Kaliningrad).

The Poles had been brave in resistance, drawing strength from a sense of identity and pride which had kept Polish nationhood alive before, even when the country was wiped off the map. In the Cold War division of Europe, however, the fate of Poland was determined by priorities set in Moscow. The military priorities first of all dictated that it must remain a loyal Soviet ally, with the Soviet Marshal Rokossovski as defence minister from 1949 to 1956, and secondly that its railway workers must not become too disaffected, since this would endanger the security of the long support chain from the Soviet Union to its front-line troops. The economic priority, accelerated industrialization, was intended to establish Poland's role in an international socialist division of labour, mainly as a heavy industrial centre.

The creation of a communist-dominated regime was accomplished with even less subtlety than elsewhere in the region, the Soviet Union being prepared to ignore Western sensibilities and guarantees of democracy to make sure that Poland was held firmly within the Soviet sphere of influence. Elections in January 1947, in an atmosphere of intimidation, were rigged to ensure a large majority for the communists and their allies (the Socialists, the Democratic Party and the Peasant Party); Bierut was confirmed as President, opposition parties were then dissolved, and opposition leaders such as Mikolajczyk forced to flee the country. In 1949 the communists absorbed their larger Socialist partners, to form the Polish United Workers' Party (PUWP).

An initial postwar economic recovery, under the three-year plan completed in 1947-49, was then distorted by an extreme Stalinist insistence on investment in heavy industry and armaments, to the exclusion of all else. After the nationalization of industry, some steps were taken towards the collectivization of agriculture, although without the full ruthlessness to carry this measure through against the resistance of the traditional Polish peasantry, and in the latter part of the 1950s the collective farming experiment was largely abandoned in Poland.

A crisis within the PUWP followed Bierut's death in March 1956. Poland's purges in the Stalinist period had been fairly mild on the scale of murderousness in the region, the party general secretary Wladyslaw Gomulka having merely been expelled and imprisoned in 1948 as the leading "right-wing nationalist deviationist". Nevertheless, the beginnings of destalinization, signalled by Khrushchev's speech at the February 1956 Soviet party congress, were taken up with some enthusiasm in Poland. An amnesty was granted, and legal limits set to the powers of the security police. Limits to this liberalization were shown quickly, when Polish troops crushed a protest in June 1956 in Poznan, involving strikes and demonstrations which turned into a riot and ended with over 50 people killed. The PUWP central committee meeting in October, however, promised more. Rokossovski and the principal Stalinists were excluded from the politburo, and Gomulka, re-elected as general secretary, stood up to Khrushchev upon the latter's unexpected and sudden arrival with a Soviet delegation on Oct. 19. Although he was careful to reassure the Soviet leader that no anti-Soviet sentiments were being kindled, and that there was no threat to the building of socialism, he went on to reaffirm the following day Poland's determination to follow its own road, and its right to build on the experience of the Soviet, the Yugoslav or any other socialist model. The Poznan riots, he said, had been a response to declining living standards, and to the party's lies on that subject; they should not be explained away as the work of "imperialist agents".

The apparently successful Polish stand gave encouragement to radically-minded reformists in Hungary, where the return of Nagy was in many ways a parallel with the PUWP's reinstatement of Gomulka. The Soviet clampdown in Hungary, and preparedness to resort to the use of overwhelming military force, sent a strong enough message to Warsaw for the Gomulka regime to be cowed into political orthodoxy. Changes which did survive were the abandonment of agricultural collectivization, and a relaxation of restrictions on religious and intellectual freedom. Although there were no longer to be Soviet 'advisers' in key Polish army and government positions, no more questions could arise over Polish loyalty to the Soviet line; this was demonstrated in August 1968 when Gomulka ordered Polish participation in the Warsaw Pact invasion of Czechoslovakia. By this time he had become reliant on the support of a strongly anti-liberal element within the party, which sought to mobilize its support around an "anti-Zionist" appeal to Polish nationalistic sentiment.

Ultimately the fall of Gomulka was linked to the failure of his leadership to deliver a sustained and sufficient improvement in living standards. The continued reliance on central planning effectively stifled the innovations which were encouraged to develop in Hungary, for example. The magnitude of Poland's economic problems was partially obscured, for ordinary people, by food subsidies on a massive scale which the economy simply could not afford. The belated attempt to cut these subsidies meant huge price increases, announced just before Christmas in 1970; riots in the Baltic ports were violently suppressed, but led to the ousting of Gomulka in favour of the Katowice communist leader with the country's best managerial record, Edward Gierek.

Gierek's economic objective was industrial development financed by borrowing, the consequence of which, however, was the rapid accumulation of a startlingly large foreign debt. Investment in new machinery was intended to improve the productivity of Polish industry and to orient that industry towards exports, which would in turn finance continuing growth. In practice the allocation of investment remained a highly centralized process, subject to bureaucratic interests and distortions, and the global recession from 1974 onwards made it more difficult to sell Polish industrial products abroad. There were serious balance-of-payments problems and shortages of consumer goods. Investment continued nevertheless to be directed towards heavy industry, displaying the critical lack of flexibility of the command economy. By the end of the decade, Gierek had already encountered resistance and strike action in 1976 over proposed food price increases; and economic growth had halted, then gone catastrophically into reverse. The other main legacy of the Gierek decade was the growth of the *nomenklatura*, the system for the appointment of a communist bureaucracy which permeated every area of public life, from government and local administration to official unions to industrial management to media, education and the arts. The *nomenklatura* provided the broad base for veniality and corruption; Gierek himself shared the predilection for hunting to which Eastern European communist leaders seem to have been especially prone, and had special facilities built in the Carpathians for the use of the privileged party elite.

The only major non-communist structure before the emergence of the Solidarity movement was the church, whose more radical elements gave important moral support to human rights activity and the emerging "workers' self-defence committees" of the late 1970s. Polish pride in nationality and catholicism received an immense boost with the October 1978 election of Cardinal Karol Wojtyla as the "Polish Pope" John Paul II, and the following June he made his first triumphal papal visit to Poland.

The wave of strikes which was to bring Gierek down in 1980 began in mid-year, in the Baltic ports and Silesian coalfields, initially in support of wage demands. Sensing the weakness of the government, which clearly had no co-ordinated response after it had rejected the resort to force, the workers then looked to preserve the unofficial union organizations which had provided the focus for their pay demands. In the "Gdansk accords" of Aug. 31, 1980, the regime conceded the right to strike and for workers to form free trade unions.

This marked in many respects a critical turning point in the protracted fall of communism in Poland. The organized workers were seen to have won, at least temporarily, the right to operate outside the communist system. They were rejecting the official unions dominated by the *nomenklatura*, and confronting the party, whose ideology was based upon its claim to represent them, the working class. Lech Walesa, who had been a leading negotiator in Gdansk, became the leader of the national Solidarity free trade union, formed the following month. The movement, overcoming legal obstacles to its registration, grew so rapidly that it could claim nine and a half million members in mid-1981; it attracted to its ranks as many as one third of the PUWP membership, and spread, too, from the ports, steelyards and mines to the countryside, Rural Solidarity being formally constituted in May 1981.

For a year it was Solidarity which dominated the political agenda, with Walesa and other leaders urging restraint upon their militant membership, as the economic situation continued to deteriorate, and the PUWP and government went through a succession of leadership changes. Gierek was replaced as PUWP leader in September 1980 by Stanislaw Kania, whose ideas for restoring party credibility through the implementation of a reform plan were under constant counter-attack from entrenched hardline interests. Kania survived a PUWP extraordinary congress in July 1981, but had to give way in October to Gen. Wojciech Jaruzelski (the prime minister since February), as industrial unrest continued.

Solidarity's national conference in September-October 1981 had revealed the strength of increasingly assertive attitudes; the conviction that, to carry through the necessary economic changes, Solidarity itself must push for explicitly political reforms, including free elections, rather than confine itself to trade union demands and worker self-management. Set against the undoubted popular strength of Solidarity, however, there was the danger of Soviet intervention. The Warsaw Pact's December 1980 summit had declared Poland's problems to be a matter of concern to all socialist countries, and this was followed in 1981 by a series of exercises by hundreds of thousands of Soviet troops near the border with Poland, and a heightened media campaign against Solidarity in the rest of Eastern Europe.

Walesa, an advocate of restraint who now risked being outflanked by militants in Solidarity, met in early November 1981 with Jaruzelski and Cardinal Glemp. There were strong indications that the party was prepared to accept some form of division of responsibilities with the unions and the church, and talks began later in the month on the formation of a broad national unity front to tackle the economic crisis. When these talks failed, the Jaruzelski government drew up a package of emergency laws, including a ban on strikes. The Solidarity response, with its threat of a general strike, prompted Jaruzelski on Dec. 13 to declare martial law; as he perceived it, this was the only course which would avert Soviet military intervention.

Martial law, in place until 1983, and the five years which followed that, were disastrous for Solidarity, for the economy, and, ultimately, for the communist regime. Jaruzelski was effectively compelled, by the fresh upsurge of strikes in August 1988, to abandon the attempt to rule against the people, and to seek a way of bringing the opposition, and the workers, together to tackle the country's overwhelming problems.

The regime's efforts to improve its image on human rights, by successive amnesties leading to a decree on the release of all political prisoners in 1986, had been damaged, irretrievably, by the kidnapping and killing in October 1984 of the pro-Solidarity priest Fr Jerzy Popieluszko. This crime, for which members of the state security forces were later convicted, provided a focus for powerful moral criticism of the regime from the church, and Popieluszko's name was repeatedly invoked, notably by the Pope on his third visit to Poland in June 1987 and by the visiting US vice-president George Bush three months later.

Solidarity's popular support in the eventual 1989 elections was remarkable insofar as it had effectively been destroyed as a mass movement under martial law. Its leaders had been arrested (although later released in a series of amnesties as the regime strove to improve its image on human rights), it was formally banned in October 1982, and many of the freedoms it had won were revoked. It nevertheless continued to organize, to mobilize demonstrations and strike action, and to urge boycotts of elections, up to and including the November 1987 referendum, by which the regime had hoped to get a mandate for its proposed economic and (modest) political reform plans.

Resentment among workers remained strong, and their grievances over pay and prices had been exacerbated as the economy deteriorated further. This was largely because its structural problems could not be tackled effectively without a national political consensus, and also because martial law had brought international condemnation and the damaging imposition (until August 1984) of US and other Western sanctions. Officially-tolerated unions had formed in 1984 a National Trade Union Accord (OPZZ), which provided an alternative to illegal Solidarity action for pressing demands on such issues as wages and price subsidies, although its close links to the ruling PUWP were illustrated controversially when its leader, Alfred Miodowicz, joined the party politburo in mid-1986.

The seriousness of the August 1988 strikes, spreading initially from the mining industry, prompted the government to offer to negotiate with the still banned Solidarity movement on trade union pluralism. (An offer by Solidarity leaders two years earlier, to end clandestine activity and open a dialogue with the government, had been rebuffed and the Solidarity leadership council immediately banned.) This agenda was enlarged, first specifically to include relegalizing Solidarity, and then more generally to extend to political reform.

The round table talks, eventually convened in February 1989, were seen at the outset as a necessary search for consensus to deal with the current crisis. The extent to which they could move on, to define the path of future political development, only gradually became apparent during the process itself. The April agreement, historic though it undoubtedly was, represented a framework for Solidarity's involvement in power-sharing under communist rule. It was not until after the partially-free June elections that the possibility of a Solidarity-led government could really be entertained. This involved separating off the two parties formerly allied to the PUWP, the Democratic Party and the United Peasants. Their responsiveness to this unexpected initiative reflected the extent to which the PUWP had been damaged by the popular vote of no confidence in its leading candidates at the election.

The formation of the Solidarity-led government under Tadeusz Mazowiecki made a reality of the formula advanced by Adam Michnik: "your president, our government". Poland thus became the only Warsaw Pact country with a non-communist government (and was careful to give reassurances that it would remain within the Warsaw Pact framework, as well as retaining PUWP members for the defence, interior and two other portfolios). This moment marked the high point of Poland's revolution, a process which really began in Gdansk nine years earlier, and whose second phase, after the long hiatus of 1982-88, had lasted just one year.

The importance of what had happened in Poland was not lost on the other countries of Eastern Europe, and had its parallels with developments in Hungary which were yet to reach fulfilment. Poland was in many ways unique; it was the only country to go through anything like the Solidarity experience of the early 1980s, and the only instance where the revolution was initiated by striking workers. The clear message which it did send out, however, was that, in the late 1980s unlike in previous decades, profound change was indeed possible without Soviet intervention. Only Ceausescu spoke for such a course of action when the Warsaw Pact met in July, underlining the hidebound nature of his own dictatorial regime, its blind resistance to the need for change, which was being recognized in Poland and, in different ways, in the Soviet Union and Hungary, as essential for economic survival.

The round table in February-April 1989, and the formation of the government in September, were the high points of the sense of national responsibility among the Solidarity leadership. The authors of the programme of economic austerity which was then introduced, and to which successive governments held fast for two difficult years, had identified the "shock treatment" as the necessary price to be paid, particularly by Solidarity's working class constituency, if Poland was to have a chance of successful conversion to a competitive free market economy. The process proved highly divisive, contributing to the splitting of Solidarity itself, and allowing a continuing role for the rival OPZZ unions as the automatic supporters of wage demands and price protests. Paradoxically, the social costs of austerity were proving so severe by the time of the elections in late 1991 that the "shock" medicine was to be renounced by the post-election Olszewski government coalition. The most right-wing of the successive governments after 1989, this coalition nevertheless included in its programme, for the sake of social peace, the maintenance of social welfare protection measures more usually associated with social-democratic than with right-wing management of the market economy. Among the challenges it faced was the resurgence of a narrow form of Polish nationalism, and the need to deal with the church's exclusion from formal politics despite its increasingly powerful voice on such divisive issues as abortion and the restitution of property.

The role of Lech Walesa remained critical for the success of Poland's experiment with democracy. It was an experiment which had not succeeded in attracting anything like the voter participation of post-communist Czechoslovakia. Perhaps not surprisingly in view of the economic hardships to which they were now fully exposed, many Poles were tempted to feel that they had merely exchanged one set of unattractive political leaders for another. Walesa, charismatic but erratic in his political impulses, was feared by many of his former colleagues for his ambition, and his impatient tendency to resort to authoritarianism. They were concerned from early on by his populist attacks on the Mazowiecki government, which prompted the formation within Solidarity of the ROAD group and the pro-government Democratic Union. They also resented his campaign, harnessing anti-communism to his desire to take over the presidency, which resulted in elections being brought forward to late 1990.

Solidarity was a trade union movement, and had never set out to be a coherent political party; its evolution into distinct political groups was a normal development under the new conditions of pluralism, but the tone of its disputes did nothing to enhance the credibility of the democratic system. The adoption of an electoral system, based on an untempered version of proportional representation, for the 1991 legislative elections, then produced a fragmented parliament where no party or natural alliance could claim a leading role. The suggestions made by Walesa at this time included the idea that he should be both prime minister and President. With his continuing emphasis on presidential powers for the new constitution (still being drafted), there were echoes of the effective abandonment of democratic processes under the Pilsudski regime in the 1920s and 1930s.

The principal personalities of Communist rule

Wladyslaw **Gomulka** (1905-1982). The man who briefly held out the hope of a reformist Polish road to socialism when he was reinstated as party leader in 1956, Gomulka had been imprisoned as a communist and union organizer in the 1930s. He escaped in 1939 and became the party's foremost wartime resistance leader, representing that element within a party soon dominated by Boleslaw Bierut and other returnees from Moscow. He held on to the post of secretary-general when Bierut took on the Presidency, but was dismissed and made to recant his "nationalist deviation" in 1948, expelled from the party the following year, and later imprisoned for five years without charge. Released amid the first signs of destalinization in April 1956, he became first secretary in the major changes that October, and initially persuaded Khrushchev to back off from a Soviet clampdown, but few of the new liberal ideas survived in the harsher climate after Soviet troops had crushed the Hungarian uprising in November. Gomulka himself became identified with the retention of tight party controls and with failure to tackle to endemic problems of the industry-oriented command economy. Worker unrest in 1970, and attempts to repress it by force, led to his downfall and replacement at the end of that year by Gierek.

Edward **Gierek** (b. 1913). Gierek made his name as party first secretary in Katowice in the 1960s, and was an increasingly influential member of the politburo, which he had joined in 1956. He took over the PUWP leadership from Gomulka in 1970 amid expectations that he would prove a more effective economic manager, and also that he would be more in tune with ordinary working people. (A miner himself, Gierek had worked in the French and Belgian coalfields before returning to Poland after the war.) His new policy of foreign borrowing, for investment in industrial plant, failed to achieve sustained export-led growth and brought the economy into ever more serious difficulties. In 1980 he had no firm response to counter the unauthorized growth of independent unions, demanding wage increases to match price rises. Ousted in September 1980 (after a heart attack), he was interned for a year under martial law after December 1981, but corruption charges against him were never pressed.

Gen. Wojciech **Jaruzelski** (b. 1923). A career soldier from a minor aristocratic family in the eastern part of Poland annexed by the Soviet Union in 1939, Jaruzelski had fought with the Polish Army in the Soviet Union in 1943-45. After 1945 his army career was combined with party posts, on the PUWP politburo from 1970, and government service, leading to his appointment in 1968 as defence minister. Named Prime Minister in February 1981 as the regime faced the Solidarity crisis, he took over as PUWP first secretary in October and introduced martial law in December 1981. In November 1985 he took the post of President, while remaining party first secretary. Never to be forgiven by the opposition as the man who imposed martial law, and distanced by a cold and rigid military manner, Jaruzelski was nevertheless the unlikely communist leader who took the party knowingly into the 1989 round-table negotiations to work out Eastern Europe's first real (if incomplete) pluralist system. The partially-free parliamentary elections in June showed the full extent of the rejection of the old PUWP, and Jaruzelski from this point took no part in shaping a future communist party. Instead he stood for the restyled post of President (having at first said he would not do so), and was narrowly elected by the parliament, where key Solidarity votes were cast in his favour in the belief that he was necessary to stability. Accepting ultimately that he would always symbolize the old regime, he had been pressured, within little over a year, into agreeing to step down and make way for the direct election of his successor, Lech Walesa.

Mieczyslaw **Rakowski** (b. 1926). The last leader of the PUWP, had been editor of the party newspaper, and had a reputation as a liberal, until Jaruzelski put him in charge of government relations with the unions in 1981. In this role he had extended contact with Solidarity leaders, which developed into mutual antagonism after the introduction of martial law. Brought into the politburo in 1987, he became in September 1988 the last prime minister of the communist regime, and was one of those rejected on the national list for the *Sejm* at the partially-free election in June 1989. When Jaruzelski bowed out of the party leadership the following month, Rakowski succeeded him as first secretary, presiding over the PUWP's dissolution and declining to stand for the leadership of its successor party in January 1990.

Alfred **Miodowicz** (b. 1929). A steel worker from Nowa Huta and first chairman of the new official All-Poland Alliance of Trade Unions (OPZZ) created in 1984, he seemed under communist rule to be accepting a trade unionism subservient to the interests of the party, whose politburo he joined in 1986. The Solidarity resurgence of the late 1980s, and the threat that this would sideline the official union structure, made him a blunt opponent of Solidarity's relegalization and a confrontational voice in the round table talks. Thereafter he saw that the OPZZ might only have a future, if it could outbid its rivals by giving automatic support to workers' wage demands. He thus opposed the economic hardship measures with which Solidarity in government was becoming tainted.

Constitutional changes

Constitutional amendments passed by the *Sejm* on April 7, 1989, gave effect to the round table agreements on the new bicameral parliament and the powers of the presidency. Laws passed at the same time guaranteed the right of free association.

Under the Mazowiecki government formed in September 1989, an early priority was the repeal of the now anachronistic Article 3 of the 1952 constitution which guaranteed the leading role of the PUWP. On Dec. 29-30, 1989, the Assembly approved another constitutional amendment, dropping the formal designation People's Republic, and renaming the country simply as the Polish Republic.

Further constitutional changes were necessary, and duly enacted in late September 1990, to allow for a change to a system of direct presidential elections every five years.

The expectation had been, at the time of the 1989 elections, that a full new constitution would be completed in time for the next elections at the end of a normal four-year term. Bringing forward the elections to 1991 meant that this process had not been completed. A government-proposed bill on a new constitution was rejected by the *Sejm* shortly before the October 1991 elections, and work done by the *Sejm*'s own constitutional committee was similarly rejected, in order to allow the new constitution to be framed by the new parliament. In December Walesa put forward, to the committee of the new *Sejm* working on the constitution, a 17-point draft intended to strengthen the executive powers of the presidency, but later in the month he withdrew it, complaining that it had been weakened unsatisfactorily by amendments.

Position and status of communists

Party name

The first Communist Workers' Party of Poland, formed in 1918 and renamed as the Communist Party of Poland in 1925, was dissolved in 1938 on Comintern orders. A Polish Workers' Party was formed in Moscow in 1941-42, with a resistance wing in Poland known as the People's Army. It was part of the provisional government in 1945 and later absorbed the Socialist Party by a formal merger. The name Polish United Workers' Party (PUWP) was used by the ruling communists from the time of this merger in 1948, until the party was wound up in January 1990. Its successor party, to which it ceded all its assets, rights and duties, adopted the name Social Democracy of the Polish Republic of Poland (SDPR). A dissident group, rejecting the continuity implied by the party's acceptance of PUWP assets, formed itself as a separate Social Democratic Union of the Republic of Poland, renamed in April 1990 as the Polish

Social Democratic Union. For the October 1991 elections the former communists set up a Democratic Left Alliance.

Legal status

After its constitutionally guaranteed status as the leading political organization was terminated by the round table agreement in April 1990, the PUWP (and its successor SDPR) operated with full legality within the multi-party framework; there were no serious moves to ban its activity.

Party assets

The *Sejm* set up commissions in late 1989 to investigate how the party had acquired its assets valued at some $700 million, and adopted on Nov. 9, 1990, a bill transferring most of them to the state on the grounds that they had been acquired illegally. The SDPR opposed this confiscation, regarding it as an act of "political revenge".

The party was embarrassed in November 1991 by disclosures which forced it to admit having received an interest-free loan from the Soviet communist party in January 1990.

Ideological orientation

New party statutes adopted by the SDPR at its founding conference in January 1990 abandoned the commitment to democratic centralism and the dictatorship of the proletariat, defining the new party as committed to parliamentary democracy; it was decided to apply for membership of the Socialist International.

Electoral significance

In the October 1991 elections the Democratic Left Alliance of former communists emerged as the second largest single group in a fragmented parliament, with 12 per cent of the total vote and 60 out of 460 *Sejm* seats (but only four out of 100 in the Senate).

Principal parties in the post-communist period

Solidarity, the movement which swept the board in the seats open for the opposition to contest in the June 1989 elections, was by this time no longer a huge mass membership organization on the scale it had reached in 1981, although it still had some two million members. Presenting itself as the electoral wing of the trade union movement, its candidates stood as the Solidarity Citizens' Committee, and its elected members formed themselves into the Citizens' Parliamentary Club. The splits in Solidarity in 1990, and the emergence of the rival ROAD/Democratic Union and Centre Alliance groups, left a rump of members of the Assembly still sitting simply as the Citizens' Committee, which in February 1991 renamed itself as the National Citizens' Committee, and was formally led by Zdzislaw Najder. In October 1991 there were 27 members elected to the *Sejm*, and 11 to the Senate, on this list.

ROAD was the acronym for the Citizens' Movement—Democratic Action group formed among Solidarity members in July 1990. It brought together those within the movement who shared the concern of influential intellectuals such as Bujak, Frasyniuk and Michnik over Walesa's ambitions and his attacks on the Mazowiecki government. By May 1991 ROAD had been integrated within the broader **Democratic Union**, together with what had been the Democratic Right Forum, and under the leadership of former prime minister Mazowiecki.

The **Centre Alliance** was formed within Solidarity in May 1990 by supporters of Lech Walesa, with Jaroslaw Kaczynski as its chairman, and was regarded as the right wing within the Solidarity movement, with Christian democratic associations. After the October 1991 elections it became part of the centre-right coalition which eventually resulted in the formation of the Olszewski government.

The **Liberal Democratic Congress** was the group most clearly associated with the economic austerity pursued by Leszek Balcerowicz as finance minister, and it remained outside the centre-right coalition government in December 1991 because of that government's intention of putting greater emphasis on "social peace" and anti-recession policies. Formed in 1988, its prominent members included the radical economist Jan Bielecki, who was prime minister for most of 1991.

The **Peasant Party** was formed in May 1990, on the basis of the United Peasants' Party (which had been a junior partner of the PUWP in government until after the 1989 elections), a revived Polish Peasant Party (banned since 1947) and some defectors from Rural Solidarity. Its leader until July 1991, the former Solidarity deputy Roman Bartoszcze, was ousted at an acrimonious congress where he pressed for the purging of those associated with the communist period. Under the new leadership of Waldemar Pawlak and Josef Zych, the party did relatively well in the 1991 elections, outpolling its main rival for the rural vote, the **Peasant Accord**. Both subsequently became coalition partners in the Olszewski government in December 1991.

A feature of the 1991 legislative elections was the success of Christian and Christian Democratic parties. In the wake of a divisive dispute over abortion (a Church-backed initiative to have it banned constitutionally in almost all cases had been rejected), the Catholic bishops had prepared pastoral letters read out the week before the 1991 election, urging the faithful to participate in the voting. The church was debarred from overt political involvement, but did take this opportunity to call for support for candidates who endorsed Christian values. The principal beneficiary of this advice was the **Catholic Electoral Action** grouping. The group's main component party, the **Christian National Union** founded in October 1989 under the leadership of Wieslaw Chrzanowski, subsequently joined the centre-right coalition in the Olszewski government, Chrzanowski himself having been elected as speaker of the *Sejm* in November 1991.

A strongly nationalistic right-wing **Confederation for an Independent Poland** (KPN) led by Leszek Moczulski emerged with 46 seats in the 1991 elections. Moczulski had originally founded this group in 1979, and had been imprisoned twice in the 1980s. His party, which had not been allowed to compete in the 1989 elections, tapped into the intolerant strain in the historical tradition of Polish cultural identity, echoes of which had emerged in the anti-Semitic campaign within the communist party in the late 1960s, but the KPN was also strongly anti-communist. The party was involved in discussions on a centre-right coalition in November and December 1991, but did not ultimately form part of the Olszewski government.

Among the proliferation of other parties in the new conditions of pluralism after 1989 were the representatives of minority groups such as the Silesian German minority cultural association led by Henryk Krol, various regional organizations, protest parties such as Stanislaw Tyminski's Party X and the Beer Lovers' Party, and also a Green party, which failed to make any national impact in the legislative elections, even though its candidate had defeated the Solidarity candidate to become mayor of Krakow in February 1990.

The post-communist political leaders

Leszek **Balcerowicz** (b. 1947). The Deputy Prime Minister and Finance Minister under the Mazowiecki government, and retained until December 1991 as a sign of commitment to Western-backed economic reforms, he was the architect and most convinced proponent of the "shock treatment" plan for a transition to a free market economy accompanied by price rises but strict controls on wage levels. His background was as an economist. He was one of those who left the PUWP during the 1981 crisis, after which he worked as a consultant to Solidarity.

Roman **Bartoszcze**. The Peasants' Party leader until June 1991, and its unsuccessful candidate in the 1990 presidential elections, Bartoszcze had been elected to the *Sejm* as a Solidarity deputy before the Peasants' Party came together. His insistence that the party should purge anyone connected with the former communist period proved predictably unacceptable to the former United Peasant's Party element in the Peasant party, and he was ousted at an acrimonious party congress in June 1991.

Jan Krzysztof **Bielecki** (b. 1951). As Mazowiecki's successor as prime minister, Bielecki retained throughout 1991 a strong commitment to the economic reform programme, keeping Balcerowicz as his finance minister. He was a member of the Liberal Democratic Congress, a centre party which negotiated with, but ultimately remained apart from, the Olszewski coalition formed after the October 1991 elections.

Zbigniew **Bujak** (b. 1955). A Solidarity activist in Warsaw in 1980 and part of its national co-ordinating committee, he was an important underground leader of the movement after martial law was imposed, and was briefly detained in 1986 but then amnestied. As proprietor of *Gazeta Wyborcza*, he was a close colleague of editor Adam Michnik, and a co-founder and leader of the ROAD group in the breach with Walesa in mid-1990.

Bronislaw **Geremek** (b. 1932). The Solidarity parliamentary leader after the 1989 elections (i.e. chairman of the Citizens' Parliamentary Club) until November 1990, he supported Mazowiecki in the presidential elections of late 1990, and in May 1991 joined the Democratic Union alliance with Mazowiecki and the ROAD group. He had been a historian, and a PUWP member until 1968, but was part of the dissident current in the late 1970s and, under martial law, was interned for his activities with Solidarity.

Jaroslaw and Lech **Kaczynski**. Twin brothers and regarded as key right-wingers in Solidarity, supporting Walesa's campaign of criticism against the Mazowiecki government in 1990, his presidential ambitions, and his insistence on speedier removal of former communists from their remaining positions of power. Jaroslaw chaired the Centre Alliance, while Lech edited the Solidarity newspaper *Tygodnik Solidarnosc*, the role which Mazowiecki had fulfilled before he became prime minister. Lech was also an interim co-chairman of Solidarity in the aftermath of Walesa's election as President.

Jacek **Kuron** (b. 1934). A historian and dissident liberal voice in the PUWP until his expulsion and detention in the mid-1960s, he was one of the intellectuals who co-founded the Workers' Defence Committee (KOR) in 1976 and the Social Self-Defence Committee (KSS) the following year, a human rights pressure group with links with the Czechoslovak Charter 77. Involved from 1980 with Solidarity, he was imprisoned under martial law, and eventually charged with conspiring to overthrow the state by force, but was then amnestied. He was one of the Solidarity delegation members in the 1989 round table talks, and regarded as a possible prime minister once Solidarity had decided in the wake of its election triumph that a communist-led government was no longer acceptable; in the event, however, he took on the post of minister of labour and social policy.

Tadeusz **Mazowiecki** (b. 1927). The first prime minister of the Solidarity-led government, Mazowiecki was hesitant in taking on this office, accepting with reservations the transition from intellectual critic and analyst to political decision-maker. An editor with a long association with independent Catholic papers, and an adviser in August 1980 who helped negotiate the Gdansk accords, he had also been the first editor of the Solidarity newspaper *Tygodnik Solidarnosc*, and was interned under martial law. He was on the Solidarity negotiating team at the 1989 round-table talks, and then resumed (briefly) the editorship of *Tygodnik Solidarnosc*. As prime minister he supported the use of the controversial "shock treatment" to overhaul Poland's economic system, encountering strong opposition from the labour movement. Walesa unexpectedly became his most damaging critic over this, and over demands that communists should be removed from government at a faster pace. Walesa's own presidential ambitions set up a direct contest between the two, and Mazowiecki's supporters in the newly-formed ROAD group were disappointed by his unexpected humiliation in the first round in November 1990. He resigned as prime minister, and became leader of the Democratic Union, a grouping which brought together ROAD and the Democratic Right Forum, and which supported the Bielecki government and the continuation of the economic programme.

Adam **Michnik**. A former historian, editor from May 1989 of the influential daily *Gazeta Wyborcza*, and co-founder in mid-1990 of the ROAD group of Solidarity members concerned about the extent of Walesa's personal ambition, Michnik was the principal representative of the social democratic strand within the Solidarity movement. He had been involved in the late 1970s with Jacek Kuron's dissident Social Self-Defence Committee, and like Kuron was imprisoned under martial law for plotting to overthrow the state, but never tried. In June 1985 he was sentenced for fomenting unrest, but amnestied again in mid-1986.

Jan **Olszewski** (b. 1930). Prime minister at the head of a centre-right coalition from December 1991, Olszewski had been Walesa's preferred candidate a year earlier (when he was unable to build a coalition behind the proposal to relax the "shock therapy" of the economy), but was accepted only very reluctantly by Walesa when he did appear to be able to put together a coalition on this basis following the inconclusive October 1991 elections. A former Solidarity member and a lawyer with a reputation for defending dissidents, Olszewski had successfully prosecuted in 1985 the four security service members who murdered Father Popieluszko.

Stanislaw **Tyminski** (b. 1948). A Polish-born emigré who had made a business career in Canada, Tyminski entered the 1990 presidential election campaign, in which he was initially regarded as a fringe candidate. He made a real impact especially in the countryside and small towns, finishing second behind Walesa, by attacking the government for mismanaging economic reform, and by claiming, however implausibly, to have radical free market solutions which would not involve the pain of austerity. The idea of bringing him to trial, for his wild charges of treason against the government, was subsequently dropped. His "Party X" was banned from the October 1991 parliamentary elections in all save four constituencies, when it was found to have entered false names of supporters on its registration lists, and he then left the country, ostensibly on the grounds that he did not wish his presence to create any "appearance of honesty" in the election process.

Lech **Walesa** (b. 1943). The President of Poland since December 1990, Walesa, a charismatic and unpredictable figure, had been the dominant figure in Solidarity since its inception in 1980. His tendency to resort impatiently to authoritarian solutions worried many of his former Solidarity colleagues after 1989 as they grappled with the difficulties of democratic politics and managing an economy in serious crisis.

Originally trained as an electrician, Walesa led a strike committee in the Lenin shipyard in Gdansk in 1970, and was dismissed in 1976 for attacking the working conditions there, but returned to join strikers in August 1980. As head of the Gdansk inter-factory committee, he helped negotiate the historic "Gdansk accords" on free trade unions, and became chairman of the newly-formed Solidarity movement's national co-ordinating commission in September. Although often attempting to hold back militant demands in the course of the next year, he made his reputation nationally and internationally as the key Solidarity leader, until the declaration of martial law.

He was then detained for 11 months, but remained head of the movement underground, while returning to work at the Lenin shipyard, and attracted further international attention to the Solidarity cause when he won the 1973 Nobel Peace Prize. The Jaruzelski regime, challenged by the wave of strikes in 1988 and attempting to achieve some political consensus, could no longer ignore Walesa (by now active leader of Solidarity again as chairman of its national executive commission), who was allowed to go on television and called for relegalization of the union.

After the round-table talks and the June 1989 elections, it was Walesa who saw and seized the opportunity to go beyond power-sharing and press for a Solidarity-led government, by proposing coalition with the parties previously allied to the communist PUWP. Keeping away from governmental responsibilities himself, he concentrated for a short period on the trade union side, attacking the very government he had helped to set up, because of the effects of its economic "shock treatment" on wages and prices—the bread-and-butter issues on which he had originally built his own career. In May 1990 he restored his somewhat fading national prestige with an unexpected intervention to dissuade railway workers from continuing a potentially crippling strike.

His presidential ambitions at this time were couched partly in terms of a desire to bring forward direct elections, to dispose of the remaining power of the former communists. Despite accusations from former colleagues in Solidarity that he was behaving "like a Caesar", he succeeded in his campaign to have the presidential elections scheduled for late 1990, and was elected in the second round; the reluctant support of the Mazowiecki camp ensured him a large majority against Stanislaw Tyminski.

As President, he demonstrated his intention of having a strong influence over the choice of government. He put forward after the inconclusive October 1991 elections the suggestion that he should himself be prime minister, and only reluctantly deferred to a centre-right coalition over the choice of Jan Olszewski, while unexpectedly now resisting this coalition's plans to relax the "shock therapy" approach to the economy.

Elections

Legislature

Under the 1952 constitution of the communist regime the legislature was a unicameral assembly, the *Sejm*, to which elections were held every four years; the 460 seats were divided in agreed proportions between the PUWP and the other two approved parties, the United Peasants' Party and the Democratic Party. The last of these, in October 1985, used a revised arrangement allowing a choice of candidates for 410 seats elected in 74 districts, while 50 candidates were elected unopposed on the list of the Patriotic Movement for National Rebirth. A turnout of nearly 79 per cent was claimed for these 1985 elections.

A new National Assembly, a bicameral legislature in which both houses would sit for simultaneous four-year terms, was created under the April 1989 constitutional amendments. The 460-seat *Sejm* (the former unicameral legislature) became the lower house, with a new 100-seat Senate as the upper house.

Direct elections for the two houses took place in June 1989. Senate seats were openly contested, but 65 per cent of the *Sejm* seats were restricted. The formula designated 35 seats for candidates on an unopposed "national list" of government and party leaders, and others for candidates from the ruling Polish United Workers' Party (157 seats), its traditional coalition partners the United Peasants' Party (65 seats) and the Democratic Party (24 seats), and three approved lay Roman Catholic organizations (16 seats). The remaining 35 per cent (161 seats) were open to be contested by candidates from opposition or independent groups (and were all won by the Solidarity Citizens' Committee—see table).

There was a requirement of a second round run-off in constituencies where no candidate won 50 per cent of the vote; these run-offs were used to decide eight Senate and 295 *Sejm* seats. Unexpectedly, this included run-offs between two new candidates, under hastily-approved new rules, to complete the elections in 33 of the 35 "national list" seats, where the original unopposed candidates had been disapproved by more than half of the voters actually deleting their names.

The first round election turnout in June 1989 was only 62 per cent, and the second round turnout only 25 per cent.

General election results

June 4 & 18, 1989: elections to bicameral National Assembly with reserved *Sejm* majority

	Sejm seats	Senate seats
PUWP (communists)	173	0
United Peasant Party (ZSL)	76	0
Democratic Party (SD)	27	0
Approved Catholic groups	23	0
Solidarity Citizens' Committee	161	99
Independent	0	1
Total	460	100

Oct. 27, 1991: first fully free elections to bicameral National Assembly

		Sejm seats	Senate seats
Democratic Left Alliance (former communists)	12.0	60	4
Catholic Electoral Action	8.7	49	9
Confederation for an Independent Poland	7.5	46	4
Liberal Democratic Congress	7.5	37	6
*Polish Peasant Party - Programmatic Alliance	8.7	48	7
*Christian National Union		,	
*+Peasant Accord	5.5	28	5
*+Centre Alliance	8.7	44	9
+Democratic Union	12.3	62	21
+Solidarity	5.1	27	11
Beer Lovers' Party	3.3	16	-
Others	21	43	24
Total		460	100

* Represented within the Olszewski government formed in December.

+ One of the groups formed from the basis of the Solidarity movement.

The October 1991 general election involved all seats being freely contested. Under a complex system of modified proportional representation agreed the previous June, the 100 Senate seats were elected in 47 two-member counties, with three members for the Warsaw and Katowice counties. For the *Sejm* 69 of the seats were elected on the basis of votes cast for party national lists. To elect the other 391 seats, the country was divided into 37 multi-member electoral districts, in which the voters cast ballots for individually named party representatives. Vote totals were then aggregated by party for each county, to determine the number of seats to go to each party. The relevant number of that party's candidates, ranked in order of the number of individual votes received, were then declared elected.

The turnout in October 1991 was only just over 43 per cent.

Presidency

Prior to 1989 the head of state under the communist regime was chosen as the chairman of the Council of State, elected by the *Sejm*. Gen. Jaruzelski was the last holder of this (ceremonial) post, from 1985.

The office of executive state President was created under the April 1989 constitutional amendments. The President was elected on 19 July 1989, supposedly for a six-year term, by a joint sitting of both houses of the National Assembly, with the members casting named ballots. Jaruzelski, rescinding a decision not to stand, was the only candidate, and, requiring over 50 per cent of the valid votes, received 270 to 233 against with 34 abstentions. Seven votes were deliberately spoiled by Solidarity members who feared the destabilizing consequences of defeating Jaruzelski. The decision to move to a directly elected presidency was reached in 1990 after a sustained campaign by supporters of Lech Walesa in particular, who successfully argued, moreover, that the elections should take place as soon as possible as part of the process of removing former communists from power. Jaruzelski agreed on Sept. 19 to resign and transfer power to a directly elected President. Voting was held in two rounds, the first on Nov. 25, 1990 (turnout 60 per cent), and the run-off on Dec. 9 (turnout 55 per cent), and Walesa was sworn in as President on Dec. 22, for a five-year term.

There had been six candidates, of whom Walesa (chairman of Solidarity) and prime minister Mazowiecki (backed by the centre-left ROAD faction) were regarded as the front runners. Candidates of the former communists, the Polish Peasants' Party and the right-wing Confederation for an Independent Poland won respectively 9.2 per cent, 7.2 per cent and 2.5 per cent in the first round. The surprise was that an apparently fringe independent candidate promising dramatic results from extreme free-market economic measures, Stanislaw Tyminski, won so many protest votes, especially in the countryside and small towns, that he finished second with 23.1 per cent, behind Walesa (39.9 per cent) but ahead of Mazowiecki (18.1 per cent). In the second round Tyminski, winning no further support, was comprehensively defeated by Walesa, who won 74.3 per cent with the (unenthusiastic) endorsement of the pro-Mazowiecki camp.

Local elections

Elections to local councils and to councils for the 49 *voivodships* (provinces, with appointed governors) were held under the communist regime most recently in June 1984 and June 1988. The 1984 election was the first at which electors were offered a choice between two approved candidates in each seat. A turnout of nearly 75 per cent was claimed on this occasion, and 55 per cent in 1988, compared with the claims of 99 per cent turnouts in the past.

Local government changes in 1990 gave greater autonomy to over 2,300 local councils, directly elected in May 1990 (the first fully free elections in the post-communist period in Poland). The turnout was only about 42 per cent. Solidarity-backed candidates won about 40 per cent of the 52,000 seats, and independents a similar number.

Governments in the post-communist period

There were three governments in the period from the first formation of a Solidarity-led administration (in September 1989) until the end of 1991. The first of these, the Mazowiecki government, lasted for rather over one year, with a reshuffle in July 1990 (completed in September) removing all but one of its communist members. The second, the Bielecki government, was formed following the presidential elections and Mazowiecki's defeat by Walesa; the third followed the National Assembly elections in October, taking nearly two months before the Olszewski centre-right coalition government was finally formed.

Principal members of governments September 1989 to December 1991				
	Sept. 89-July 90	July-Dec 90	Jan.-Oct 91	Dec. 1991
Prime minister	Tadeusz Mazowiecki	Mazowiecki	Jan Krzysztof Bielecki	Jan Olszewski
Finance	Leszek Balcerowicz	Balcerowicz	Balcerowicz	Karol Lutkowski
Interior	Lt.-Gen. Czeslaw Kiszczak	Krzysztof Kozlawski	Henryk Majewski	Antoni Macierewicz
National defence	Gen. Florian Siwicki	Vice-Adml. Piotr Kolodziejczyk	Kolodziejczyk	Jan Parys
Foreign affairs	Prof. Krzystof Skubiszewski	Skubiszewski	Skubiszewski	Skubiszewski

Security and human rights issues

A well-known Catholic journalist and Solidarity member, Krzysztof Kozlawski, was responsible for overseeing the disbanding of the communist secret police, as Deputy Interior Minister in the Solidarity-led coalition government formed in September 1989. In May 1990 he took charge of a new security service, the Office for Protection of the State. He became interior minister in a June 1990 cabinet reshuffle.

The most celebrated case of human rights abuse, the murder of Father Popieluszko in 1984, remained in the public eye in early 1992 as two senior generals were brought to trial for their alleged involvement. The 1985 trials had involved only those who actually planned and carried out the kidnap and murder.

CHRONOLOGY

January 1947. The communists and their allies dominate the general election and claim an overwhelming parliamentary majority.

July 1947. An initial decision to accept Marshall Plan assistance is rescinded under pressure from the Soviet Union.

September 1948. Gomulka is replaced as general secretary of the communist party and recants his "national deviationist" errors; Boleslaw Bierut, the communist President, reassumes the party leadership.

December 1948. The Socialist Party is merged with the communists to form the Polish United Workers' Party (PUWP).

January 1949. Poland officially incorporates the territories formerly part of Germany; mass expulsions of Germans to the west follow in March 1950, and in June of that year East Germany formally accepts the Oder-Neisse line as its border with Poland.

November 1949. The PUWP central committee is purged with the removal of Gomulka and his main "nationalist deviationist" associates, while the Soviet Marshal Rokossovski is brought into the politburo and becomes Minister of Defence.

March 1954. The second PUWP congress brings in a collective leadership on the post-Stalin Soviet model.

June-October 1956. In the face of strikes originating in Poznan and a growing demand for liberalization, there is no intervention by Soviet forces, Rokossovski is dismissed as defence minister, and Gomulka is reinstated as general secretary of a PUWP with hopes of a reformist image, until the Soviet invasion of Hungary in November demonstrates that this will not be allowed to develop, and across Eastern Europe more hardline policies are resumed.

January 1960. Church and state reach an accord, reportedly after a secret meeting between Gomulka and Cardinal Wyszynski.

November 1968. The Soviet party leader Leonid Brezhnev, speaking at the PUWP congress in Warsaw, supports the theory that socialist states have limited sovereignty and that other socialist countries may have an "internationalist obligation" to intervene in the defence of socialism. This doctrine, already set out in a *Pravda* article in September, is elaborated by Brezhnev at the Soviet party congress on March 30, 1971, and becomes generally known as the "Brezhnev doctrine"; its implications overhang the Solidarity crisis of the early 1980s and its subsequent abandonment under Gorbachev is a major factor in creating the conditions in which revolutions could take place, in Poland in the first half of 1989 and thereafter across Eastern Europe.

December 1970. Poland and West Germany sign the Warsaw treaty, with explicit recognition of the Oder-Neisse line as the border between Poland and (East) Germany.

December 1970. Price increases are countered by strikes and rioting in coastal cities, in which hundreds are killed, the dead becoming martyrs honoured by the Solidarity movement a decade later.

December 1970. Gomulka is replaced by Edward Gierek; party and government changes continue over the next six months as the regime, shaken by the December riots, places increasing stress on the importance of improving living standards; by December 1971 the party congress has endorsed this as the party's "supreme goal", but Gierek's pursuit of economic growth built on foreign investment fails to deliver the export-led boom for which he had hoped.

June-July 1976. Riots force the government to back down on proposed food price increases.

October 1978. The election of the "Polish pope", John Paul II (Cardinal Karol Wojtyla), is welcomed enthusiastically by the Polish people.

June 1979. The Pope makes his first of a series of visits to Poland.

February 1980. Prime Minister Jaroszewicz, who has held the post for ten years under Gierek's regime, is dismissed in a dispute over economic policy; he is succeeded, briefly, by Edward Babiuch and then Jozef Pinkowski.

31 August 1980. Strikes are ended by the government's concession, in the historic Gdansk accords, of the right to strike and the right to form free trade unions. (The registration of independent unions is validated by legislation on Oct. 8.)

September 1980. Gierek, having suffered a heart attack, is replaced as PUWP leader by Stanyslaw Kania.

24 September 1980. Solidarity applies for legal registration, after a meeting of independent unions in Gdansk two days earlier chaired by Lech Walesa. After disputes in the courts the registration is granted on Nov. 10.

February 1981. The defence minister Gen. Jaruzelski becomes prime minister.

28 May 1981. Cardinal Wyszynski dies; his funeral on May 31 draws 250,000 mourners including President Jablonski and Lech Walesa. He is succeeded as Archbishop of Gniezno and Warsaw, and thus as Primate of Poland, by Cardinal Jozef Glemp.

September 1981. Walesa is elected as Solidarity chairman at the first national delegate conference, but the meeting is dominated by radical demands for political action.

October 1981. Gen. Jaruzelski succeeds Kania as PUWP first secretary.

13 December 1981. Martial law is declared in a clampdown on the Solidarity opposition, which has taken up a confrontational position and is calling for political change including free elections. Solidarity's leaders, including Walesa, are arrested, and the Gdansk accords revoked, with a ban on strikes and the suspension of trade unions.

8 October 1982. A new trade union act is passed under which Solidarity is effectively dissolved; for the next six years it maintains an underground existence.

12 November 1982. Walesa is released after eleven months in detention.

30 December 1982. Martial law is suspended.

June 1983. The Pope, on a visit to Poland, calls for dialogue between the authorities and the people.

22 July 1983. Martial law is formally lifted.

October 1983. Walesa is awarded the Nobel Peace Prize.

30 October 1984. The body is discovered of the kidnapped pro-Solidarity priest Fr Jerzy Popieluszko; 250,000 people attend his funeral on Nov. 3, and members of the state security forces are convicted of the murder on Feb. 7, 1985.

January 1985. Price increases are announced for basic goods, but are then modified in the face of protests from the new official trade unions and to avert a general strike called by the (illegal) Solidarity union.

13 October 1985. Official results claim a turnout of nearly 79 per cent in legislative elections where votes can choose between two approved candidates.

6 November 1985. Jaruzelski adds the office of head of state (succeeding Henryk Jablonski) to his position as PUWP first secretary, but gives up the post of prime minister to Zbigniew Messner.

September 1986. Solidarity leaders, released in amnesties affecting over 13,000 detainees, propose to end clandestine activity and open a dialogue with the government, but their new leadership council is immediately banned.

June 1987. The Pope on his third visit gives particular emphasis to the importance of human rights, repeatedly invoking the name of the murdered Fr Popieluszko, and expressing at a mass in Gdansk on June 12 his unequivocal support for the right to form free trade unions; the previous day he has given Walesa a private audience.

26-29 September 1987. US Vice-President Bush visits Poland, meeting not only with Jaruzelski and senior government leaders, but also with Walesa and other Solidarity leaders, and laying a wreath at Fr Popieluszko's grave.

29 November 1987. Seeking endorsement in a national referendum for a programme of economic reforms drawn up on Oct. 10 (involving "radical curing" and two to three years of austerity) and for limited political liberalization and decentralization, the government gets less than the 50 per cent minimum support it had sought. The turnout is only 67 per cent, of whom only about two-thirds vote "yes" on each proposition.

June 1988. Local elections, held after two months of widespread strikes over price rises, are recorded as attracting only a 55 per cent turnout as Solidarity urges a boycott.

August-October 1988. Industrial unrest, focusing around the eighth anniversary of the Gdansk accords and the demand for relegalization of Solidarity, leads to talks between the government and Walesa, at which the government holds out the promise of round table talks; the intention of starting these talks in October is postponed and there is outrage over a government decision to close the Lenin shipyard in Gdansk.

September-October 1988. Messner is replaced as prime minister by Mieczyslaw Rakowski and a new government is formed.

30 November 1988. The threat to the power of the official trade union organization, from the re-emergent but still formally banned Solidarity movement, is dramatized in a live debate between Walesa and the OPZZ leader Alfred Miodowicz.

17-18 January 1989. An acrimonious PUWP plenum approves Jaruzelski's proposal to hold round talks on relegalizing Solidarity, to "take into account pluralism of interests" within the trade union sphere and in political life.

6 February 1989. Round table talks begin in Warsaw, involving the government, the PUWP, the other two official parties and approved social organizations, their umbrella Patriotic Movement for National Rebirth, the official OPZZ trade union, Solidarity, and the Church. The talks then break up into working groups on unions, economic reform, and political change.

7 March 1989. The Polish government openly places the blame for the 1940 Katyn massacre on the Soviet Union, for the first time, when spokesman Jerzy Urban says that a historical commission has found all the evidence to indicate that "the crime was committed by the Stalinist NKVD" rather than by the Nazis when they overran the area the following year.

5 April 1989. Comprehensive agreements are signed in a historic agreement marking the successful conclusion of the round table talks. They provide for the holding of multi-party elections under a complex formula protecting the PUWP majority (and for free multi-party elections four years later), other constitutional changes, the relegalization of Solidarity, and the introduction of a package of economic reforms.

17 April 1989. Solidarity is legalized, as is Rural Solidarity three days later.

8 May 1989. The independent daily newspaper *Gazeta Wyborcza* edited by leading Solidarity activist Adam Michnik is published for the first time, under the round table agreement on press freedom.

17 May 1989. The Roman Catholic Church is accorded a status unparalleled in Eastern Europe under a new legal framework for church-state relations which guarantees freedom of conscience and of religious belief. It recovers extensive rights to run schools and provide a social welfare framework for its adherents, and wins the restoration of its property confiscated in the 1950s; it is allowed to have its own press and broadcasting organizations, and to run its religious and lay functions without central government supervision.

23 May 1989. A Warsaw court refuses registration of the Independent Students' Union (NZS), finding that its demand for the right to strike puts it in contravention of the law on rights of association passed in April in fulfilment of the round table agreement. Protests and sit-ins spread in the ensuing week. The NZS finally wins legal recognition in September, eight years after its 1981 banning.

29 May 1989. Parliament pardons those convicted since the 1980 Gdansk accords for strikes, demonstrations and supporting banned organizations.

4 and 18 June 1989. The election of the new bicameral National Assembly produces a humiliating result for the ruling PUWP and other approved organizations, which win only the seats reserved for them in the 460-seat *Sejm* (lower house) and no seats at all in the freely-elected Senate. Even on the unopposed "national list" for

35 seats, 33 top government and party leaders are rejected because a majority of voters cross out their names. The Solidarity Citizens' Committee wins all 161 seats open to it in the *Sejm* and 99 of the 100 Senate seats.

6 June 1989. Gen. Jaruzelski offers to include Solidarity in a coalition government in the light of its election triumph, although Solidarity leaders restate their intention of remaining in opposition (as they will do again in July), and on the following day Jaruzelski accepts publicly that the PUWP would relinquish power in 1993 if it were defeated in the free elections due to be held in that year.

30 June 1989. The PUWP fails to agrèe on a candidate for the Presidency. Jaruzelski has proposed interior minister Gen. Czeslaw Kiszczak, but later agrees to stand himself, despite his original statement that the Polish people associate him too closely with the imposition of martial law in 1981.

19 July 1989. Gen. Jaruzelski, as the only candidate, secures election to the new post of President at a joint sitting of both houses of the Assembly. Influential Solidarity figures including Walesa regard this outcome as preferable to a destabilizing political crisis, and seven leading Solidarity members spoil their ballots to ensure that he is returned but with only the narrowest possible majority of 50 per cent plus one.

29 July 1989. Outgoing prime minister Mieczyslaw Rakowski succeeds Jaruzelski as PUWP first secretary, and politburo and secretariat changes strengthen the position of reformers; Leszek Miller is among those promoted.

1 August 1989. Food prices rise by up to 500 per cent after the abolition of state price controls

2 August 1989. Kiszczak is elected by the *Sejm* as prime minister but proves unable to put together a government because the PUWP's traditionally subservient allied parties, the ZSL and SD, are by now discussing a possible coalition with Solidarity, as suggested publicly by Walesa on Aug. 7.

19 August 1989. Faced with a crisis over its possible exclusion from government, the PUWP agrees to join a Solidarity-led coalition provided it is adequately represented, with more than just the defence and interior ministries.

24 August 1989. The Solidarity candidate Tadeusz Mazowiecki is elected by the *Sejm* as prime minister.

12 September 1989. The *Sejm* swears in Mazowiecki's Solidarity-dominated government. It contains four PUWP members, but is the first government in Eastern Europe since the 1940s which is not under communist control.

15 September 1989. The PUWP at a meeting of its central committee receives Leszek Miller's highly critical report warning that it faces marginalization unless it can transform itself into an effective and vote-winning "party of the Polish left".

29 September 1989. The ZOMO riot police units of the civic militia are disbanded.

12 October 1989. Government plans for a rapid transition to a market economy are published, bearing the hallmark of finance minister Leszek Balcerowicz's

prescription of "shock treatment", and despite Walesa's warnings of the civil unrest which may result.

9-14 November 1989. West German Chancellor Helmut Kohl, in the name of Polish-German reconciliation, pays a six-day visit which includes the site of the Auschwitz / Oswiecim extermination camp. He signs a declaration on West German acceptance of the post-1945 Polish frontiers.

29-30 December 1989. Both houses of the National Assembly approve the dropping of the formal designation People's Republic, renaming the country simply as the Polish Republic.

2 January 1990. Dramatic price increases begin under the IMF-backed austerity package of "deep surgical cuts", as approved in the budget four days earlier. The package, accompanied by a devaluation, is designed to tackle rampant inflation notably by limiting wage increases to one fifth of the rate of inflation; it provokes strikes in mid-January in the Silesian coalfield.

27-30 January 1990. The PUWP's last congress, at which it dissolves itself on Jan. 28, becomes the founding congress of a successor party which chooses the name Social Democracy of the Polish Republic (SDPR) and elects Aleksander Kwasniewski as its chairman and Leszek Miller as its general secretary. The SDPR abandons democratic centralism and commits itself to parliamentary democracy, but accepts the PUWP's assets ceded to it, a controversial decision which prompts protest demonstrations and the formation of a breakaway Social Democratic Union.

5 February 1990. Formal approval of the IMF agreement is followed by World Bank loans and the rescheduling on Feb. 16 of $9 billion of Poland's $41 billion foreign debt.

9 February 1990. Krakow, severely affected by heavy industrial pollution especially from the giant Nowa Huta steelworks, elects a Green Party mayor in preference to the Solidarity candidate.

19-25 April 1990. Solidarity's national conference in Gdansk re-elects Walesa as chairman, supports prime minister Mazowiecki's call for free parliamentary elections to be brought forward from 1993 to early 1991, but also comes out in favour of political changes more rapid than Mazowiecki is advising, notably including direct election of the President.

13 April 1990. A statement by the Soviet news agency Tass marks the long-awaited official Soviet admission that the Katyn massacre of Polish officers was carried out by the Soviet NKVD secret police in early 1940, not by the Nazis in 1941.

27 May 1990. The first fully free elections, for 2,300 local councils to replace the existing communist-dominated local authorities, give Solidarity a clear lead and control of the main cities, but the turnout is only 42 per cent. This degree of disaffection with electoral politics is attributed to the unpopularity of economic austerity measures. The elections are overshadowed by a strike by railway workers, mounting the first major industrial challenge to these policies. However, Walesa intervenes unexpectedly and boosts his prestige by persuading them on May 27 to return to work.

29 June-1 July 1990. The Solidarity citizens' committees, as urged by Walesa, reject government proposals for restructuring the movement and tying it in to a permanent representation committee which would provide formal support for the government. Walesa himself, pressing for the expulsion of former communists from the cabinet and for direct presidential elections to be held in autumn 1990 rather than spring 1991, and already nominated as a candidate by a newly-formed Centre Alliance, is urged by Adam Michnik to step back from confrontation with the government. Michnik, having accused Walesa of behaving "like a Caesar", has resigned (together with Zbigniew Bujak and Henryk Wujek) from the Solidarity national committee on June 24.

6-7 July 1990. Mazowiecki replaces three former communist ministers, including interior minister Kiszczak, but refuses Walesa's challenge that he should debate policy with him at the Gdansk shipyard; at a meeting in Warsaw, however, the two men promise to work together, for economic reconstruction "preserving social peace".

13 July 1990. Passage of the privatization bill, which allows workers to buy shares in their enterprises at half price, opens the way for the sale of state holdings amounting to 80 per cent of the economy.

27 July 1990. The Centre Alliance urges that Jaruzelski should step down as President and that Walesa should take his place pending direct elections.

28 July 1990. The first congress is held of a newly-formed group, the Citizen's Movement for Democratic Action (ROAD), representing those within Solidarity most suspicious of Walesa's ambitions, including Adam Michnik, Zbigniew Bujak and Wladyslaw Frasyniuk.

1 October 1990. Jaruzelski, having agreed to step down, signs legislation passed by the National Assembly in late September to amend the constitution and arrange direct presidential elections.

14 November 1990. A border treaty with Germany is signed by the German and Polish foreign ministers in Warsaw, formally abandoning German territorial claims dating from the end of World War II.

25 November 1990. Walesa tops the poll in the first round of the presidential elections, winning 40 per cent of the vote in a 60 per cent turnout. The unpopularity of the economic reform programme is reflected in a vote of only 18 per cent for Mazowiecki, who is beaten into third place by the flamboyant and erratic emigré businessman Stanislaw Tyminski.

9 December 1990. Walesa wins three quarters of the vote to defeat Tyminski in the second round run-off, having received the endorsement of Mazowiecki; he resigns as chairman of Solidarity on Dec. 12.

22 December 1990. Walesa is sworn in as President, symbolically receiving the insignia not from outgoing former communist president Jaruzelski, who is excluded from the inauguration, but from the head of the Polish government-in-exile.

12 January 1991. A new government is sworn in under Jan Krzysztof Bielecki, nominated as prime minister by Walesa the previous Dec. 29.

15 March 1991. Poland wins agreement on the rescheduling of 50 per cent of its public sector foreign debt (which accounts for over two thirds of the total of some $48 billion).

1-9 June 1991. The Pope pays his fourth visit to Poland, amid fears that this will lend weight to the idea of a more overt church involvement in Polish political affairs; on June 4 he makes controversial comments linking abortion with the genocide of the holocaust.

14-15 August 1991. Over a million young people at Czestochowa hear the Pope's call for the building of a new world "based on truth, justice, solidarity and love".

27 October 1991. Poland's first fully free multi-party election since the beginning of the communist period ends without any party establishing a clear claim to form a government; there is a turnout of only 43 per cent, and considerable support for joke protest candidates.

23 December 1991. A centre-right coalition government is finally sworn in, nearly two months after the elections, after Walesa has on Dec. 5 agreed reluctantly to the nomination of Jan Olszewski as prime minister.

ROMANIA

The official name of the country was the Socialist Republic of Romania _(Republica Socialista Romania)_ until Dec. 28, 1989, when it was renamed simply as Romania.

Romania, with a land area of 229,000 sq. km and population of some 23,200,000, is only slightly smaller than Yugoslavia, its neighbour to the west, and it is more than twice as large as Bulgaria to the south or Hungary to the north-west. Romania has a coastline on the Black Sea

in the south-east (the Dobruja region east and south of the Danube). It has three principal historical regions—Walachia, Moldavia and Transylvania. Walachia, the southern third of the country, is rich low-lying land with the Danube delimiting it in the south along the border with Bulgaria, and the southern range of the Carpathian mountains to the north. Bucharest, the capital, is Walachia's major centre of population. Moldavia in the east is rural but densely populated in the north towards the border with Ukraine; it is drained from north to south by tributaries of the Danube. Romania's eastern border separates this Romanian region of Moldavia from Bessarabia, which now comprises the independent former Soviet republic of Moldova. The north-western third of what is now Romania comprises Transylvania, whose population of some seven million is in ethnic terms 60 per cent Romanian but with a large Hungarian minority.

Bucharest is a city of some two million inhabitants, apart from which the largest urban centre is Brasov (350,000) and only four other towns have populations above 300,000, namely Constanta, Timisoara, Iasi and Cluj. The population is classified, however, as over 50 per cent urban.

In ethnic terms something under 90 per cent are Romanian, speaking a Romance language written with the Latin script. (The same language, across the border in Moldova, is written with the Cyrillic script imposed there by Stalin.) The Hungarian minority is variously given as 1,700,000 (in Romanian census figures) and over two million (Hungarian estimates). There are small minorities of German-speaking Saxons, Ukrainian-speakers, Serbs, Croats, Russians and Turks, and a large Roma (gypsy) travelling population numbering several hundred thousand.

The main religion is Christianity. There are only about 15-30,000 Jews (the majority of a Romanian Jewish community ten times this size having been allowed to emigrate from 1953 onwards) and 40,000 Muslims. Most of the Christians belong to the Romanian Orthodox church. Uniate Catholics were banned in 1948 and required to join the Romanian Orthodox church. Smaller Roman Catholic, Calvinist, Lutheran and Baptist churches remained distinct, the Protestant churches in particular sometimes coming into conflict with the Ceausescu regime which exercised tight control over them.

The Romania (or more accurately Rumania) of the inter-war period, benefiting from having fought on the Allied side from August 1916, was substantially larger than its current (or pre-1914) size; it included the formerly Hungarian area of Transylvania, and also Bessarabia and part of what is now Bulgaria (southern Dobruja). The nominally democratic system under the monarchy was notorious for the corruption of its politics, which were dominated mainly by the National Liberal Party in the towns and the National Peasants' Party in the countryside, and for the competition for influence between communists (banned from 1924) and an increasingly powerful fascist 'Iron Guard'. King Carol in 1938 established a royal dictatorship. Under heavy pressure from the alliance between the Soviet Union and Nazi Germany, Romania ceded territory in 1940 first to the Soviet Union and then to Bulgaria and Hungary. The Iron Guard then mounted its own coup, compelling King Carol to abdicate in favour on his son Michael, and in November 1940 the government led by Gen. Ion Antonescu joined the Tripartite Pact, undertaking to co-operate in a Nazi-dominated "new order" in Europe. The following year Romania entered the war on the German side against the Soviet Union, hoping thereby to recover Bessarabia. When the tide of the war turned against the Axis powers, however, and Soviet troops reached the Romanian border, King Michael on Aug. 23, 1944, dismissed Antonescu and changed sides, a major blow to the retreating Germans in south-east Europe. A wartime coalition government included the Romanian Communist Party (RCP), increasingly in control after March 1945.

The peace treaty concluded in September 1947 restored to Romania all of Transylvania, at Hungary's expense, but neither Bessarabia nor Southern Dobruja.

With Soviet troops in occupation (they were withdrawn in 1958), the immediate postwar political scene was dominated by the Communist Party out of proportion to its membership or electoral support. The National Democratic Front, of which it was a leading component, claimed a comprehensive victory in the much-criticized 1946 elections. Opposition parties and other Front member parties (Social Democrats, Liberals, Ploughmen's Front, National people's Party and part of the National Peasant Party) were progressively eliminated or coerced into mergers, and in 1948 the communists (known as the Romanian Workers' Party, until 1965, to denote the "merger" with the Social Democrats) became the sole legal party. Meanwhile in December 1947 King Michael had been forced to abdicate, and the official title of the country became the People's Republic of Romania.

After a series of large-scale purges in the party, agricultural collectivization began in earnest in 1948-50, as did the nationalization of major industries, to which the regime ascribed a major importance for the country's future. This "Romania first" policy ran counter to the Soviet idea that Romania would concentrate on a food-producing role in the international socialist division of labour. Gheorghe Gheorghiu-Dej, a leading "nationalist" within the party and its first secretary (and prime minister from June 1952), succeeded in controlling Romania's ruthless version of the Stalinist show trials of this period, with the unusual outcome that it was the "Muscovites" in the party who were purged. Playing the nationalist card, he promoted Romania's independence from the Soviet line, particularly on foreign policy, where it remained neutral on the Sino-Soviet dispute.

When Gheorghiu-Dej died in March 1965, Nicolae Ceausescu became first secretary (restyled as general secretary at the July congress when the name change to RCP was approved); he added in December 1967 the post of President. His regime, in power for nearly 25 years, cultivated the good opinion of the West. This was achieved on the basis of a maverick foreign policy, an anomaly in the otherwise monolithic stance of the "Soviet bloc" countries. Romania retained links with China, and with Israel after the 1967 war. Even more striking, although Romania in the end accepted the renewal of the Warsaw Pact, it refused to participate in the 1968 invasion of Czechoslovakia, which Ceausescu condemned, as he later condemned the Soviet invasion of Afghanistan in 1979. This critical independence was probably tolerated by Moscow only because of Romania's relative strategic unimportance; in 1968, and again in 1971, there was tension and fear of a possible Soviet intervention.

Ceausescu was widely feted in the West, notably in the USA and the UK, and Romania was admitted as a member of the international financial community from the early 1970s. This assisted with access to foreign funds for investment in the continuing development of a heavy industrial base. However, Ceausescu made an unexpected decision, with far-reaching consequences, in 1982; the foreign debt was all to be paid back, to avoid compromising the country's independence. To do this, it was necessary to achieve and sustain a large export surplus, which was made possible partly by diverting agricultural output (already affected by under-investment in the drive to industrialize) from meeting internal food needs.

The Romanian people were exposed to tremendous hardship over the rest of the decade (although the debt was indeed cleared by 1989), with food rationing and shortages, and wholly inadequate availability of electricity even for basic heating in winter. Scarce resources went on grandiose planning projects, the vast steel and petrochemical complexes, and the construction schemes like the Bucharest "Avenue of the Victory of Socialism" and the uncompleted "Palace of the Republic" with no purpose other than the glorification of the regime's self-proclaimed "golden age". It was privation which earned Ceausescu the resentment of the working classes, which had come into being largely because of communist industrialization policies, but which, with the exception of a miners' strike in 1977, had not been a source of opposition in the past. As the price of Ceausescu's economic policies became more apparent, the regime relied increasingly on its huge security police apparatus, whose elite *Securitate* divisions were inculcated from their youth with the doctrine of unswerving loyalty to Ceausescu. (Recruitment from orphanages was a characteristic technique, to ensure maximum psychological "bonding" to the leader-figure.) The Ceausescu version of communist rule was also highly centralist, concentrating power within a narrow circle (including his wife Elena) and frequently reshuffling the government and party leadership in the classic ploy to prevent the emergence of powerful rivals.

The changing Soviet stance under Gorbachev from 1985 was not much felt in Romania in terms of the influence of ideas of *perestroika* and *glasnost*. Reformist ideas were screened out by censorship, although there continued to be occasional (and quixotic) opposition to Ceausescu within the RCP leadership, as had been the case when in 1979 Constantin Pirvulescu stood against him for the post of general secretary. (Denounced and expelled, Pirvulescu reappeared in March 1989 as one of six signatories of a letter attacking the regime for violating human rights and discrediting socialism.) However, the international climate in which Romania enjoyed Western favour was one where the Soviet Union was seen as an inflexible opponent. With Gorbachev in power, there were now more promising direct avenues for the West to explore. Coinciding with the descent of the Ceausescu regime into repression and human rights abuses on a greater scale than before, this led to increasing international criticism and the growing isolation of his regime.

Repression took the form, in part, of economic deprivation. In part in meant the suppression of wage demands and protests, as with the use of troops in 1987 against workers in Brasov incensed by shortages and by the imposition of a seven-day working week. In part it was the denial of individual freedoms in social policy, the criminalization of abortion, the requirement that women should use no birth control unless they had five children, so that Romania could reach a 30 million population "target". A special feature was misdirected social engineering on the national scale. The "Romanization" campaign in Transylvania brought in settlers to the towns to support policies of anti-Hungarian discrimination, and above all, the notorious "systematization" policy sought to impose a more "modern" pattern of habitation in the rural areas and villages.

In March 1988 Ceausescu announced the intensification of the "systematization" drive, with the aim of demolishing half of the country's 13,000 villages by the end of the century, and resettling their inhabitants in agro-industrial centres. Condemnation was most vocal in Hungary, where it was keenly felt that this erasing of the past was directed especially at the Hungarian minority community.

The unlikely spark for an uprising was the detention of a Hungarian-speaking pastor, Father Lazlo Tokes, in Timisoara, the major town of western Transylvania, and the use of brutal force to suppress a protest by his supporters there. Many were killed, and the numbers were then inflated by the rumour mill. In Bucharest the talk was of thousands massacred in Timisoara, and the anger all the greater when Ceausescu seemed to brush it aside. When protestors dared to shout Ceausescu down, the Securitate responded with killings in the capital.

The revolution came with astonishing suddenness on Dec. 22; the army changed sides, and Ceausescu and his wife tried to flee, all on the same day. It was violent, as the Securitate fought back desperately over the succeeding days, and Ceausescu and his wife were shot after summary trial. This degree of violence was conspicuously absent from the revolutions of 1989 in other East European countries, but several analysts had already predicted that it was the only way that Ceausescu could be dislodged from power.

As the National Salvation Front moved immediately into the power vacuum, it became even more apparent that there had been no real organized opposition movement. It was outrage which had brought the people on to the streets. The army, which decisively threw its weight on the side of the uprising, had been starved of the sophisticated weapons and prestige accorded to his more trusted Securitate; it had even, in 1986, faced personnel cuts for which Ceausescu got endorsement in a national referendum. The suspicion grew afterwards, although the only evidence was circumstantial, that what sceptics began calling "the events" of December had been manipulated, or even planned in advance, by senior communist party and army leaders.

It was a suspicion which dogged the ex-communist President Iliescu, and the NSF, itself dominated by former communists. This sense, of a revolution hijacked, was further fuelled by the haste with which former communist officials throughout the Socialist Republic now became officials of the new post-communist Romania. Even the Securitate secret police were not fully rooted out, their members forming a ready basis for a burgeoning state police machinery under NSF rule. No opposition party was in any position to challenge the NSF at the 1990 elections, once it had gone back on its original statement that it would not be a party itself. Student-led protestors sustained an eight-week demonstration, before and after the elections, complaining that former communists in the NSF had "stolen" the revolution and demanding that they be ousted. They were denounced as "fascists" by Iliescu, who subsequently thanked miners who came to Bucharest in force in mid-June (not the first time they had turned up to show support for the beleaguered government) and terrorized the city, beating up anyone they took to be against the government.

This crude dependence on intimidation greatly damaged the Iliescu regime's image internationally. It subdued temporarily, but did not end, the protest campaign by students and intellectuals (later grouped in the Civic Alliance). Drawing attention at every opportunity to the NSF's communist connections, the protestors were affronted by the series of court judgments in which Ceausescu's former party leaders, security officials and family had "genocide" charges against them dropped, or received comparatively short sentences even when they were convicted on lesser counts.

This unsavoury aspect of the Iliescu regime certainly contributed to the lack of confidence in it, both domestically and internationally. It was perhaps less critical for its prospects of survival, however, than its inability to win acceptance of the need for economic austerity measures. In this respect the regime itself was divided. Roman, as prime minister, repeatedly put forward proposals for the removal of price subsidies, whereas Iliescu and a "centre-left" element in the NSF attempted to preserve a greater degree of social protection. Ironically, it was a second violent intervention by the miners on the streets of Bucharest, in September 1991 and this time in confrontation with the government, which provoked the downfall of the embittered Roman.

The formation of an interim coalition government in October, and the scheduling of fresh parliamentary elections in 1992, reflected the extent to which the NSF had failed to provide credible national leadership for a genuine transition from communist rule. At the same time, however, the strengthening of presidential powers in the new constitution (adopted in December) suggested a disposition on Iliescu's part to resort to more authoritarian solutions.

The principal personalities of Communist rule

Gheorghe **Gheorghiu-Dej** (1901-65). The first leader of the Romanian communist regime, he was a party activist in the 1930s and was imprisoned under the wartime Iron Guard regime. As party first secretary in the immediate postwar period, he was the dominant figure in the Front government and thereafter tightened his grip on power by the intimidation of opponents outside the party, and merciless purges of rivals within it. His control of the party machinery, and his adeptness at playing on strong Romanian nationalistic sentiments, enabled him to use these purges to remove the pro-Moscow faction in the party, whereas elsewhere in Eastern Europe it was the "nationalists" like himself who faced denunciation in the late 1940s and early 1950s. He launched Romania on the independent foreign policy pursued by his successor Ceausescu, securing the removal of all Soviet troops from Romania by 1958. His stance of "Romania first" also involved insisting that Romania must modernize and develop its own heavy industrial base, rather than be food supplier to the Soviet bloc. After his death from cancer there was a brief and rather half-hearted attempt to discredit him; his brutal purges were criticized, and some of his surviving victims were rehabilitated.

Nicolae **Ceausescu** (1918-89). The Romanian party leader from 1965 until his violent overthrow in December 1989, and head of state for all but two of those years, had begun his political life as a teenage communist activist from a peasant family; he was imprisoned under King Carol and again by the Iron Guard during the war. Associated closely with Gheorghiu-Dej's nationalist group in the party, he succeeded his mentor as general secretary, and played the patriotic card riskily but successfully. Besides maintaining contacts with China and Israel, he condemned the Warsaw Pact's 1968 invasion of Czechoslovakia, and declared all-out resistance against the threat of Romania suffering the same fate. Although he kept Romania within the Warsaw Pact, he offered western governments the possibility of an intermediary, and enjoyed the attention and foreign honours which he (and his high-profile wife Elena) received in return. His economic schemes were geared to notions of Romania's grandeur, and a pride in what modern man could do to his environment, but his lifestyle was remote from the hardship which such policies entailed for ordinary people. The Ceausescu nepotism was unpopular in the upper echelons of the party, but strict censorship and a pervasive personality cult stifled dissonant voices as he proclaimed his rule to be the "golden age", and he seemed genuinely astonished to encounter protest and even hatred from his people in the days when he and Elena were overthrown, captured and shot.

Constitutional changes

Interim constitutional arrangements, incorporating radical changes to the 1965 constitution, applied for the first two years of the NSF regime following the overthrow of Ceausescu. The new constitution came into effect on Dec. 13, 1991, when President

Iliescu announced the results of a Dec. 8 referendum endorsing it by 77 per cent to 23 per cent. Parliament had approved it the previous month, in the face of opposition criticism that it vested too much power in the executive President.

Position and status of communists

Party name

The ruling party was known from 1965 as the Romanian Communist Party, the name under which it had originally been founded in 1921. Between 1948 (when it formally absorbed the Social Democratic Party) and 1965 it used the name Romanian Workers' Party.

The communist party re-emerged in November 1990 under a new name, the Socialist Labour Party (SLP). A former prime minister, Ilie Verdet, was confirmed as the SLP executive president at the party's first congress in Bucharest on Aug. 11, 1991. A veteran dissident communist who had been a founder member of the RCP and stood against Ceausescu for the party leadership in 1979, Constantin Pirvulescu, was SLP honorary president.

Membership

The RCP was a mass membership organization under communist rule, claiming a membership of 3,640,000 in 1986 and over 3,800,000 in 1989; this was the largest figure for any country of Eastern Europe.

Legal status

In the immediate aftermath of the overthrow of Ceausescu, the ruling NSF was momentarily pressured in mid-January 1990 into announcing the banning of the party, but retracted this decision almost immediately, proposing a referendum on the issue but never holding one. The NSF repeatedly denied the frequent charge that it had connections with the former RCP, and resisted pressure from opposition demonstrators for effective action to eliminate former communists from power and to ban communist parties.

Party assets

The RCP's assets were nationalized in January 1990.

Electoral significance

Under communist rule the party-dominated broad front organization monopolized Assembly seats and claimed over 97 per cent support. There was no communist party at the time of the May 1990 elections.

Principal parties in the post-communist period

The **National Salvation Front** (NSF) dominated the political scene in the aftermath of the overthrow of Ceausescu; set up during the uprising as an ad hoc body, it moved rapidly to fill the power vacuum, and soon rescinded its early promise not to become a political force for the longer term. The dominance of former communists and senior army men in the NSF leadership came under attack as early as January 1990. Those few people with longer-standing dissident credentials, like Doina Cornea, broke with the NSF and accused it of seeking to keep its tainted leadership in power by "stealing" the revolution. Its programme for the May 1990 elections called for "a complete and irreversible break with the communist system and its ideology", and set itself out to be a centre-left party, advocating a gradual transition towards a market economy, while preserving a minimum wage and unemployment benefits and retaining much state ownership in industry and agriculture. Despite its overwhelming May 1990 election victory, public confidence in the NSF was progressively eroded. Failing to meet the challenge to do more to root out those who held and abused power under Ceausescu, the NSF regime became dependent on the brute force of pro-government miners to break up the continuing demonstrations and intimidate its opponents. It was also divided between those believed in the necessity of severe austerity measures, notably prime minister Roman, and those more committed to the social welfare element of its programme. Roman became the NSF leader when Iliescu became Romania's President in June 1990 (Iliescu having been endorsed as leader by a 71-member council elected at the first NSF national conference on April 7-8, 1990). On March 16-17, 1991, he won the backing of an NSF national convention, by 988 votes to 58, for a social democratic programme, "A Future for Romania," and was re-elected as leader, in the face of attacks by two small splinter groups (respectively on the radical and conservative wings). A new steering college was set up, consisting of government ministers and others appointed by the party leader. By April 1991, however, when the NSF-dominated Assembly rejected two of Roman's government appointments, there were indications that the unpopularity of his economic policies would undermine his position unless he could reach some broad agreement with his critics. Roman was eventually sacrificed when the miners used the power of their violence in September 1991 to counter what they regarded as his government's attack on their living standards.

The most effective and cohesive group in parliament apart from the NSF itself was the **Hungarian Democratic Union of Romania** (HDUR), with the writer and publisher Geza Domokos as its president. The HDUR stood for the protection of the interests of the minority Hungarian population. It sought to maintain, in the face of the hostility of a newly-created nationalist Romanian Hearth Movement (*Vatra Romaneasca*—UVR), the agreement on ethnic and cultural rights reached by the NSF and the Hungarian government immediately after the overthrow of Ceausescu, which had promised Hungarian language education, local autonomy, and an end to the forced settlement of Romanians in Hungarian-inhabited areas of Transylvania.

Two "historic" parties, revived after being banned for over 40 years of communist rule, put up candidates in May 1990 both for the presidency and for the parliamentary elections. Neither provided much challenge to the NSF's dominance, the **National Liberal Party** (NLP) led by Radu Campeanu winning only 29 assembly seats (and subsequently affected by party splits), and the **Christian Democratic National Peasants' Party** (CDNPP), whose president was Corneliu Coposu, winning 12.

The acute pollution problems caused in particular by unregulated industrial emissions provided a basis for campaigns by two **ecological parties** which won 21 seats between them.

The **National Convention for the Restoration of Democracy** was formed on Dec. 16, 1990, in an attempt to unite the parliamentary opposition parties; six of them joined—the HDUR, the NLP, the CDNPP, both ecological parties and the small Romanian Social Democratic Party, but not the Socialist Democratic Party, the Romanian Unity Alliance or the Agrarian Democratic Party (ADP, close to the NSF). In an increasingly unstable political situation the NLP, the Romanian Ecological Movement and the ADP joined the coalition government formed in October 1991, but the HDUR held out unsuccessfully for the creation of a ministry for national minorities.

An extraparliamentary opposition group, the **Civic Alliance**, was formed on Dec. 16, 1990, chaired by Marin Munteanu, and maintained a high profile in protest demonstrations in Bucharest in particular, both against the continuing power of former communists and against the impact of economic liberalization on living standards. In July 1991 it decided to transform itself into a political party, with a view to contesting elections in 1992. Its membership remained largely confined to students and intellectuals, however, and the more powerful opposition on economic issues continued to come from the unions, including the powerful and violent miners' groups from the Jin valley. A new umbrella **National Advisory Council of Romanian Unions** was formed in November 1991, claiming a membership of four million in its affiliated unions, and signed a co-operation agreement with the Stolojan government over the negotiation of work contracts and pensions.

The post-communist political leaders

Ion **Iliescu** (b. 1930). The directly elected President of Romania since May 1990, and previously the head of the NSF and of its interim administration, Iliescu was the son of a communist railway worker, an engineer by profession, and a communist youth leader, who rose to ministerial rank and then became party propaganda secretary. After 1971 he was sidelined to regional party leadership, in Timisoara and then Iasi, and then to lesser technical postings, having offended by lack of enthiusiasm for the burgeoning Ceausescu personality cult. Visible from early on in the December uprising as one of the NSF leaders, he had become its dominant figure by early January 1990. His victory in the May 1990 presidential election appeared overwhelming, despite charges of irregularities and intimidation. His image was soon badly tarnished, however, by his dependence on the violent intervention of pro-government miners, to break up protestors who were charging his regime with perpetuating the rule of former communists. Iliescu himself, although no longer officially part of the NSF once he became President, was a powerful influence among those who wanted to cushion free market reforms with maximum social protection. The way he abandoned prime minister Roman in September 1991, faced with the hostility of the powerful miners to the government's austerity programme, strengthened the view that his regime lacked the capacity to build a national consensus for real change. The nature of the presidential powers allowed under the new constitution in December 1991 held out the prospect of a descent into authoritarianism if no clear policy direction emerged from the 1992 elections.

Ion **Ratiu** (b. 1917). A former diplomat who returned to Romania in January 1990 as leader of the revived Christian Democratic National Peasant Party, Ratiu had lived in Britain since 1940, built a successful business career, and set up an anti-Ceausescu exile group, the World Union of Free Romanians, in 1984. He came a poor third in the May 1990 presidential election, although he got one of his party's 12 seats in the Assembly.

Radu **Campeanu** (b. 1924). The former exile who returned to lead the revived National Liberal Party in the 1990 elections (standing unsuccessfully for the presidency), Campeanu had been imprisoned in 1947-56 and spent his exile years mainly in Paris. The divisiveness of exile politics made it impossible for him to agree a united candidacy, thus splitting the opposition vote with his old rival, peasant party leader Ion Ratiu. He was elected, however, to the Senate and became its deputy speaker. His leadership of the party, which ultimately joined the October 1991 coalition government, was not sufficiently flexible to prevent splits as the historic party sought to adapty to the new conditions.

Silviu **Brucan** (b. 1928). A former diplomat and editor of the communist party newspaper *Scienteia*, Brucan became identified as a reformist and was detained after signing the March 1989 critical letter to Ceausescu. When the December uprising began he immediately emerged as an NSF leader, its chief spokesman and foreign affairs expert, but became one of its most vocal critics when it transpired that the NSF intended to consolidate itsown political power by contesting the elections. He retired from politics himself, but later added his voice to the charge that the December revolution was really a form of coup, plotted in advance by figures within the Ceausescu regime.

Doina **Cornea**. One of Romania's few dissident intellectuals, she had been a professor of French, but suffered arrest and repeated harassment in a "one-woman campaign" against Ceausescu's abuses of human rights. An early member of the NSF, she was also one of the first to leave, in January 1990, when the Front leaders changed their position on contesting elections and keeping themselves in power.

Marian **Munteanu** (b. 1964). A student leader in Bucharest and participant in the December 1989 uprising, he then became the most visible anti-communist opponent of the NSF, leading the University Square occupation in May-June until the miners arrived, when he was beaten up and arrested. Released six weeks later after sustained protests, he became chairman in December 1990 of a new extraparliamentary Civic Alliance, and by mid-1991 was set to convert this into a political party, in a bid to offer more effective opposition than could be achieved in street protests.

Petre **Roman** (b. 1944). The prime minister of the NSF regime until the miners compelled his resignation by their opposition to economic austerity measures in September 1991, Roman was a professor of engineering in Bucharest, and a long-standing communist party member (the son of a veteran activist), until he became involved in the December 1989 uprising. Interim prime minister in a regime soon accused of being too much under the control of former communists, he nevertheless led the NSF to its victory in the May 1990 elections. Thereafter he was increasingly identified with the need for price increases and other austerity measures, as part of his government's attempts to create a free market economy. Iliescu, more disposed to mollify the miners, backed down and effectively sacrificed his prime minister in September 1991.

Theodor **Stolojan**. The prime minister from October 1991, at the head of the coalition government formed following the resignation of Roman, Stolojan was chosen as a non-party figure with a commitment to economic reform; he had been finance minister under Roman until April 1991 and then director of the privatization agency.

Elections

Legislature

Nominally, political authority under communist rule was defined by the 1965 constitution as residing in the 369-member unicameral Grand National Assembly. This body was elected for a five-year term from a list of party-approved candidates, most recently in 1985, and turnouts were regularly given as nearly 100 per cent, with over 97 per cent voting for the official candidates. A choice of approved candidates was offered in some seats from 1975 onwards (185 seats in 1985). The lists were put forward in the name of the communist-dominated broad front organization, known successively as the National Democratic Front, the People's Democratic Front (1948-68), the Socialist Unity Front and the Socialist Democracy and Unity Front.

The legislative elections of May 1990 were held under interim constitutional arrangements and an electoral law approved on March 17, providing for a multi-party democratic election using modified proportional representation in 41 multi-member constituencies.

General election results

May 20, 1989: elections to bicameral parliament				
	National Assembly		Senate,	
	percentage	seats	percentage	seats
NSF	66.3	263	67.0	92
HDUR	7.2	29	7.2	12
NLP	6.4	29	7.1	9
CDNPP	2.6	12	2.5	1
Romanian Ecological Movement	2.6	12	2.5	1
Romanian Ecological Party	1.4	8	1.4	1
Romanian Unity Alliance	2.2	9	2.2	1
Agrarian Democratic Party	1.6	9	1.6	0
Socialist Democratic Party of Romania		5	1.1	0
Independent				1
Other smaller parties		11		
Allocated: national minorities and other groups		11		
Total		400		119

Presidency

Under the 1965 constitution the President of the Republic was elected by the Assembly and also presided over the 21-member Council of State (again elected by the Assembly). Ceausescu held this post himself from 1967.

Direct presidential elections were held concurrently with the parliamentary elections on May 20, 1990, and were won by Ion Iliescu of the NSF with 85 per cent of the vote in an 86 per cent turnout; the two defeated contenders were returning exiles who represented "historic" parties of the pre-communist period, Radu Campeanu of the NLP (10.2 per cent) and Ion Ratiu of the CDNPP (4.3 per cent). The electoral law provided that, once elected, the President could not be a member of a political party. Iliescu was sworn in on June 20.The constitution of December 1991 provided for stronger powers for the executive presidency.

Governments in the post-communist period

There were four governments in 1990-91; a provisional government formed in late January 1990, the Roman government formed in June 1990 following the May elections, Roman's reshuffled government formed in April 1991, and the Stolojan administration formed in October 1991.

Principal members of governments January 1990 to December 1991				
	Jan.-May 90	June 90-April 91	April-Sept. 91	Oct. 1991
Prime minister	Petre Roman	Roman	Roman	Theodor Stolojan
Finance	vacant	Theodor Stolojan	Eugen Dijmarescu	George Danielescu
Interior	Col.-Gen. Mihae Ghitac*	Doru Viorel Ursu	Ursu	Victor Babuic
Defence	Gen. Nicolae Militaru*	Col. Gen. Victor Stanculescu	Gen. Nicolae Spiroiu	Spiroiu
Foreign affairs	Sergiu Celac	Adrian Nastase	Nastase	Nastase

*Ghitac and Militaru came under attack in February from junior army officers who complained that they were associated with Ceausescu's crimes, and that Ghitac in particular had been directly involved in the Timisoara massacre. Ghitac kept his post until the May elections, but Militaru was ousted and replaced by Stanculescu on Feb. 16.

Human rights issues

An amnesty was announced on Jan. 5, 1990, for all political prisoners detained since 1947 for protests against the communist regime. On Jan. 8 Romanians were allowed the freedom to travel abroad, without the requirement of exit visas or restrictions on their return, although the applicability of this freedom was severely circumscribed by the lack of hard currency for those wishing to travel.

The regime's very limited willingness to bring prosecutions for abuses of power under the Ceausescu regime, and the attitude of the courts when such cases did come to trial, became a major issue. In Timisoara there was an especially sustained campaign, backed by serious strikes in December 1990 and January 1991, around the belief that the truth had never been told about the December 1989 massacres.

Ceausescu and his wife had of course been shot on Dec. 25, 1989. This was justified at the time as much in terms of a civil war necessity, to remove any sustaining hope of a counter-revolution, as in terms of retributory justice. It was subsequently seen as having conveniently removed the biggest single reason for a more thorough assessment of the burden of guilt. The judge at the Ceausescu "trial" himself committed suicide in March 1990.

The treatment of captured Securitate members was one part of the problem. Less symbolic but more fundamental, for a society which had been so thoroughly suffused with a network of spies and police informers, was the issue of what happened to the huge numbers of "ordinary" Securitate personnel, and to the information accumulated by them over the years. In this respect three decisions stood out; the creation on April 25, 1990, of a new Romanian Intelligence Service (RIS), albeit accountable to parliament and without powers of arrest, but which would not abjure the recruitment of former Securitate staff; the revelation on July 30, 1991, that an "important number" of former Securitate staff had been removed from the RIS; and the approval on Oct. 7, 1991, of a new law on the RIS which controversially included the right to use Securitate archives.

Religious freedoms

An estimated 15 million people, the great majority of Romanian Christians, were of the Romanian Orthodox faith. The Orthodox Church, a key repository of cultural nationalism, and a social reality with which the atheistic Ceausescu regime had come to terms—greatly assisted by the subservient and uncritical attitude of the church hierarchy. Patriarch Teoctist, however, having resigned over this in January 1990, was reinstated by the synod three months later. The regime had by this time set up a Ministry of Religious Affairs, to consult on framing laws which would restore the full freedoms and role of the Church. The bishops began to press for the early resumption of religious education in schools.

The Uniate (Catholic Eastern Rite) Church, banned in 1948 (when it was said to have had as many as 1,700,000 adherents among the Hungarian ethnic community) and required to merge with the Roman Catholic church, was legalized fully on April 24, 1990. Decrees lifting the 1948 ban had already been issued in January, and on March the Pope had appointed five Eastern Rite bishops as well as seven Roman Catholic bishops. Diplomatic relations between Romania and the Vatican, broken off in 1950, were resumed on May 15, 1990. Uniates and Roman Catholics (many of them ethnic German or Hungarian) were estimated by the Vatican to number 2,800,000.

The appointment of Lazlo Tokes as Bishop of Oradea on March 29, 1990, reflected his transition from persecuted dissident to prominent leader of the Hungarian ethnic community in Transylvania.

The Jewish community, of only some 15,00 and mainly in Bucharest, became during 1990 an increasingly frequent target of anti-semitic attacks, including desecration of graves. This racism was associated with the rise of extremist nationalism, and in August 1991 Iliescu condemned the publication of anti-semitic articles in the nationalist weekly *Romania Mare*—the US government having warned that anti-semitism in the Romanian media would be a barrier to economic assistance.

Nationalities and minorities issues

The Hungarian and German minorities in Romania

Romania's ethnic Hungarian minority, living principally but not exclusively in the region of Transylvania which had once been Hungarian territory, numbered between 1,700,000 and 2,000,000. The mistreatment of ethnic Hungarians under the Ceausescu regime had been a major source of friction with Hungary, and prompted much of the emphasis on human rights abuses which latterly determined the regime's international image. In the post-1989 period there was a continuing demand from ethnic Hungarians for a full exposure of the record of the Ceausescu regime (including the Timisoara massacre).

The cohesive voting of ethnic Hungarians in May 1990 made their party, the HDUR, the second largest in parliament. Its programme was principally concerned with obtaining fulfilment of the minority rights guarantees which the NSF had immediately promised in December 1989—including local autonomy, an end to forced settlement of Romanians in the mainly Hungarian areas, and education in the Hungarian language. Rights of this nature were contested by Romanian nationalists, whose activism was co-ordinated in Transylvania by a new Romania Hearth movement which played effectively on popular anti-Hungarian sentiment. There were a series of violent clashes in Tirgu Mures during March 1990, in which several people were killed and hundreds injured before a state of emergency was declared (and an inquiry set up by President Iliescu, which reported the following January in a manner intended to place the blame on the former communist regime). An appeal by Hungary for UN intervention, and the Hungarian decision to allow dual Romanian-Hungarian nationality, was taken by the Romanian nationalists as evidence of Hungarian irredentist aspirations. It was estimated in 1991 that 30,000 ethnic Hungarians with Romanian citizenship had gone to Hungary as refugees since mid-1987.

The number of German-speaking Saxons, once as many as 350,000, declined rapidly with assisted emigration to West Germany; in the first six months of 1990 nearly 100,000 obtained German citizenship, and the number remaining in Romania was put as low as 80,000.

Romanians outside Romania: the separate existence of Moldova

Romanian-speaking people form the majority population of Moldova. A Soviet republic of Moldavia had been created in Bessarabia after the annexation of this territory by Stalin after World War II. Its people renewed contacts enthusiastically with Romanians across the border as an expression of their cultural identity, as their aspiration for independence became increasingly plausible. Some 500,000 (out of nearly three million) were allowed to cross into Romania for one day on June 16, 1991, and in meetings at the highest government level both sides expressed the desire for a treaty arrangement between them, although making it clear that borders would not be called into question. With Moldova's passage to full independence within the post-Soviet structure of the Commonwealth of Independent Republics at the end of 1991, the possibility of reunification became, however, a topic of open discussion.

CHRONOLOGY

23 August 1944. King Michael dismisses the pro-German regime of Gen. Ion Antonescu and Romania changes sides in the war, allying with the advancing Soviet forces.

31 August 1944. The Red Army arrives in Bucharest

6 March 1945. A Soviet-backed regime is set up under Petru Groza.

May 1946. Romania's territory as defined by the Paris peace conference agreement includes Transylvania, at Hungary's expense, but not southern Dobruja (returned to Bulgaria), while Bessarabia and north Bukovina are incorporated into the Soviet Union.

July 1946. The peace treaty with the Soviet Union confirms the loss of territory and requires war reparations to be paid.

November 1946. The communist-dominated National Democratic Front claims to have won over two thirds of the vote in a disputed general election.

October 1947. The merger of the social democrats into the Communist Party lays the basis for the Romanian Workers' Party.

30 December 1947. King Michael is forced to abdicate, the monarchy is abolished and the Romanian People's Republic proclaimed.

1948. The Social Democratic Party is merged into the communist party to form the Romanian Workers' Party, a name it will use until 1965.

1953-54. Leading members of the Jewish community are tried for Zionism.

August 1953. Gheorghiu-Dej signals a shift away from the emphasis on heavy industrial development and the allocation of more resources to consumer goods, as well as efforts to improve food supplies. Under his regime the drive for industrialization nevertheless continues, whereas the Soviet vision for the international division of labour would allocate Romania primarily a food-producing role.

July 1958. Soviet troops withdraw under a Warsaw Pact agreement.

June 1964. Political prisoners imprisoned in the last three years are released.

19 March 1965. Gheorghiu-Dej dies, and is succeeded by Nicolae Ceausescu as party first secretary.

1965. A new constitution is introduced, and the RWP reverts to using its pre-1948 name of Romanian Communist Party.

May-June 1966. Ceausescu attacks the Soviet seizure of Bukovina and the existence of hostile blocs in the world, reinforcing the perception that he is distancing his regime from the Soviet line in international affairs; Romania has in recent years offered itself as a mediator in the Sino-Soviet dispute, rather than as a loyal Soviet acolyte. Brezhnev visits Bucharest unexpectedly in May, as does the Chinese premier Zhou Enlai the following month, but Zhou later attacks Romania's stance while on a visit to Albania.

January 1967. Responding to West German overtures, Romania becomes the first East European country to grant that country formal recognition.

August 1968. Romania condemns the Warsaw Pact invasion of Czechoslovakia.

August 1969. US President Nixon visits Romania, where huge crowds turn out to greet him.

December 1970. Ceausescu visits the United States.

1971-72. Romania becomes a member of GATT, the IMF and the World Bank.

June 1973. Ceausescu visits West Germany.

March 1975. The United States grants most favoured nation trading status to Romania.

April-July 1978. Ceausescu visits the USA and the UK, the first communist head of state from Eastern Europe to pay a state visit to London.

March 1980. Romania and the UK issue a joint statement criticising the Soviet invasion of Afghanistan.

December 1982. Ceausescu resolves to pay off the country's foreign debt by the end of the decade, by means of a sustained export drive. A series of harsh austerity measures are introduced including rationing of food (much of which is now earmarked for export) and of energy.

September 1983. US Vice-President Bush visits Romania and afterwards describes Ceausescu as "one of Europe's good communists".

October 1985. A state of emergency is declared in the energy industry.

15 November 1987. Major riots in Brasov mark the most serious challenge to the Ceausescu regime; the trouble is forcibly suppressed. After the 1989 revolution the rioters attain heroic status; their convictions for "hooliganism" are annulled and finally, in March 1991, they are reclassified as having been political prisoners.

5 April 1988. Plans are announced for the forcible "systematization" policy, with the aim of demolishing half of Romania's villages by the year 2000, releasing land for the use of collective farms, and imposing a more "modern" pattern of agro-industrial centres. Hungary expresses particular concern that the destruction of villages will be targeted against the 1,700,000 ethnic Hungarians, and on April 19

accuses Romania of a policy of forcible assimilation. The "systematization" plan is widely condemned internationally, marking a pronounced change in the generally favourable Western attitude towards the Ceausescu regime, which had been based on its independence from the Soviet line in foreign policy, but which is now increasingly affected by concern about violations of human rights.

March 1989. In an unprecedented sign of criticism of Ceausescu from within his regime, six formerly prominent figures, all still party members, accuse him in an open letter of discrediting socialism, ruining the economy, and earning international condemnation over human rights issues. The six, who are reportedly detained for interrogation by the security police, are former foreign minister Corneliu Manescu, three party veterans, a former first deputy premier, and party newspaper editor Silviu Brucan, already marked out as a critic since the Brasov riots of 1987.

April 1989. The completed repayment of foreign debt is announced proudly in Bucharest.

July 1989. A fence which the Romanians had begun to construct along the northern border, to prevent the departure of ethnic Hungarians, is dismantled after international criticism, but the controversy over the mistreatment of the Hungarian minority continues.

July 1989. The Warsaw Pact meets in Bucharest. Ceausescu reveals the extent of his isolation in the changing climate of Eastern Europe when he proposes military intervention in Poland to prevent the establishment of a non-communist government led by Solidarity.

20-24 November 1989. The 14th party congress, at which Ceausescu is unanimously re-elected as general secretary, records the regime's "achievements" over the past five years. The Soviet communist party sends a message calling for an "exchange of experiences" among socialist countries, suggesting implicit criticism of the regime's anti-reform stance.

15-17 December 1989. A demonstration in Timisoara, called to protest over the removal of the ethnic Hungarian priest Father Lazlo Tokes, swells to a march of several thousand chanting "Down with Ceausescu". It is suppressed, although the army commander apparently refuses to shoot the unarmed protestors. On Dec. 17, when the demonstrators return in defiance, the army troops do fire on the crowd under the direction of the Securitate secret police; about one hundred people are killed. Reports spread that there has been a major massacre, running into thousands. Timisoara becomes the symbol of the brutality which has finally provokes large-scale public repudiation of the Ceausescu dictatorship.

20 December 1989. Ceausescu, returning from a brief visit to Iran, dismissively blames the trouble on foreign agents and traitors.

21 December 1989. Ceausescu appears at midday to address a crowd which has been called to hear his speech from the balcony of the party headquarters in Bucharest, and is bewildered when demonstrators shout him down, an unprecedented act of defiance which he attempts to counter by announcing pay increases. A large crowd,

including many students, reassembles in the evening and the Securitate forces then open fire; the bodies of the dead are disposed of secretly.

22 December 1989. The Romanian revolution begins as a popular uprising. Ceausescu, having once again tried to address the crowd, is overthrown when the armed forces change sides in Bucharest and join the demonstrators. The "suicide" of defence minister Gen. Vasile Milea, reported earlier in the day, is now explained as his having been shot by a presidential bodyguard for refusing to order the army to fire on demonstrators. Ceausescu and his wife Elena escape dramatically by helicopter from the roof of the party headquarters as it is being stormed.

23 December 1989. An ad hoc "National Salvation Front" put together by the army and the opposition protestors, effectively based at the television station, declares itself to be "in charge" and calls for free elections. Elite units of the Securitate forces fight back, killing indiscriminately, in an effort to preserve the Ceausescu regime.

25 December 1989. Ceausescu and his wife Elena, captured near Tirgoviste, are given a summary trial, in which they refuse to be held accountable to their accusers, are sentenced to death, and then shot repeatedly.

26 December 1989. A video recording showing Ceausescu's corpse is broadcast on television. The fighting in Bucharest and elsewhere begins to subside. (The death toll in the December events, originally widely cited as running into many thousands, is revised downwards and the eventual official total is 1,033.) Ion Iliescu is declared President of the NSF and a government is formed under Petre Roman, both men being former communists.

28-29 December 1989. NSF decrees are announced, and constitutional amendments then published, to change the country's name (from the Socialist Republic of Romania, to just Romania), to guarantee the rights of national minorities, to allow freedom of worship, and to provide for the conversion to a free market economy. Other announcements include the abolition of the ban on abortion and birth control, abolition of the death penalty, and the promise of free elections in April 1990.

5 January 1990. All political prisoners imprisoned since 1947 are released under an amnesty.

12-13 January 1990. Demonstrators at a day of national mourning shout down Iliescu and Roman with cries of "down with the communists" and "death for a death". After a meeting between the NSF executive bureau and the demonstrators' leaders, NSF vice-president Dumitru Mazilu announces the abolition of the communist party and a referendum later in January on restoring the death penalty. Iliescu, however, announces the following day the reversal of the ban on the communist party; this too, he says, should go to referendum, but the plans for both referendums are later cancelled.

23 January 1990. The NSF confirms its reversal of its original promise to dissolve itself in the transition to democratic rule, insisting that it will contest the elections as a political party.

24 January 1990. Leading dissident Doina Cornea resigns from the NSF, claiming that it is dominated by former communists.

26 January 1990. Dumitru Mazilu, the NSF's first vice-president, resigns after a campaign against him, based on the allegation that he had been closely involved with the Securitate.

1 February 1990. Pending the election of a legislature, a Provisional Council of National Unity is formed, on which the NSF has 105 seats and the 35 registered political parties three each.

2 February 1990. Four former communist leaders are sentenced to life imprisonment with hard labour for "co-authorship of genocide".

19-20 March 1990. Several people are killed in the predominantly ethnic Hungarian town of Tirgu Mures in clashes revealing continuing hostility towards the Hungarian minority.

April 1990. Romanian Orthodox Patriarch Teoctist Arapas is reinstated by the church synod, having previously retired (in January) in the face of criticism of his compliant attitude towards the Ceausescu regime.

11 April 1990. Former King Michael is refused admission for a proposed visit to Romania.

May 1990. Diplomatic relations are restored with the Vatican following the legalization of the Catholic church in Romania.

20 May 1990. Elections are held, a month later than originally scheduled, and result in an overwhelming NSF victory in both houses of the new Assembly (whose main task is to draft a new constitution), while Iliescu wins 85 per cent of the vote in the presidential election.

May 1990. Petre Roman is named as prime minister, but demonstrators sustain a protest in Bucharest and claim that the revolution has been "stolen" by former communists in the NSF.

15-16 June 1990. Miners arriving from the provinces take over the streets of Bucharest, intimidating and breaking up the anti-NSF demonstrations with great brutality. International condemnation is followed by the decision of the European Communities to suspend the planned association agreement with Romania.

20-28 June 1990. Roman is renominated as prime minister; he forms a new government, stressing the "clean past" of his nominees, and presents a programme for a rapid transition to a market economy.

20 July 1990. Roman presents legislation on the legal framework for a free market economy and the development of the private sector, initially involving small and medium-sized enterprises.

August 1990. Former NSF members Silviu Brucan and Gen. Nicolae Militaru claim that the overthrow of Ceausescu had been plotted by opponents within his regime.

21 September 1990. The former dictator's son Nicu Ceausescu, 39, is sentenced to 20 years in prison for incitement to murder, in connection with the attempted counter-revolution by Securitate forces; he is released the following week for medical treatment, and in June 1991 his sentence is reduced to 16 years. Nicu's elder brother and sister have already been released in August 1990, but the

dictator's younger brother Andruta Ceausescu has been sentenced on June 21 to 15 years' imprisonment.

November-December 1990. Prices rise dramatically as subsidies are removed in line with the Roman government's economic reform policy; protestors mount large demonstrations, union leaders demand a greater emphasis on social protection measures, and continuing strikes force the government on Dec. 11 to defer price liberalization.

16 December 1990. Opposition parties in parliament form a National Convention for the Restoration of Democracy, while an extraparliamentary Civic Alliance at its first congress elects student protest leader Marin Munteanu as its chairman.

25-26 December 1990. Former King Michael is again refused a visa and expelled the day after his arrival.

13 February 1991. Romania applies formally for associate membership of the European Communities, having cultivated the support of France and Italy in particular for such a development.

16-17 March 1991. The NSF at its first national convention endorses Petre Roman as its leader, approves new party statutes and backs Roman's "A future for Romania" programme for a market economy and social democratic principles. Small dissident factions threaten a split, with a radical former demonstrator speaking of "the total collapse of the Front".

18 March 1991. Former Securitate chief Col.-Gen. Iulian Vlad is convicted of illegally arresting demonstrators on Dec. 21, 1989, and sentenced to three and a half years. Charges of complicity in genocide had originally been brought, but were dropped after testimony that he had formally approved Ceausescu's orders only out of fear. In May he receives a four-year sentence for a similar offence, having been convicted along with 11 others, but the government's critics remain dissatisfied that so few charges are successfully brought.

25 March 1991. A court convicts 13 former politburo members on the reduced charge of having "favoured the criminal" (i.e. Ceausescu), rather than "participating in genocide", in supporting the violent suppression of December 1989 demonstrations in Timisoara and Bucharest. On Dec. 12 the appeal court overturns the convictions.

1 April 1991. Prices of basic goods are doubled by cuts in public subsidies under the second stage of a liberalization programme, although attempts are made to mitigate the impact by increased social security benefits and compensation payments to workers and pensioners.

5 April 1991. A Soviet-Romanian treaty of friendship is signed by Iliescu and Soviet President Gorbachev in Moscow, specifying respect for existing borders and consultation and co-operation on security issues.

29 April 1991. Roman reorganizes his government in an effort to overcome resistance to radical economic reform.

14 August 1991. Iliescu signs a law on a major privatization programme. Opposition to the sell-off of industry to foreign capital is partially countered by a requirement

that 30 per cent of shares be set aside for acquisition by Romanian nationals, to whom free ownership certificates will be allocated.

3 September 1991. The Romanian parliament supports Moldova's declaration of independence, and Iliescu later suggests readiness to consider unification.

27 September 1991. Petre Roman resigns as prime minister, describing himself as the victim of "those who want to maintain the old system", after three days of rioting (and five deaths) in Bucharest. The unrest has been instigated by miners from the Jiu valley, who had taken over the capital a year earlier to cow the opponents of the Iliescu government, but who are this time protesting gainst the austerity policies identified with Roman.

October 1991. Theodor Stolojan, a non-party technocrat who had been finance minister until April 1990 and then in charge of the state privatization programme, becomes prime minister in a coalition government committed to pursuing free market economic reforms, although he soon promises to retain price controls on basic goods for a further six months.

21 November 1991. A new constitution receives parliamentary approval, giving substantial powers to an executive presidency and enshrining guarantees of pluralism, respect for human rights, and a free market economic system.

8 December 1991. A referendum approves the new constitution, which takes effect on Dec. 13.

9-12 December 1991. Eight officials and former Securitate officers are imprisoned for the "aggravated murder" of the demonstrators at Timisoara in December 1989.

YUGOSLAVIA

Since 1963 the official name of the country has been the Socialist Federal Republic of Yugoslavia (*Socijalisticka Federativna Republika Jugoslavija*). The independence of Slovenia and Croatia gained wide international recognition in January 1992, by which time declarations of independence had also been made by Bosnia-Hercegovina and Montenegro.

Until its effective disintegration in 1991, Yugoslavia, meaning land of the south Slavs, was the largest country in the Balkans. It was somewhat bigger than Romania both in terms of its population (nearly 24 million) and its land area (255,800 sq. km). Three quarters of the country was mountainous, with the highest peak in the Slovenian Alps in the north, and with rugged terrain extending parallel with the Adriatic coast to the Albanian border, and across into southern Serbia, Kosovo and Macedonia. The main lowland areas, including fertile arable land, were the Sava valley from Zagreb to Belgrade (the city built at the confluence of the Sava and the Danube), the narrower valley of the Morava valley which flowed north to join the Danube downstream from Belgrade, and, most importantly, the Danube plain itself, extending north and north-west of Belgrade to the Romanian and Hungarian borders. (West of the great river, the Danube plain was part of Slavonia in Croatia;

the rest was in Vojvodina, which had the status of an autonomous province within Serbia.)

There was a pronounced trend of population movement from rural to urban areas, with some 47 per cent of the population classified as urban in 1990. Belgrade, the federal and Serbian capital, was by some way the largest city with a population of about 1,500,000. The largest cities in Croatia (respectively second, third, fourth and fifth largest in Yugoslavia) were the Dalmatian port of Split, Osijek in Slavonia, and the republican capital Zagreb (all with populations of approaching one million) and Rijeka, formerly Fiume (over half a million). Other substantial centres were the republican capitals Skopje (Macedonia), Sarajevo (Bosnia-Hercegovina) and Ljubljana (Slovenia), the city of Nis on the Morava, Novi Sad in Vojvodina on the Danube upstream from Belgrade, and Pristina in Kosovo.

Yugoslavia conducted its full censuses every ten years, but that of April 1991 was badly affected by boycotts by disaffected nationalities. According to the 1981 figures, the total population was 22,425,000 of whom over 40 per cent lived in Serbia (9,314,000 including 2,035,000 in Vojvodina and 1,584,000 in Kosovo, the two autonomous provinces within Serbia). Croatia accounted for over 20 per cent (4,601,000), Bosnia-Hercegovina 18 per cent (4,124,000), Slovenia and Macedonia each about 8.5 per cent (1,892,000 and 1,909,000 respectively) and Montenegro 2.6 per cent (584,000).

Distribution by ethnic groups is shown on the accompanying map. Linguistically, Serbo-Croat was most widely used, as a single spoken language but written separately as Serbian (Cyrillic script) and Croatian (Roman script); other official languages of

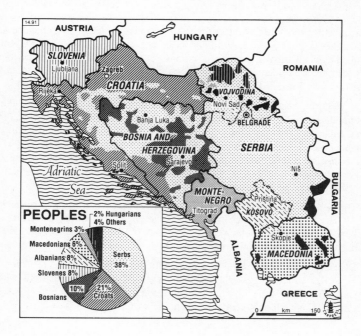

Yugoslavia were Slovenian, and Macedonian (akin to Bulgarian). The largest minorities were Albanians, mainly concentrated in Kosovo and officially recorded as numbering over 1,700,000 but rapidly increasing due to high birth rates, and Hungarians (426,000) mainly in Vojvodina.

The history of Yugoslavia as an entity had its origin in the disintegration of the Ottoman empire and, in the 1914-18 war (when Serbia fought on the side of the Allies against the Central Powers), the defeat of Austro-Hungarian expansionist ambitions in the Balkans. Its first existence was as the Kingdom of Serbs, Croats and Slovenes, proclaimed in December 1918 under King Alexander of Serbia. It was renamed Yugoslavia in 1929, when Alexander ended its brief and fractious democratic experiment and imposed a royal dictatorship.

The assassination of Alexander in France in October 1934, by Croats who resented Serbian dominance of the unitary state, illustrated violent rivalries which were even more bloodily expressed during World War II. A German invasion in April 1941 terminated the brief reign of the 17-year-old King Peter, who had been put on the throne only the previous month (ending the six-and-a-half year regency of the pro-German Prince Paul) by a pro-Allied group which tried to refuse to let German troops through to attack Greece. The Germans then set up a puppet fascist regime, the notorious *ustashi*, in Croatia and much of Bosnia-Hercegovina, where the subsequent massacres of Serbs established a legacy of fear that was still powerful when Croatian independence was declared fifty years later.

Most of Slovenia was annexed to the *Reich*; neighbouring countries allied with Germany took the opportunity to expand their territory at defeated Yugoslavia's expense; and the rump of Serbia was occupied by German forces. Wartime resistance to the German occupation was begun immediately by Serbian royalist *chetniks* under Draza Mihailovic, linked to the Yugoslav (and mainly Serb) government-in-exile. A separate guerrilla struggle was built up by communist partisans led by Josip Broz Tito, a Croat. The royalist hatred of communists (their guerrilla adversaries since the 1920s), and disagreement over whether a postwar Yugoslavia should be unitary (as the royalists presumed) or federal, made co-operation impossible.

In 1943 the western Allies transferred their support to the partisans, on the advice of intelligence agents that they represented the more effective anti-German force, and that Mihailovic was by now more preoccupied with civil war against the partisans than with driving out the Germans. This pro-Tito Western attitude, the collapse of the Croat *ustashi* regime, and the presence of the Soviet Red Army alongside the partisans in expelling the Germans in 1945, left Tito and the communists in a position to take control of the immediate postwar situation.

The Federal People's Republic of Yugoslavia was proclaimed in November 1945, with Tito as prime minister, following communist-dominated elections to a provisional assembly. The country had a succession of constitutions, in 1946, 1953, 1963 (adopting the present name) and 1974.

Decisive in its future development was the break with the Soviet Union in June 1948, after which Yugoslavia was anathematized by Stalin. Relations were "normalized" in 1955, but with Yugoslavia outside the Warsaw Pact and at arm's length from the Soviet bloc's economic planning in Comecon (of which it became an associate member, however). The friction arose because Tito rejected the idea of Soviet hegemony, and because the Yugoslav party had sufficient independent credibility. With the national prestige of its resistance successes, it could not be dominated, and purged of "nationalists", by a faction of returned exiles from Moscow; unlike parties elsewhere in Eastern Europe [but see also Romania], it was the "Cominformists" who fled or were purged.

The breach, and the blockade which followed, deprived Yugoslavia of much-needed assistance with its ambitious first five-year plan for economic centralization and industrialization. High growth rates were nevertheless sustained, paralleled by the development of the "self-management" which was presented as characteristic of the Yugoslav road to socialism. This idea was progressively extended from industrial workers' councils to broader social and administrative self-management, with a concomitant reduction in centralized authority. Making the system responsive to market signals, a specific objective from the mid-1960s, involved in practice a high level of reliance on the directors of the individual enterprises. There was insufficient overall co-ordination, however, to control the growth of foreign borrowing which, particularly in the 1970s, appeared as the only available means of sustaining a high level of economic growth.

Tito died in May 1980, leaving behind a tradition of international non-alignment, and a series of distinctive experiments in market socialism. The complex state structure evolved under his regime was designed to withstand the mutual suspicions of the component republics, by the delegation of powers and the rotation of federal posts, but it had also created cumbersome procedures and bureaucracies which impeded change.

The first year after his death appeared to confound many dire predictions, as a new collective leadership began to tackle balance-of-payments problems and an economy in crisis. The following year, however, there was a major outbreak of nationalist agitation among Albanians in Kosovo, forcibly put down by the Army, killing several hundred, according to unofficial accounts. Over the succeeding years, Serbians became increasingly hostile to the prospect of Albanians taking over power in what they regarded as the Serb mediaeval heartland of Kosovo, where the difference in birth rate, and an exodus of Serbs, had further strengthened the Albanian numerical dominance. Their eventual resort, in 1989-90 and again with the Army to enforce their will, was to amend the Serbian constitution and thereby reduce the powers of the autonomous provinces.

Ultimately, the denouement of the Yugoslav crisis, from the late 1980s, was not precipitated by the continuing but apparently peripheral problem of Kosovo's Albanians and their relationship with Serbia. This issue did nevertheless contribute in important measure to the central questions, because it pointed up the extent to which the federal state structure, or since 1974 more properly the confederal structure, left the Serbs themselves with the feeling that their own national interests were threatened.

It was economic failure which weakened the structure of Yugoslavia to the point where its strong centrifugal forces would pull it apart. That economic failure, when its consequences could no longer be masked by the high level of foreign borrowing sustained through most of the 1980s, rebounded on the claims of the communist party to have found a way of combining socialism with the market economy. In attempting to devolve responsibility, the state structure compounded the problems because it gave planning vetoes to the bureaucracy at the level where special interests were dominant. Without Tito to moderate the process, the effect was strangulation. The federal government in 1989-90 made what turned out to be a last attempt to grapple with the economic situation, as prime minister Ante Markovic declared war on hyperinflation. A currency reform pegged the new dinar to the Deutschmark, wages were held down and prices allowed to rise, a balance of payments surplus achieved to reduce the foreign debt, and a package of reform measures pushed through to try to encourage a more genuine free market. The effect on inflation was dramatic in 1990, but it did not change the fact that so many of Yugoslavia's economic units were operating in an unrealistic environment, behind the protection of the web of special interests.

A substantial body of intellectual pressure had built up, from 1985, not only for economic reform but for serious attention to the structure of the political system. Within the different republics, there were varying levels of permissible debate, and Slovenia, the most prosperous province but also one of the worst affected by the economic crisis, had reached by 1989 the point where opposition groups could emerge. The first independent political party in Eastern Europe, calling itself the Democratic Alliance, was founded in Slovenia in January 1989, and the proliferation of groups had been recognized in the republic by the end of the year, when a law on political pluralism was introduced in Slovenia.

The federal communist party itself, the League of Communists of Yugoslavia (LCY), had accepted at a turbulent party plenum in February 1989 the need to bring forward its 14th congress, now scheduled for December but not actually convened until Jan. 20, 1990. By the time it was held, the revolutions across Eastern Europe had strengthened the current of opinion which held that the party had been part of the problem, and that it had no role to play in seeking a solution. However, a policy declaration was presented, as approved in advance by the League of Communists in each republic, entitled *For a New Outline of Democratic Socialism for Yugoslavia"*, to end the authoritarian role of the party and allow for an undefined form of political pluralism.

The congress was acrimonious. It was clear that the Slovene LC leadership's conception of pluralism, allowing full multi-party systems in the republics, with the LCY reduced to a loose confederation of those republican parties which affiliated to it, was incompatible with the retention of democratic centralism, the position demanded by the hardline Serbian LC leader Slobodan Milosevic. The congress voted on Jan. 22, 1990, overwhelmingly in favour of removing the party's constitutionally guaranteed leading role; but it then collapsed because the Slovenes walked out, when their proposals on restructuring the party were rejected. The Slovene LC leaders declared the suspension of links with the LCY, but their declaration was superfluous; in practical terms, the LCY had collapsed.

With or without the LCY, Markovic said, "Yugoslavia continues to function"; but, as preparations went ahead for changing the federal Constitution, it was in the republics that the key decisions were being made. In 1990, the multi-party elections were held in all six republics which defined the stance that each would take on the future of Yugoslavia. For all that Markovic had won some respect with the impact of his austerity measures, his federal government ceased to have a real role beyond its attempts at preserving some stewardship of the overall economic administration. His formation of a federal party, the Alliance of Reform Forces, was launched in mid-1990 as soon as the federal legislation had caught up with the tide towards pluralism, but the federal elections for which it was intended never took place.

The results of the republican multi-party elections in 1990, held in April in Slovenia, in April-May in Croatia, and in November-December in the other four republics, crystallized out the divergence of their paths. Persuaded that the federal structure of the Yugoslav state could not provide the appropriate policies for their recovery from the current economic crisis, Slovenia, Croatia, and then Bosnia-Hercegovina and Macedonia, all opted for centre-right or right-wing nationalist governments. The communist or post-communist formations fared badly in three out of these four cases, but performed respectably in Slovenia, where the communist leadership had shown itself determinedly reform-minded and independent of the federal party, and where its leader Milan Kucan was returned to office as republican President.

In Serbia and tiny Montenegro, by contrast, the communists (retitled in Serbia as the Socialist Party) won convincingly in the republican elections. The Serbian leader Milosevic had claimed at the LCY congress that a multi-party system would allow nationalists to exploit the political system, and to fragment the country. In reality, under his own leadership the Serbian League of Communists had taken up a strongly nationalistic position, both as regards Kosovo and, in the larger sense, in seeking to preserve a federal structure which would remain responsive to Serbian aspirations as by far the largest component of the federal state. This stance served him well in electoral terms, enabling his party to defeat the challenge from nationalists of the right-wing persuasion. It was incompatible, however, with the acceptance of the kind of loose federation which Slovenia and Croatia might at that late stage have been prepared to accept.

The stages of Yugoslavia's eventual fragmentation in 1991 are recorded in the chronology which ends this chapter. The civil war has become the dominant factor. Until it is ended, and political life can be restored in peaceful circumstances (in what, as seems clear by the beginning of 1991, will be the several rather than the single successor states to communist Yugoslavia), it will be impossible to attempt any sensible summary of the changes occasioned by the abandonment of the Tito system.

Position and status of communists at federal level

Party name

Yugoslavia's ruling communist party operated under the name League of Communists of Yugoslavia (LCY) from 1952 to 1990. It had previously been called the Communist Party of Yugoslavia (CPY), since 1920, and had first been set up in 1919 under the name Socialist Workers'Party of Yugoslavia (Communist).

The LCY's 14th Congress, held in Belgrade from Jan. 20, 1990, broke up on Jan. 23 in disagreement and the Slovene LC announced that it was leaving the LCY (the Croat LC later following suit). The congress eventually resumed in order to close formally on May 26, 1990. A 15th Congress proposed for September 1990 to relaunch the LCY never took place. On Nov. 19, 1990, an attempt was made to resurrect the party in the form of a new League of Communists—Movement for Yugoslavia (LC—MY), declaring the goal of preventing the disintegration of the country, and seeking to preserve its 1974 constitutional structure. This formation was regarded widely as the "party of the generals" because of its dominance by retired senior officers. In effect, however, the main communist party in Yugoslavia by this time was the hardline Serbian party, retitled in mid-1990 as the Socialist Party of Serbia, the dominant political force in the Serbian republic which in turn, by the end of 1991, was the principal element of what remained of a federal Yugoslavia.

Legal status

The LCY, and the LC party organizations in the republics and provinces, were the sole legal political parties until the proliferation of pluralist arrangements in the different republics introduced in 1989-90. The LCY itself approved at its 14th congress on Jan. 22, 1990 (i.e. the day before its effective collapse) the ending of its constitutionally guaranteed "leading role".

Electoral significance

Under the 1974 Constitution, candidates for the communal assemblies (which elected the republican and federal assemblies) were required to be subject to screening by the LCY-dominated broad front organization, the Socialist Alliance of the Working People of Yugoslavia (SAWPY).

Nationalities and minorities issues

The tragedy of 1991 dramatised the problem, particularly but not exclusively in Croatia, that fissions along ethnic lines are scarcely ever neatly along administrative boundaries. The Serbs within Croatia fear what may happen if they become a minority group in an independent state; in the highly charged atmosphere of crisis and civil war, they have no faith that they will in future be well treated with that status; and their reaction in turn fuels the spiral of tension. The process of disintegration in Yugoslavia took on a momentum, similar to that which was occurring simultaneously in the Soviet Union, where the movement of a given republic, towards independent status, brought in its wake separatist declarations by minorities within that republic.

The Albanians of Kosovo, the major ethnic division which does not have a corresponding republic, is a particular case and needs some mention here; for the rest, it is beyond the scope of this book to chronicle what is in any event a rapidly changing story.

The Albanians of Kosovo

The anti-Yugoslav line taken by the Hoxha regime in communist Albanian left the Albanian people divided by what was intended to be an impermeable border. Within Yugoslavia there were some 1,700,000 Albanians, a small proportion of whom lived in Montenegro and some in Macedonia (amounting to nearly 20 per cent of the population there), while the great majority were in Kosovo. They were recognized as a distinct national group, Albanian had official language status and there were Albanian schools, but there were nevertheless repressive policies directed against

Albanians in Kosovo, notably through the Serb-dominated state security police, due to the rivalry between the two communities in the Kosovo region.

Serbian political leaders were anxious that the mainly Muslim Albanian majority should not diminish the Serb identity of the Kosovo region, whichthey regardedas the mediaeval heartland of Serbia and its Orthodox Church. The high Albanian birthrate, and an exodus of Serbs, nevertheless threatened to do just that. A campaign for separate republic status, launched in the late 1960s, resulted in the 1974 constitution's compromise whereby Kosovo was upgraded to the status of an autonomous province within Serbia. Massive nationalist demonstrations broke out in 1981, and were suppressed by the federal Army at a cost believed to be as high as several hundred dead. The Army again intervened after the Serbian Assembly had in March 1989 passed constitutional changes to limit Kosovo's autonomy; there were further deaths, widespread arrests, and the detention of Albanian nationalist leaders, notably Azem Vllasi.

The intense Serbian nationalist feeling around the celebrations of 1989, six hundredth anniversary of the Battle of Kosovo, and the domination of the republic's subsequent political development by the Serbian nationalism espoused by its president Slobodan Milosevic, has intensified the alienation of the Albanians of Kosovo. They boycotted the December 1990 Serbian elections, and remained as a serious further destabilizing factor in the disintegration of a federal Yugoslavia.

Without an official republican structure to make a formal declaration of independence, the Kosovo Assembly (declared dissolved by the Serbian authorities in mid-1990) arranged an unofficial referendum in September 1991 on sovereignty for Kosovo. It claimed a turnout of 87 per cent, and an almost unanimous yes vote, and went on to form a "provisional government", which was recognized by Albania on Oct. 22.

The Hungarian minority

A Hungarian minority mainly in Vojvodina, numbering in excess of 400,000, which had enjoyed effective minority rights under the communist regime since 1945, found its position seriously destabilized by the resurgence of Serbian nationalism from 1988, and more dramatically by the outbreak of civil war and protracted fighting in nearby Croatia from mid-1991.

Hungary took an active position in opposing the Serbian-dominated Army mobilization against Croatia, and in calling upon Serbia and the federal Yugoslav authorities to observe a ceasefire. Members of the Hungarian minority in consequence felt their security threatened, and some 20,000 had crossed the border into Hungary itself as refugees by the end of 1991.

CHRONOLOGY

June 1948. The Comintern, meeting in Budapest, denounces Titoism as a nationalist deviation.

June 1950. Workers' Councils are established in industry.

May 1951. New measures in agriculture allow farmers to sell produce on the free market.

May 1955. Khrushchev visits Belgrade, and a joint agreement the following month formally ends the rift between Yugoslavia and the Soviet Union.

August 1957. Milovan Djilas's controversial analysis of how Yugoslav socialism is creating powerful interest groups among party cadres and managers, *The New Class*, is deemed an unacceptable thesis and he is sentenced in October to a seven-year prison term for propaganda.

July 1966. Alexander Rankovic, the Interior Minister and widely seen as Tito's most likely successor, is removed as part of a purge of his faction.

April 1973. An agreement on economic co-operation is concluded with West Germany during a visit by Willy Brandt.

October 1973. Improved relations with the Soviet Union are marked by the signature of an agreement on non-interference and industrial co-operation, during a visit by Soviet prime minister Kosygin.

December 1973. Croat nationalists are purged from the party leadership and from the government.

February 1974. The promulgation of the fourth constitution since the war increases the powers of workers' councils and creates more complex confederal arrangements whose effect is to give republican administrations the power to block change.

June 1976. Tito, for the first time for 19 years, attends the conference in East Berlin of Soviet and European communist parties, at which the breach between Euro-communists and the Soviet bloc is clear.

4 May 1980. Tito dies, after four months in hospital for much of which he has been in a coma. Mechanisms for a rotating federal presidency, in preparation since 1971, take effect smoothly.

March-April 1981. A state of emergency is declared in Kosovo in the face of widespread unrest among ethnic Albanians.

March 1987. A year of serious industrial unrest is ushered in by a government wage freeze, part of its attempts to combat rampant inflation.

August 1987. The Agrokomerc scandal in Bosnia-Hercegovina, involving the illegal issue of promissory notes, undermines confidence in the banking system and exemplifies the problem of mismanagement and corruption in the decentralized system of economic administration.

May 1988. An LCY emergency conference proposes economic and political reforms.

June-October 1988. Protests mount in Belgrade over the effects of government economic austerity measures.

December 1988. The federal government of Branko Mikulic falls when it is defeated in the Assembly over its budget proposals.

February-March 1989. The ethnic Albanian Azem Vllasi is dismissed from the federal party central committee, and arrested the following month for promoting unrest in Kosovo over a wave of strike protests against Serbian modification of the province's autonomy status.

March 1989. A new government takes office under Ante Markovic and begins urgent efforts to tackle the country's economic crisis and persisting hyper-inflation.

May 1989. Slobodan Milosevic becomes Serbian President.

27 September 1989. The Assembly in Slovenia approves constitutional changes which include the republic's right, as an "independent, sovereign and autonomous state", to secede from Yugoslavia.

October 1989. Vllasi goes on trial amid protests across Kosovo.

December 1989. The border between Serbia and Slovenia is effectively closed, after the Slovene authorities ban a planned rally by Serbs, and Serbia retaliates with an economic blockade; the actions of both sides are condemned as unconstitutional by the federal government. The assemblies of both Slovenia and Croatia endorse the calling of multi-party elections in their respective republics the following April.

20-23 January 1990. The federal League of Communists of Yugoslavia, having convened its 14th congress and voted to abolish its constitutionally guaranteed leading role, nevertheless collapses when the Slovene LC walks out over the defeat of its proposals to change the party structure to one of a loose confederation of republican parties.

5 February 1990. Serbian President Milosevic provokes a fresh upsurge in the continuing unrest in Kosovo by proposing a campaign of Serbian settlement there, to remedy the demographic effects of their exodus since 1967.

19 March 1990. Announcement of the approval of a credit agreement with the IMF gives some international support for Markovic's attempt at economic reform.

April 1990. Vllasi is acquitted and released, to popular acclaim in Kosovo, but protests are revived the following month over Serbian constitutional proposals.

8 April 1990. Slovenia holds the first multi-party elections to take place in Yugoslavia since the beginning of the communist period. The elections for the republican Assembly are won by the centre-right DEMOS coalition, while a direct presidential election (completed in a second round on April 22) is won by the popular reformist leader of the Slovene LC (renamed LCS-Party of Democratic Renewal), Milan Kucan.

May 6-7, 1990. Croatia completes its multi-party elections (begun on April 22), producing a clear victory for the right-wing nationalist Croatian Democratic Union.

May 15, 1990. The annual rotation of the federal presidency between the republics brings the Serbian representative Borisav Jovic into office as head of state, with Stipe Suvar of Croatia as deputy.

16 May 1990. A Slovene government is formed under the leadership of Lojze Peterle, whose Christian Democratic Party was part of the DEMOS electoral alliance.

May 30, 1990. The Assembly in Croatia elects Franjo Tudjman of the Croatian Democratic Union as President, and Stjepan Mesic forms a new republican government.

2 July 1990. A referendum in Serbia approves constitutional changes, provoking a declaration by ethnic Albanians in the Kosovo assembly that their province (whose autonomous status is seriously curtailed by the Serbian changes) now regards itself as having the status of a separate Yugoslav republic. There is serious unrest in the province in September, as Serbia's constitution comes into force, and police arrest Kosovo assembly deputies who have reasserted their claim to republican status.

2 July 1990. The assembly in Slovenia issues a formal proclamation of the republic's sovereignty.

25 July 1990. Leaders of the Serbian minority in Croatia react by proclaiming their own sovereign and autonomous status after the approval of constitutional changes in the republic, notably on its name, flag and presidential system and on the derecognition of the Cyrillic alphabet used by Serbs.

25 July 1990. Federal legislation is passed to allow the free formation of federal, as against republican, political parties. Prime minister Markovic on July 29 launches the Alliance of Reform Forces, in the expectation of multi-party federal elections being held within the year.

19 August 1990. Voting begins in a two-week referendum process organized by leaders of Croatia's Serbian minority to demonstrate support for the proclamation of their autonomy. The Croatian government condemns as an "armed uprising against the Croatian state" the confrontations in Knin, where Croat police are impeded from preventing the referendum. There are alarmist reports of the Serb-dominated federal Army being called out if the referendum is not allowed to proceed.

24 August 1990. The nationalist Mesic replaces the communist Suvar as Croatia's representative on the federal State Presidency.

1 October 1990. The "Serbian National Council" formed by Serbs in Croatia declares the existence of an "autonomous region" in areas of majority Serb population, and Milosevic calls for federal intervention to defend them from Croatian repression.

November-December 1990. The holding of multi-party elections in Bosnia-Hercegovina, Macedonia, Montenegro, and finally Serbia, completes the process begun with the April polling in Slovenia and Croatia. Nationalist victories in Bosnia-Hercegovina and Macedonia confirm the trend towards disintegration of the federal state. However, Serbia (whose LC has renamed itself the Socialist Party—SPS) returns the incumbent hardline President Milosevic with a large majority, relegating his right-wing nationalist challenger Vuk Draskovic to a poor second place, and Montenegro likewise elects a communist president and a communist-dominated assembly.

21 December 1990. The Croatian Assembly promulgates the republic's new constitution, including the assertion of Croatia's sovereignty and right to secede.

23 December. In Slovenia a referendum overwhelmingly approves a mandate for the republic's government to declare full independence, if Yugoslavia's six republics have not reached agreement within six months on the restructuring of the federal state.

9 January 1991. An order by the federal presidency, apparently directed at the measures by Slovenia and Croatia to place their territorial defence forces under republican leadership, requires the surrender of arms within ten days by all "unauthorized" units. The federal Army is placed on alert on Jan. 23 to enforce the order; the acute tension over possibly imminent civil war is reduced, however, when on Jan. 25 the Croatian government agrees to demobilize its new paramilitary police units and indicates that it will disarm nationalist paramilitary groups.

25 January 1991. The Macedonian assembly declares the republic's sovereignty and right to secede.

20-21 February 1991. Both the parliament of Slovenia and that of Croatia support resolutions that the federal state of Yugoslavia be dissolved into sovereign and autonomous states.

15-16 March 1991. Borisav Jovic resigns the federal collective state presidency, the representatives of Vojvodina and Montenegro also resign, and the Kosovo representative is recalled for "anti-Serbian activities", all apparently in a ploy devised by Milosevic to render the collective state presidency inquorate and to demonstrate the need for an intervention by the Army. When the armed forces reject the suggestion of such involvement, however, and accept the legitimacy of the residual collective state presidency, Jovic's resignation is rescinded.

11 April 1991. The third in a series of weekly summit meetings of the six republican presidents agrees that each republic should hold a referendum by the end of May (except that Slovenia has already had a referendum the previous December) on the country's future structure. Slovenia, however, reaffirms its schedule to declare independence on June 26, and Croatia declares that it will do likewise unless there is agreement by the end of June.

15 May 1991. Serbia and its allies (Montenegro and the autonomous provinces of Kosovo and Vojvodina within Serbia itself) refuse to support the election of the Croat Stipe Mesic as president of the collective state presidency. Mesic, the current deputy president, was the automatic choice according to the annual rotation principle in use since 1974. This development marks the breakdown of the formal structure of federal government, already barely papering over the cracks in the increasingly overt hostility between Croatia and Serbia in particular; Mesic is eventually elected to the post, on June 30, only in a CSCE-mediated attempt to retrieve the situation after both Croatia and Slovenia have declared full independence.

19 May 1991. A referendum in Croatia records an 83 per cent turnout and a 94 per cent majority for independence, but in the Serb-inhabited areas, where unrest and violence are increasing, a vote the previous week has called for separation from Croatia and union with Serbia.

29 May 1991. Croatia unilaterally proclaims its sovereignty.

25 June 1991. Croatia and Slovenia proclaim their independence and dissociate themselves from the Yugoslav federation.

27-30 June 1991. Up to 40 people die in fighting in Slovenia as the Serbian-dominated Yugoslav federal army, the JNA, attempts to take control of the republic in the name of securing Yugoslavia's borders. A ceasefire is declared on June 30, and both Slovenia and Croatia are persuaded to suspend for three months their unilateral declarations of independence, as a result of diplomatic intervention under the newly-agreed CSCE conflict prevention mechanisms, which includes the despatch to Belgrade and Zagreb of the so-called "troika", the foreign ministers of Italy, Luxembourg and the Netherlands.

5 July 1991. Slovenia agrees to release captured JNA federal soldiers and to lift the siege of their barracks, where Slovene forces have driven them in the course of fighting in the first few days of July. (The federal presidency announces on July 18 the withdrawal of the JNA from Slovenia following CSCE mediation.) The death toll for the Slovene conflict is given as 67. The European Communities, hitherto taking the stance that Yugoslav federal unity must be preserved, now imposes an arms embargo, freezes aid and implicitly threatens that its member countries may recognize Slovene and Croat independence if the JNA conducts further offensives.

7 July 1991. The European "troika" mediators persuade Serbian, Slovene, Croatian and federal leaders to sign a joint declaration in Brioni calling for an immediate ceasefire; JNA forces are to withdraw to barracks, and the postponement of the Slovenian and Croatian independence declarations is confirmed.

22-31 July 1991. The focus of violent unrest switches to Croatia, and particularly its majority Serb-populated regions, Slavonia and Banija south of Zagreb. JNA units join Serb militants in running battles with Croat security forces, and over a hundred people are killed; fighting of a similar intensity continues throughout August in the face of repeated attempts to procure a lasting ceasefire.

2 September 1991. An EC peace plan, put forward on Aug. 27 and envisaging a conference in the Hague as well as EC ceasefire monitors in Croatia, is accepted after protracted discussions in Belgrade involving the federal government and the leaders of the six republics. The Hague conference, chaired by former UK foreign secretary Lord Carrington, opens on Sept. 7 even though hostilities are still continuing in Croatia (as they do, increasingly bloodily and interrupted only briefly by a succession of unsuccessful ceasefires, throughout the next three months).

15 September 1991. Macedonia becomes the third of the six republics to proclaim its independence, supported by a 95 per cent vote in a referendum on Sept. 8.

25 September 1991. The UN Security Council imposes an embargo on arms sales to Yugoslavia, but does not pass a French proposal for the dispatch of an emergency peacekeeping force.

15 October 1991. The parliament of Bosnia-Hercegovina declares the sovereignty of the republic, with ethnic Serbian deputies walking out and organizing referendums within their own communities to demonstrate their opposition.

8 November 1991. The EC imposes sanctions.

18 December 1991. The UN Security Council agrees to send 20 military observers to monitor the situation in Croatia. The UN special envoy Cyrus Vance, who has conducted repeated peace missions, has on Dec. 8 ruled out any despatch of a UN peacekeeping force unless and until both sides (i.e. Croatia, and the ethnic Serbs and the JNA) comply with the most recent ceasefire agreement, that of Nov. 23.

ORGANIZATIONS AND LINKAGES IN THE NEW EUROPE

The roles of many of Europe's international organizations came under review in 1990 and 1991 as they faced the challenge of responding to the radical political reshaping of the continent. In this new scenario, East Germany's position was unique among the former East European communist bloc countries. Its reunification with West Germany had resulted in its automatic absorbtion into the Council of Europe, EC, NATO, Western European Union and other bodies of which West Germany was already a member.

Of all the other East European political leaders, it was the Czechoslovak President Vaclav Havel who had been the most persistent in articulating his desire for a "return to Europe". The government progressively withdrew from communist organizations, demanding in October 1990 the closure of the headquarters of the communist-dominated World Federation of Trade Unions and other international communist "front" organizations in Prague. Instead the government took an active part in developing the role of the **Conference on Security and Co-operation in Europe (CSCE)**. At the November CSCE summit in Paris it was agreed that the CSCE secretariat should have its headquarters in Prague. In 1991 the Czechoslovak government was among the promoters of the use of CSCE conflict prevention mechanisms in seeking a solution to the crisis and civil war in Yugoslavia.

Along with Czechoslovakia, the other two countries in what has become known as the "Visegrad Three", Hungary and Poland, have been most successful in integration with such previously solely western organizations as the **Council of Europe**, the EC and EFTA. Hungary was the first to join the Council of Europe in November 1990, followed by Czechoslovakia in February 1991 and by Poland in November 1991. The membership applications of Albania, Bulgaria, Romania and Yugoslavia were all still pending as of early 1992.

Similarly Czechoslovakia, Hungary and Poland have successfully negotiated association agreements with the **European Communities (EC)** (signed in December 1991), which they hope will eventually lead to membership. The EC is very much seen as the motor of European economic integration, although East European countries recognise that membership can only be realized in the medium to long term.

The EC itself, while heavily occupied with negotiations on its own economic and monetary union and on EC political union, has also been forced to consider the prospect of the accession of many new members. By the end of 1991 negotiations had been all but concluded on an agreement between the EC and the **European Free Trade Association (EFTA)** on establishing a European Economic Area (EEA), which would establish the world's largest common market of 380 million people from the 12 EC and the seven EFTA countries. The applications for EC membership by both Austria and Sweden, and the expectation that other EFTA countries would shortly follow suit, reinforced the perception that EFTA could serve as a form of "antechamber" for countries which would subsequently move on to membership of the EC itself. East European countries have shown themselves keen to develop relations with EFTA, with this idea of an "ante-chamber" evidently having its appeal.

In seeking to aid the **restructuring of the economies of Eastern Europe** the Group of Seven industrialized countries agreed at their Paris summit in July 1989 to set up a programme, administered by the EC Commission, which at first channelled assistance to Hungary and Poland. It has since been extended to Bulgaria, Czechoslovakia, Yugoslavia and East Germany (until unification), to Romania, and finally in January 1992 to Albania and the Baltic states. Subsumed within this programme is the EC's own "operation phare" (the acronym initially intended to refer, in French, to aid for economic restructuring in Poland and Hungary). Germany is by some way the largest investor in the emerging East European market economies while the United Kingdom has promoted its own "know-how" fund to export expertise to Eastern Europe. The western countries also set up the **European Bank for Reconstruction and Development (EBRD)** in April 1991 to assist further with the channeling of funding for this reconstruction.

It is, however, the strategic balance of power within Europe which has already changed most radically, leaving the **North Atlantic Treaty Organization (NATO)** to restructure itself in a world without its traditional enemies.

In the "two-plus-four" negotiations on German unification Gorbachev had initially fought hard for a unified Germany outside NATO, but in the end, in conceding a unified Germany's right to choose its own alliances, he settled for a good strategic bargain. Under treaties regulating German unification, Soviet troops were allowed to remain in (eastern) Germany until December 1994, while Germany (i) confirmed its final acceptance of its borders (notably the Oder-Neisse border with Poland); (ii) its renunciation of nuclear, biological and chemical weapons, and (iii) undertook to reduce its troop levels to 370,000 within three to four years. The new unified Germany and the Soviet Union signed a 20-year bilateral treaty of good neighbourliness and co-operation, and Germany committed itself to substantial financial assistance in the upkeep of Soviet troops remaining in Germany in the building of housing for returning Soviet soldiers.

While western organizations have sought to adapt to the changing shape of Europe their eastern counterparts have withered away as Gorbachev's application of the policy of *perestroika* to Eastern Europe has lifted the Soviet hold on its neighbours. The introduction of hard currency trade among **Comecon** countries from January 1991 and the resulting collapse of traditional markets in the Soviet Union has obliged all the East European countries to look westwards for new markets and to seek to negotiate preferential terms for their economies which would otherwise be unable to compete. Comecon was dissolved in June 1991.

Central and eastern Europe in 1991

Similarly the **Warsaw Pact** found its raison d'être undermined as the eastern bloc states progressively negotiated the withdrawal of Soviet troops from their soil. Soviet troops (which had not been in either Bulgaria or Romania since the 1950s) left Czechoslovakia and Hungary in mid-1991 and were scheduled to complete their withdrawal from Poland by December 1993 and from Germany by December 1994. The Warsaw Pact was dissolved in July 1991.

CHRONOLOGY

December 1945. Soviet and western troops leave Czechoslovakia. Soviet and western forces remain in Austria and Germany; there are also Soviet troops still in Bulgaria, Hungary, Poland and Romania.

27 December 1945. The IMF and World Bank come into existence.

5 October 1947. Cominform, the Communist Information Bureau, is established by the communist parties of Bulgaria, Czechoslovakia, France, Hungary, Italy, Poland, Romania, the Soviet Union and Yugoslavia.

December 1947. Soviet troops leave Bulgaria.

April 1948. The Marshall Plan is launched to implement the European Recovery Plan; the eastern European countries, under Soviet pressure, decline to participate.

28 June 1948. Cominform expels the Yugoslav communist party.

25 January 1949. Comecon is set up by Bulgaria, Czechoslovakia, Hungary, Poland, Romania and the Soviet Union. Albania becomes a member in February 1949 but then withdraws in 1961. East Germany joins on 1 October 1950. Yugoslavia is an associate member after 1965.

4 April 1949. NATO is set up under the North Atlantic Treaty.

23 October 1954. NATO countries sign a treaty to allow the accession of West Germany.

14 May 1955. The Warsaw Pact is signed by Albania, Bulgaria, Czechoslovakia, East Germany, Hungary, Poland, Romania and the Soviet Union. Albania ceases to participate in 1961 and leaves formally in September 1968.

25 February 1956. Khrushchev criticises many of Stalin's policies at a secret Communist Party congress. His public denunciation of the execution of innocent people under Stalin does not come until the 22nd party congress in October 1961.

18 April 1956. Cominform is dissolved, having "exhausted its function".

November 1956. Soviet troops crush the Hungarian uprising.

25 July 1958. The last Soviet troops leave Romania.

30 September 1961. The Organization for Economic Co-operation and Development (OECD) is founded. None of the East European countries is a member, although Yugoslavia participates in certain aspects of the OECD's work. By 1991 Czechos-

lovakia, Hungary and Poland are participating in a co-operation programme with the OECD resulting in the publication of OECD reports on Hungary in July 1991, on Czechoslovakia in January 1992 and on Poland in February 1992.

24 April 1965. Yugoslavia becomes an associate member of Comecon.

20-21 August 1968. Soviet, Polish, East German, Hungarian and Bulgarian troops invade Czechoslovakia, invoking the principle which comes to be known as the "Brezhnev doctrine" on intervention where socialism is threatened.

16 October 1968. Czechoslovakia has to accept the "temporary" presence of Soviet troops.

11 August 1975. The permanent Conference on Security and Co-operation in Europe (CSCE) is set up under the Helsinki Final Act signed by 35 countries including Bulgaria, Czechoslovakia, East Germany, Hungary, Poland, Romania, and Yugoslavia.

1978. The Alpen-Adria grouping is established for regional co-operation on tourism, energy, environment, transport, sport and culture. It brings together five Austrian provinces, three of Hungary's western regions, four northern regions of Italy, Bavaria (Germany), Croatia and Slovenia.

19-20 June 1978. Yugoslavia and EFTA agree on a joint committee to improve economic co-operation.

2 April 1980. Yugoslavia signs a preferential trade and co-operation agreement with the European Communities, which comes fully into force in April 1983.

6 May 1982. Hungary joins the IMF.

12 June 1986. Poland rejoins the IMF.

12 June 1986. An apostolic pro nuncio is appointed in Yugoslavia following the establishment of diplomatic relations with the Vatican. (The Vatican subsequently recognizes Croatia and Slovenia in December 1991.)

7 December 1988. Mikhail Gorbachev announces unilateral troop withdrawals, involving 50,000 troops and 5,000 tanks then based in Czechoslovakia, East Germany and Hungary by the end of 1991. By late 1989 this move is overtaken by independent calls for the withdrawal of Soviet troops from Czechoslovakia, East Germany and Hungary, although Poland is less keen until the terms of German unification are settled.

24 April 1989. European Community Foreign Ministers announce a new "dynamic approach" to economic relations with Comecon countries. EC-Comecon meetings are held over subsequent months but the EC is keen to stress bilateral links with the countries concerned.

14-16 July 1989. The Group of Seven industrialized countries set up a programme to assist Poland and Hungary in "transforming their economies in a durable manner". The programme, which is administered by the European Commission, is extended on 4 July 1990 to Bulgaria, Czechoslovakia, Yugoslavia and East Germany (until unification), on 30 January 1991 to Romania, and on 1 January 1992 to Albania and the Baltic states. As of November 1991 the aid totals US$ 32,000 million.

18 December 1989. The EC "operation phare" plan comes into effect, to assist the economic development of east European countries.

17 July 1989. Poland and the Vatican re-establish full diplomatic relations.

26-27 October 1989. Warsaw Pact foreign ministers confirm the effective renunciation of the "Brezhnev doctrine"; in what is popularly known as the "Sinatra doctrine" eastern European countries can now "do it their way".

9 February 1990. Hungary and the Vatican re-establish full diplomatic relations; an apostolic pro nuncio is appointed on 28 March 1990.

26-27 February 1990. Czechoslovakia and the Soviet Union sign an agreement providing for the withdrawal of the 73,500 Soviet troops in Czechoslovakia by July 1991.

March 1990. Balkan government representatives agree at a conference in Athens to strengthen regional economic and technological co-operation. Albania, Bulgaria, Greece, Romania, Turkey and Yugoslavia are all represented at this meeting and at a second session in Tirana on 24-25 October 1990.

March 1990. Romania and the Vatican re-establish diplomatic relations.

10 March 1990. Hungary and the Soviet Union sign an agreement providing for the withdrawal of two-thirds of the 49,700 Soviet troops stationed in Hungary by the end of 1990 and the remainder by July 1991.

9 April 1990. Czechoslovak, Hungarian and Polish leaders meet in Bratislava to discuss their "return to Europe". The Austrian, Italian and Yugoslav foreign ministers also attend the meeting as observers.

May 1990. Regions bordering on the river Danube establish a working community (*Arbeitsgemeinschaft*) on regional co-operation and exchange of expertise. Bavaria (Germany), four Austrian provinces, Bohemia and Slovakia, seven Hungarian counties, Serbia and Croatia, provinces in Bulgaria, the Romanian district of Giurgiu, and the Soviet Republic of Moldova are all involved.

8 May 1990. The EC signs trade and commercial and economic co-operation agreements with Bulgaria and Czechoslovakia, which take effect on 1 November 1991.

7 June 1990. The Moscow summit of the Warsaw Pact seeks to transform the organization into a "political-military" body instead of a "military-political" one and to work out a "new, pan-European system of security" involving closer co-operation with NATO, non-aligned and neutral states.

13 June 1990. Czechoslovakia, Hungary and Poland sign declarations on co-operation with EFTA; these are scheduled to lead to the signature of free trade agreements in the first half of 1992.

26 June 1990. Hungary withdraws from the Warsaw Pact.

31 July-1 August 1990. Leaders from Austria, Czechoslovakia, Hungary, Italy and Yugoslavia meet to promote economic and cultural co-operation. This "Pentagonale" group, first suggested in November 1989 in Budapest by Italian foreign

minister Gianni De Michelis, becomes the "Hexagonale" group on 27 July 1991 when Poland joins, and is renamed from 28 January 1992 as the Central European Initiative.

24 September 1990. East Germany withdraws from the Warsaw Pact shortly before unification with West Germany on Oct. 3.

25-27 September 1990. Bulgaria and Czechoslovakia join the IMF. Czechoslovakia had been an IMF founder member but withdrew in 1954. Albania is now the only non-member in Eastern Europe.

12 October 1990. Germany and the Soviet Union sign a treaty providing for the withdrawal from eastern Germany by December 1994 of all Soviet troops (which have been there since the War, regulated since 1957 by a bilateral treaty). A treaty signed three days earlier provides for Germany to meet most of the costs. Both treaties complete the ratification process by April 1991.

22 October 1990. Romania and the European Communities sign a five-year agreement on trade and economic co-operation.

6 November 1990. Hungary joins the Council of Europe, the first former communist country to do so.

19 November 1990. Warsaw Pact and NATO countries sign the Treaty on Conventional Armed Forces in Europe (CFE) five days after jointly declaring that they no longer regarded each other as adversaries.

1 January 1991. Trade accounts between Comecon member countries are henceforth to be settled in hard currency.

24-25 January 1991. The Council of Europe holds a ministerial-level conference in Vienna to co-ordinate government immigration policy. It is attended by all CSCE countries in the face of growing concern over the influx of migrants and asylum seekers from the Soviet Union and eastern Europe (especially Poland and Romania). By July 1991 an OECD report finds, however, that fears of a large-scale influx have not been realised.

February 1991. A meeting at Visegrad, near Budapest, between leaders of Czechoslovakia, Hungary and Poland (the "Visegrad Three") discusses mutual co-operation.

13 February 1991. Romania applies formally for associate membership of the EC.

21 February 1991. Czechoslovakia joins the Council of Europe.

25 February 1991. Warsaw Pact member countries agree to disband the Pact as a military alliance from 31 March.

16 March 1991. An apostolic pro nuncio is appointed in Bulgaria following the establishment of diplomatic relations with the Vatican.

15-17 April 1991. The European Bank for Reconstruction and Development (EBRD) is inaugurated. Bulgaria, Czechoslovakia, Hungary, Poland, Romania, and Yugoslavia are founder members. First proposed by French President François

Mitterrand in November 1989, the EBRD's founding charter has been signed in May 1990.

June 1991. The last Soviet troops leave Czechoslovakia and Hungary.

12-14 June 1991. Havel hosts a conference in Prague to discuss the idea of a "European confederation".

19 June 1991. Albania joins the CSCE as its 35th member, having been given observer status in November 1990.

20 June 1991. Albania establishes full diplomatic relations with the European Communities.

28 June 1991. Comecon is formally dissolved after its 46th session in Budapest. Its full liquidation is, however, delayed as member countries are unable to agree on the distribution of assets.

1 July 1991. The Warsaw Pact is formally dissolved at a meeting in Prague.

5 July 1991. EC financial aid to Yugoslavia is frozen.

11-12 July 1991. Countries around the Black Sea (Bulgaria, Romania, the Soviet Union and Turkey, with Greece and Yugoslavia as observers) meet to begin negotiations on an economic co-operation agreement.

29 August 1991. Meeting in Weimar, Germany, the foreign ministers of Germany, France and Poland declare their commitment to mutual co-operation and agree to meet at least once a year.

7 September 1991. Albania and the Vatican establish diplomatic relations.

5-6 October 1991. The "Visegrad Three", Czechoslovakia, Hungary and Poland, sign a co-operation treaty in Krakow. They declare their commitment to a united Europe and affirm that their security interests are best served by integration within NATO.

8 October 1991. Poland and the Soviet Union initial an agreement providing for the withdrawal of all Soviet combat troops stationed in Poland by 15 November 1992 and for the withdrawal of all remaining personnel by 31 December 1993. Soviet troops have been in Poland since the War, regulated since December 1956 by a bilateral treaty on their status. 4,387 of the 50,000 military personnel stationed in Poland have already left by the end of October.

26 November 1991. Poland becomes the third east European country to join the Council of Europe after its democratic elections in October. Albania, Bulgaria, Romania and Yugoslavia have all applied for membership and have been given "special guest status"; Yugoslavia's status has been withdrawn since mid-1991, however, because of the civil war.

10 December 1991. Bulgaria, Romania, Estonia, Latvia and Lithuania sign joint declarations on co-operation with EFTA.

16 December 1991. Czechoslovakia, Hungary and Poland sign association agreements with the EC after negotiations in progress since February 1991. The agreements provide for free trade within 10 years and possibly eventual EC membership.

17 December 1991. The European energy charter is signed in The Hague by 45 countries and organizations including Albania, Bulgaria, Czechoslovakia, Hungary, Poland, Romania, Yugoslavia. The charter is intended to secure supplies of oil and gas from the Soviet Union and "unlock the resources of the former Soviet bloc countries". A legally binding agreement is scheduled to be drafted in the first half of 1992.

20 December 1991. The North Atlantic Co-operation Council holds an inaugural meeting in Brussels to discuss security co-operation. It is attended by Foreign Ministers from the 16 NATO countries, the Soviet Union, eastern European countries, Estonia, Latvia and Lithuania.

BIBLIOGRAPHICAL NOTE

The speed and scope of change has been such that a conventional bibliography of the region would seem largely irrelevant in this book. What follows are merely some suggestions which will give at least some starting points, for general interest and academic study; in the latter case, the student will need to watch the academic journals on regional and international politics, where the research will only now be appearing on history so recent that it is still very much in the current affairs category.

For the pre-communist background, a point of reference is *Eastern Europe between the Wars 1918-41* by Hugh Seton-Watson. Surveys of the subsequent years are *The Socialist Regimes of Eastern Europe; their establishment and consolidation* by Jerzy Tomaszewski (Routledge, London, 1989); *Eastern Europe 1968-84* by Olga Narkiewicz (Routledge, 1986) and the series *Marxist Regimes*, ed. Bogdan Szajkowski (Pinter Publishers, various dates). The major work on the economic developments and problems of the region is Michael Kaser's multi-volume *The Economic History of Eastern Europe* which takes 1919 as its starting date.

Covering the period 1985-89, with a perspective centring on the Soviet role and consequences, is *Eastern Europe, Gorbachev and Reform: the great challenge* by Karen Dawisha (Cambridge University Press, 2nd edition 1990).

The drama of the revolutions of 1989 came over strongly in news coverage of those historic events. Books based on the reporting of Western journalists include *Tearing Down The Curtain; the people's revolution in Eastern Europe* by an Observer newspaper team, edited by Nigel Hawkes (Hodder and Stoughton, 1990), *Lighting the Night* by the US journalist William Echikson (Sidgwick and Jackson, 1990), and *The Times Guide to Eastern Europe: the changing face of the Warsaw pact* edited by Keith Sword (Times Books, 1990). An impassioned more recent addition is *The Life and Evil Times of Nicolae Ceausescu* by John Sweeney (Hutchinson, 1991).

Written with less sense of immediacy, but offering insights in the interpretation of the action, are *The Rebirth of History; Eastern Europe in the Age of Democracy* by Misha Glenny (Penguin Books, 1990) and *The Patriots' Revolution* by Mark Frankland (Sinclair-Stevenson 1990). The pre-1989 opposition movements of Central Europe are depicted in *The Uses of Adversity* by Timothy Garton-Ash (Granta Books, 1990), while more oblique portraits of Hungarian and Polish political life are in *Europe, Europe* by Hans Magnus Enzensberger (published in 1987 in German; English edition Hutchinson Radius, 1989).

There are many centres of discussion on the implications of seeking to convert to free market economics. The OECD has set up a Centre for Co-operation with the European Economies in Transition. The World Bank has published a report from its late 1990 conference *Reforming Central and Eastern European Economies; Initial*

Results and Challenges. A a more succinct Western economists' assessment of the major strategies and their problems is *Reform in Eastern Europe* by Oliver Blanchard, Rudiger Dornbusch et. al. (MIT Press, 1991).

The strategic dimension of the change in Europe, and above all of the reunification of Germany, is itself a massive subject and well beyond the scope of this bibliographical note. On the Balkan dimension, although it predates the war in Yugoslavia, *Remaking the Balkans* by Christopher Cviic of the Royal Institute of International Affairs (Chatham House Papers, Pinter Publishers, 1991) analyses the political and security implications, the old rivalries, and possible international responses.

The task of keeping abreast of the continuing changes may be assisted by reference to the monthly news summaries in *Keesing's Record of World Events*, edited by Roger East (Longman, Harlow). The same publisher's reference list contains a *Political and Economic Encyclopaedia of Eastern Europe and the Soviet Union*, edited by Stephen White (Longman, 1990), a directory of *New Political Parties of Eastern Europe and the Soviet Union* , edited by Bogdan Szajkowski (Longman, 1991) and a *Handbook of Reconstruction in Eastern Europe and the Soviet Union* edited by Stephen White (Longman, 1991).

INDEX

This index seeks to combine a number of functions.

1. It provides a comprehensive index of personal names.

2. References to political parties are given (under the full English-language name) to indicate an entry on that party in the relevant section of each country chapter. The index does not aim to cover every mention of every party; it is hoped that the text itself is sufficiently clearly structured to make that irrelevant for most readers.

3. Additional index terms assist with investigation of common themes across the different countries. In many cases these references are to the specific section headings in each chapter. Other themes are dealt with by means of comprehensive index references to key words (for example atheism, destalinization, pollution, purge).

4. It provides comprehensive references to international organizations.